NO VISIBLE BRUISES

BY THE SAME AUTHOR

What We've Lost Is Nothing: A Novel

*Fugitive Denim: A Moving Story of People and Pants
in the Borderless World of Global Trade*

NO VISIBLE BRUISES

What We Don't
Know About
Domestic Violence
Can Kill Us

RACHEL LOUISE SNYDER

BLOOMSBURY PUBLISHING

NEW YORK · LONDON · OXFORD · NEW DELHI · SYDNEY

BLOOMSBURY PUBLISHING
Bloomsbury Publishing Inc.
1385 Broadway, New York, NY 10018, USA

BLOOMSBURY, BLOOMSBURY PUBLISHING, and the Diana logo are
trademarks of Bloomsbury Publishing Plc

First published in the United States 2019
Copyright © Rachel Louise Snyder, 2019

Certain portions from this book first appeared in the *New Yorker* in
slightly different form.

This is a work of nonfiction. However, the author has changed the names and redacted
identifying characteristics of certain people to protect their privacy.

LIBRARY OF CONGRESS CATALOGING-IN-PUBLICATION DATA

Names: Snyder, Rachel Louise, author.
Title: No visible bruises : what we don't know about domestic violence
can kill us / Rachel Louise Snyder.
Description: New York, NY : Bloomsbury Publishing Inc., 2019. |
Includes bibliographical references and index.
Identifiers: LCCN 2018053597 | ISBN 9781635570977 (hardback) |
ISBN 9781635570991 (ebook)
Subjects: LCSH: Family violence—United States. |
Victims of family violence—United States.
Classification: LCC HV6626.2 .S59 2019 | DDC 362.82/920973—dc23
LC record available at https://lccn.loc.gov/2018053597
6 8 10 9 7 5

Typeset by Westchester Publishing Services
Printed and bound in the U.S.A. by Berryville Graphics Inc., Berryville, Virginia

To find out more about our authors and books visit www.bloomsbury.com
and sign up for our newsletters.

Bloomsbury books may be purchased for business or promotional use. For
information on bulk purchases please contact Macmillan Corporate and
Premium Sales Department at specialmarkets@macmillan.com.

For Barbara J. Snyder

CONTENTS

PREFACE

Idrive my rental car from downtown Billings to a four-story house far outside of town, perched up on a hill, where the man inside can view anything that might come at him. Telescopic observation of the world outside: mountains, plains, escape routes to everywhere in Montana and beyond. The man I'm here to see has avoided me for a long time. Passive avoidance. I've come to Billings from my home in Washington, D.C., talked to his daughters, his ex-wife, caseworkers. Returned again. I know the town now. Some of the police, some of the prosecutors, advocates, hotel workers, and even the printer whose wife runs a basement museum dedicated to women. And now, finally, on this maybe my third visit, he has agreed to see me.

I talk to a lot of people who don't want to talk to me. People who've murdered their families, people who've nearly been murdered, people who've arrested those murderers, people who've grown up with people who nearly murdered them. Men like Paul Monson are always reluctant to talk, reluctant to voice the magnitude of what they've lost, because what they've lost skirts the very limit of their imaginations.

When I arrive I hear shuffling inside the house, and think for a moment that Paul won't answer, that he's changed his mind about the interview. I've been in Billings for several days already; he knew I was coming. His ex-wife, Sally Sjaastad, has spent many hours with me, but could not get him to agree to meet me the first time she asked. Or the second or the third. I'm surprised, frankly, that he agreed at all. The windowless front door is gray and full of dents.

Finally, the door opens. Paul barely looks at me. He's a little hunched over, white hair receding, face drawn. He looks his age, early sixties. Paul opens the door wider, gestures me inside without meeting my gaze. He wears a blue shirt, buttoned up, jeans. Looks like he's clenching his jaw.

*   *   *

1

THE HOUSE, WHICH PAUL built himself, has a just-moved-in feel to it. Not much decoration, opened boxes here and there in a couple of corners. A telescope points toward the carpet, like it's resigned its mission. Mountains dominate the view outside. Paul is reserved, quiet, meticulous. We sit at his dining room table and he runs his fingers along the smooth edge, watching his own hands. The table is covered in piles of paper. I make an off-handed comment about my rental car, and it sets us on a safe course.

My father taught me about cars, how to change oil and tires, instructions on measuring fluids and swapping air filters. The mechanics of a piston. Basic stuff, but it's enough. Paul is an electrical design technician—an engineer type—and so cars are a comfortable topic for him, the familiarity of the machine. An equation that adds up—wires atop plugs create a spark, which fires an engine. They're predictable. Fixable. Something goes wrong, it's a mystery that can be solved. I let him talk. He tells me he bought all of his daughters their first cars. Alyssa's was a Honda Civic. Michelle's a white Subaru. He says Melanie is "kind of a car eater," so he's bought her several. He knows we're not yet talking of the thing I came to talk about, and I can feel the tension in the room, palpable as humidity.

Rocky was into cars, too. Paul remembers Rocky's first car, a little green thing. An Opel, he thinks. Rocky was his son-in-law, married to his middle daughter, Michelle. "The first memory I have of him is pulling up to my curb," Paul says, to come and see Michelle. The car first, then the man. Later, Paul would get the impression Rocky spent half his time working on a Mustang. "He had one he was building, and the other one was a parts car," Paul says. "That was his interest and it looked like to me that he spent a lot of time in the garage by himself."

Paul says he and Rocky never really bonded like a typical father and son-in-law. For nearly a decade Michelle and Rocky were together, but Paul can only remember having one conversation with Rocky, about that Mustang. Rocky had once asked Paul's advice on paint color. "White's the way to go if you don't really know what you're doing," Paul tells me. The most forgiving of colors. You can screw up with white and the result will still be decent. "White's a color all by itself," he says.

IN NOVEMBER OF 2001, Rocky Mosure bought a gun from the *Thrifty Nickel*, the classified paper where you can buy everything from a ferret to a tractor to a piano. Then he went home, where Michelle had just fed the kids dinner. A neighbor saw Rocky peering in the windows. Sometime after, one by one, he shot them. Michelle, Kristy, Kyle. Then himself.

It was a case that shocked the entire state. Michelle was young, twenty-three, her kids six and seven. In first and second grade. Learning to read. Drawing stick people and lollipop trees. Paul found Kyle slumped on the stairs, Rocky at the bottom, his face all twisted, scribblings on his arms in what looked like Magic Marker. Michelle's car was there, and for a few minutes, Paul thought maybe she was alive. He ran to the backyard, then the garage. He saw Rocky's Mustangs. A bag of family videos. Then the police came. And they found Michelle.

I'D ARRIVED AT PAUL Monson's house as most journalists arrive at their most pivotal stories: through a tangled series of people and geographies and years of research. In the summer of 2010, I'd been standing on my friend Andre Dubus's driveway in New England when his sister, Suzanne, drove up. She and the rest of the family were all going on a holiday. The next few hours would turn out to chart the following decade of my life.

Less than a year earlier, I had returned to the States after living and traveling abroad on and off, most recently in Cambodia, where I had spent six years. The adjustment had been difficult. I sat in faculty meetings at the university where I was a new assistant professor, feigning knowledge in matters of bureaucracy and pedagogy that felt like a foreign language to me. During my time in Cambodia, I had written about gang rape and post-genocide society, poverty and workers' rights, stories that felt palpably about survival in a way that nothing in my new life did. Our expat dinner conversations in Phnom Penh had revolved around the war crimes tribunal,[1] sex trafficking, ongoing violence, political corruption. Once, while I was walking my dog in a local park, a moto taxi driver who knew me from our shared neighborhood sped up beside me, tossed me across the seat behind him, balancing my dog in my lap, and zoomed away from Hun Sen Park as fast as he could. A man had been shot seconds earlier just fifteen feet away from where I'd been walking, and Sophal, the moto driver, had taken it upon himself to get me to safety. Another time (again with my dog), a man set himself on fire in that same park, and I froze in panic, watching him burn. My friend Mia, who also lived in Phnom Penh, used to say that she sometimes felt we were living on the front lines of humanity.

In the United States, it wasn't that there were no problems—poverty, disease, and natural disasters all happened here, too—but I'd forgotten how possible it was to live where, if you had the desire and the means, you could fairly easily insulate yourself from a lot of these problems. And my new life insulated me from the kinds of issues and stories I'd covered for decades in a way I hadn't anticipated. I wasn't unhappy. Just restless. I'd studied fiction in graduate school, but gravitated toward nonfiction soon after because I understood almost immediately that nonfiction was a more direct source of change. I was pulled toward hidden corners of the world, to disenfranchised people, because I knew in some small measure what it felt like to be an unseen, unheard person, what it felt like to grieve beyond what you thought your body could absorb.

Suzanne and I exchanged small talk on her brother's driveway that day in 2010. She and the family were still in preparation-and-packing mode for their annual camping vacation into the hinterlands of Maine, and Suzanne had been greeted by her brother, Andre, with a long shopping list. She told me she worked for a domestic violence agency in town, that they had recently developed a new program that she was calling the Domestic Violence High Risk Team. Their primary aim was simple, she said: "We try to predict domestic violence homicides before they happen, so we can prevent them."

It sounded immediately implausible. So implausible in fact that I thought I'd misheard some elemental piece of it.

"Predict?" I remember saying. "You said *predict* domestic violence homicides?"

I had come across domestic violence in my reporting over the years, not only in Cambodia, but also in places like Afghanistan, Niger, and Honduras. But it had never been a focus for me; instead it was always adjacent to whatever other story I was writing, so much so that it was practically banal. The young girls jailed for love crimes in Kabul; the Indian child brides who gave interviews only in front of the men who controlled them; the Tibetan women forcibly sterilized by the Chinese government; the teenage brides in Niger cast from their villages after post-pregnancy fistulas made them pariahs; the Romanian women forced to birth multiple children under Ceaușescu and who now, in their early thirties, were grandmothers fated to poverty; the Cambodian street workers beaten and gang-raped for weekend sport by well-heeled Khmer teenagers. All of these women, in every country, were brutalized and controlled by men as a matter of routine. Men made the rules, primarily through physical violence. It was there lurking in practically every story I'd ever covered across the world, a shadowy background so obvious I didn't even have to ask about it most of the time. It was as common as rain. Until that moment in the driveway with Suzanne Dubus, if I thought of domestic violence in the States at all, I saw it as an unfortunate fate for the unlucky few, a matter of bad choices and cruel environments. A woman hardwired to be hurt. A man hardwired to hurt. But I never envisioned it as a social ill, an epidemic we could actually *do* something about. Now here was Suzanne Dubus talking about preventative measures for a type of violence that, for the first time, I saw operating along a continuum. The young girl in India married as a child, the Tibetan woman sterilized, the Afghan woman jailed, the housewife in Massachusetts brutalized by her husband—all shared a common privation, what domestic violence victims across the world lacked: agency in their own lives. The forces that brought a Cambodian prostitute to the brink of death were the same forces that killed thousands of women and children and men (but mostly women and children) across America, and the entire globe, every year. An average, in fact, of 137 women each and every day are killed by intimate partner or familial violence across the globe.[2] This does not include men. Or children.

Everything in my body suddenly came alive that day. I saw all the faces of women around the world from over two decades of work, and I realized how rarely I'd gazed inward, at my own country, at what we got wrong and what it meant. At how it connected to those years of other stories and other faces. The universality of domestic violence and how it crosses geographical, cultural, and linguistic barriers. Maybe all those other stories were in preparation for the day I'd meet Paul Monson and look at the mountains from his living room windows.

I ended up following Suzanne to the farmers' market, and then to the grocery store, and then to the liquor store as she prepped for her camping trip. I helped her carry ice and peaches and hamburger meat. I asked question after question while she drove and while her mother, Pat, sat in the passenger seat chiming in here and there. *How did it work? How many have you stopped? What else can you predict?* My questions were vast and endless. Like many people who hold a casual acquaintance with a problem, I believed all the common assumptions: that if things were bad enough, victims would just leave. That restraining orders solved the problem (and that if a victim didn't show up to renew a restraining order, the problem had been solved). That going to a shelter was an adequate response for victims and their children. That violence inside the home was something private, unrelated to other forms of violence, perhaps most notably mass shootings. That a lack of visible injury signaled a lack of seriousness. And, perhaps most of all, that unless we stand at the receiving end of a punch, such violence had nothing at all to do with us.

Over the next few years, Suzanne Dubus and her colleague, Kelly Dunne, patiently taught me about the scope and history of an issue that still today is too often hidden. I learned why past approaches had failed, and what we could do more effectively today. Between 2000 and 2006, 3,200 American soldiers were killed; during that same period, domestic homicide in the United States claimed 10,600 lives. (This figure is likely an underestimate, as it was pulled from the FBI's Supplementary Homicide Reports, which gather data from local police departments, and participation is voluntary.) Twenty people in the United States are assaulted *every minute* by their partners. Former United Nations Secretary-General Kofi Annan called violence against women and girls the "most shameful human rights violation"[3] and the World Health Organization called it a "global health problem of epidemic proportions." A study put out by the United Nations Office on Drugs and Crime cited fifty thousand women around the world were killed by partners or family members in 2017 alone.[4] *Fifty thousand women.* The UNODC report called home "the most dangerous place for women."[5] And despite growing awareness that men, too, can be victims of domestic violence, the overwhelming majority of victims—about 85%—are still, today, women and girls.[6] And for every woman killed in the United States from domestic violence homicide, nearly nine are almost killed.[7] The story of how Suzanne Dubus and Kelly Dunne created a program to predict domestic violence homicide became my first piece for the *New Yorker*, in 2013.

It also became the seed for this book when I realized so much more needed to be said. Several years into my reporting, domestic violence began to seem like something we could actually address if we just started to pay attention. Over the next eight years, I would go on to learn more and more, including how domestic violence sits adjacent to so many other problems we as a society grapple with: education, economics, mental and physical health, crime, gender and racial equality, and more. Those who push for prison reform butt up against domestic violence over and over as perpetrators go to jail for a time, get little or no treatment, return to civilian society, and repeat the cycle. Private violence has such vastly profound public consequences. I met people in Florida,

California, Maryland, Ohio, New York, Massachusetts, Oregon, and elsewhere trying to survive their own private war, and I saw, through them, how much it costs us personally and collectively, in fractured communities, families, people. In severed lives and lost opportunities. In enormous financial burdens to victims, to taxpayers, to the criminal justice system. Domestic violence health and medical costs top more than $8 billion annually for taxpayers and cause victims to lose more than eight million[8] workdays each year. It is a direct cause of homelessness for more than half our homeless women and is overall the third leading cause of homelessness in our country. The overwhelming majority of incarcerated men today first witnessed or experienced violence as children in their own homes, and children who grow up in violent homes are at far greater risk for developmental disorders.[9] And those mass shootings that seem to plague us more with each new year?

Most of them, too, are domestic violence.

In April of 2017, the advocacy group Everytown for Gun Safety published a report that claimed 54% of mass shootings in America today involved domestic or family violence.[10] The statistic traveled far and wide across the media. The link between mass shootings and domestic violence made its way into news articles and op-eds across the country, with one small alteration. Instead of "involved" the media began to use the word "predicted." As in, "domestic violence predicts mass shootings more than half the time." When a reporter from the website *PolitiFact* called the Everytown statistic into question, citing a much lower percentage from the research of Northeastern University professor James Alan Fox,[11] the most important point was buried halfway down the piece in a quote by Fox, who told the *PolitiFact* reporter, "You could certainly say about half the cases of mass shootings are extreme incidents of domestic violence."

In other words, it's not that domestic violence *predicts* mass shootings. It's that mass shootings, more than half the time, *are* domestic violence.

Consider, for example, Adam Lanza of Newtown, Connecticut, who began his killing spree at home with his mother before making his way to Sandy Hook Elementary School. Devin Patrick Kelley tied his wife to their bed with handcuffs and rope before driving to the First Baptist Church in Sutherland Springs, Texas.[12] You can go further back to what is widely considered to be the United States' first mass shooting—when in August of 1966 Charles Whitman opened fire on students at the University of Texas at Austin and killed sixteen people. What many people have forgotten is that his rampage began the night before, with his wife and his mother.

But domestic violence lurks in the other 46% of mass shootings, too. It's there, in the backgrounds of so many of the shooters. Omar Mateen, who killed 49 people at the Orlando Pulse nightclub in June of 2016, had strangled his first wife—an act that is a felony in the state of Florida, where he lived, and could have put him behind bars for a decade according to federal law. Yet he was never charged. Then there were the three terrifying weeks in October of 2002 when a sniper named John Allen Muhammad kept Virginia, Maryland, and Washington, D.C., under siege, shooting people seemingly at random. Elementary schools had indoor recess during those weeks; gas stations hung tarps to conceal customers. In fact, Muhammad had a long history of abuse against his estranged wife, Mildred. The attacks had been a cover. He told police he thought killing random strangers would conceal his ultimate plan—to kill Mildred. And what if we'd provided services and support for a young Dylann Roof, witness to years of alleged extreme abuse by his father to his stepmother?[13] Might that have saved nine people at the Emanuel African Methodist Episcopal Church in Charleston, South Carolina, in June of 2015?

These, sadly, are just the incidents that linger in the public consciousness. There are many, many others. In the United States, we generally define mass shootings as four or more victims, which means the overwhelming majority of mass shootings get coverage only in local or regional news, if any. And they disappear after a day or two, the thousands of women, men, and children killed each and every year. Cases like these and so many others make clear that domestic violence, rather than being a private problem, is a most urgent matter of public health.

ALL OF THIS EVENTUALLY brought me to the dented front door of Paul Monson in the spring of 2015. I had known most of his family for several years by then and had heard Michelle and Rocky's story from Michelle's mother and sisters. Paul found it nearly impossible to talk about the murders. To me his pain seemed overwhelming, the guilt sometimes suffocating. Domestic violence is hard to talk about. It is also, I learned in the course of this research, among the most difficult of subjects to report on. It is vast and unwieldy, but it's also utterly hidden. As a reporter, you can stand in the middle of a war zone and describe what you're seeing. You can go to the site of a famine or a plague and report on it in real time. You can visit an HIV/AIDS clinic, a cancer center, a refugee camp, an orphanage, and you can write about the struggles. You can write about what these social and environmental and public health and geopolitical problems look like from the inside out as they're happening in front of you. Even if you're writing about a postwar issue, as I so often was in Cambodia, you can assume a degree of safety for the interviewees simply by dint of the war or the natural disaster or whatever the disruption that brought you there having ended.

One of the most difficult aspects of writing about domestic violence is that you're writing about a situation of such intense volatility that you risk endangering victims who are already right in the middle of an explosive and dangerous situation. Yet the ethics of journalism mandate that everyone has a chance to tell their side of the story—victims and abusers alike. This meant, in several cases, that I spent months or even years interviewing victims, only to have to toss all those hours of interviews because to even ask the abusers for an interview would have compromised a victim's safety. One woman I spent over a year interviewing, for example, had to withdraw from our talks for her own protection. She'd spent years with her abuser, and he used to hold her up naked to the heating pipes in their apartment or toss a blanket over her head and duct tape her around the neck. Her story of abuse and eventual freedom was among the most chilling stories I'd heard. Even now, writing this of her, I can include just these details because they don't identify her, and the particulars of her story—the heating pipes, the blanket—appear in so many others' stories, too.

With domestic violence, often there is no end date for the victims. Women who do manage to break free of their abusers still spend their lives negotiating with them if they share custody of children. And even if children are not involved, many victims remain on the lookout long after they escape abuse—particularly if incarceration was a result of the abuse. If they find a new partner, it can put both of them at risk. One woman I interviewed called it keeping her "head in the swivel"—at least until their children were grown. Visitations and drop-offs are notoriously dangerous even for victims who manage to get away. One woman I know had her face smashed into a stone wall while her children were watching from the backseat of their car during a custody drop-off. She'd been divorced for years by then. Indeed, as I write this, six people in Bakersfield, California, including the shooter's ex-wife and her new boyfriend, were killed just yesterday, September 12, 2018 (a Google search for "estranged husband" and "killed" brings up more than fifteen million results). Escaping an abusive relationship hardly ensures that the danger is over. As a result, I have tried, wherever possible, to balance the ethics of journalism with the safety of the people brave enough to let me interview them. As often as possible I've interviewed multiple people about any given incident or relationship, but there were times when it was simply too dangerous for a victim to allow me to seek out her abuser. In several cases, other participants or witnesses were no longer alive. Some of the names of interviewees have been changed and their identities kept secret for their own safety and privacy. My methodology was to redact information rather than alter it, with the exception of names. I have noted all these instances in the text.

DOMESTIC VIOLENCE IS LIKE no other crime. It does not happen in a vacuum. It does not happen because someone is in the wrong place at the wrong time. Our homes and families are supposed to be sacred territory, the "haven in a heartless world," as my college sociology teacher drilled into me. (Her class was the first place I'd ever heard the phrase.) This is part of what makes it so untenable. It's violence from someone you know, from someone who claims to love you. It is most often hidden from even one's closest confidantes, and on many occasions the physical violence is far less damaging than the emotional and verbal violence. I can't tell you how many abusers I've heard bemoaning their inability to stop loving the same women they assaulted so severely it landed them in prison. It is, perhaps, a powerful aphrodisiac, the idea that someone is gripped by love so intensely he or she is powerless in the face of it. Though the intellectual coercion required to make a man believe that his love and his violence stem from the same place inside himself is of course utterly duplicitous. I came to learn that there is a high incidence of narcissism in perpetrators. And a high incidence of other factors that can make duplicity a matter of survival—addiction, poverty, and other acts of desperation can be particularly deadly when combined with a certain toxic masculinity.

We live in a culture in which we are told our children must have a father, that a relationship is the ultimate goal, that family is the bedrock of society, that it's better to stay and work out one's "issues" in private than to leave and raise kids as a single mother. Michelle Monson Mosure said this over and over when she insisted to her mother that she didn't want to raise her children in a "broken home." As if a home with one adult abusing another adult isn't broken, as if there are degrees of brokenness. The messages are insidious and they are consistent. We see those messages when our politicians wrangle over reauthorizing the Violence Against Women Act, and then fund it so sparingly it's practically a hiccup in the federal budget. VAWA has an entire budget of just under $489 million at present.[14] To give a frame of reference, the entire annual budget for the Department of Justice, which oversees the Office of Violence Against Women, is currently $28 *billion*.[15] Another way to think about it might be this: the wealthiest person in the world, Jeff Bezos, who is estimated to be worth $150 billion, could fund VAWA's current budget for *three hundred years* and still have millions upon which to carve out a meager subsistence.[16]

But we give victims the message to stay in other ways, too. When our court system puts them on the defensive, asks them to face a person who may have tried to kill them, a person they know only too well may kill them for real next time. We see it in court rulings that give violent perpetrators a mere slap on the wrist, a fine, maybe. A few days in jail after a brutal assault. We get the message when law enforcement treats domestic violence as a nuisance, a "domestic dispute," rather than the criminal act that it is. I have to believe if the tables were turned, if women were beating and killing men in such vast numbers—*fifty* women a month in the United States are killed by their intimate partners using guns alone—the problem would be the front page of every newspaper in this country. Vast pools of funding would surface for researchers to figure out what's wrong with women today.

And, after all of this, we have the audacity to ask why victims stay.

The reality is that many victims like Michelle Monson Mosure and her children are actively and stealthily trying to leave, working within the system that exists and step by step, with extreme vigilance, doing everything they can to escape. In so many cases, including hers, we mistake what we see from the outside as her choosing to stay with an abuser, when in fact it's we who don't recognize what a victim who is slowly and carefully leaving actually looks like.

NONE OF THIS IS surprising, given that we didn't recognize domestic violence as wrong for most of human history. Jewish, Islamic, Christian, and Catholic religions all traditionally believed it was within a husband's purview to discipline his wife in more or less the same manner as he might discipline and control any other of his properties, including servants, slaves, and animals; of course, the holy texts—Koran, Bible, and Talmud—from which such beliefs stem were simply interpretations by (of course) men of the time.[17] Some of these interpretations even gave instruction on the manner of wife beating, such as avoiding direct blows to the face, or making sure not to cause lasting injury. In the ninth century, the Gaon of Sura believed assault by one's husband was less traumatic than a stranger's assault since a wife was, according to the law, subject to her husband's authority.[18] In the United States, the Puritans had laws against wife beating, though they were largely symbolic and rarely, if ever, enforced. Instead, abused wives were believed to have provoked the violence of their husbands—and this belief threads through hundreds of years of literature on domestic violence, nearly everything written about spousal abuse, in fact, prior to the 1960s and '70s. On those very rare occasions when a case of private violence did make it to a courtroom, the rulings tended to side in favor of the man so long as the wife's injuries were not permanent.[19]

It's only been in the last century or so that laws against wife beating have been written in the United States, and even those early states—Alabama, Maryland, Oregon, Delaware, and Massachusetts—that began writing legislation against spousal abuse in the late nineteenth century rarely enforced their own laws.[20] The American Society Against the Cruelty of Animals predates laws against cruelty toward one's wife by several decades, meaning, I suppose, that we held our dogs in higher regard than we held our wives. (Pet shelters in the 1990s outnumbered domestic violence shelters by nearly three to one.[21]) In the fall of 2018, as I write this, there are still more than a dozen countries where violence against one's spouse or family member is perfectly legal—which is to say that no specific laws against domestic violence have been written. These include Egypt, Haiti, Latvia, Uzbekistan, and the Congo, among others.[22] And then there's Russia, which in 2017 decriminalized any domestic violence that doesn't result in bodily injury.[23] There's also, of course, the United States, whose first appointed attorney general under the Trump Administration believed domestic abuse was not grounds for asylum and that such an "alien" merely suffered the fate of "misfortune."[24] In other words, these days if you have the good luck to be terrorized outside your home by your own government's forces, you can claim asylum, but if that terror exists behind closed doors? Well, that kind of bad luck means you're on your own.

So much of what exists in the United States around domestic violence today in terms of legal precedent happened very, very recently. It wasn't until 1984 that Congress finally passed a law that would help women and children victims of abuse; it was called the Family Violence Prevention and Services Act, and it helped fund shelters and other resources for victims.[25] Stalking wasn't identified as a crime until the early 1990s and still today is often not seen for the threat it truly is—not by law enforcement, abusers, or even by the victims actually being stalked, despite three-quarters of women killed in America having been stalked beforehand by these same partners or ex-partners.[26] Nearly 90% of domestic violence homicide victims were both stalked and beaten in the year prior to their deaths.[27] A national hotline for victims of domestic violence was not established in this country until 1996.[28]

Suzanne Dubus taught me that there were essentially three movements across the country revolutionizing how we address domestic violence today. One was her program begun in 2003—the advent of High Risk Teams within domestic violence agencies that try to quantify the dangerousness of any given domestic violence situation and then build protections around victims. Another was the 2002 opening of the country's first family justice center; begun in San Diego by a former city attorney named Casey Gwinn, family justice centers put victim services under one roof—police, attorneys, victim compensation, counseling, education, and dozens of others. (San Diego's opened with thirty-five different agencies. Other geographies have varying numbers of partners.) And the third was the Lethality Assessment Program, begun in Maryland in 2005 by a former police officer named Dave Sargent, which primarily addressed how law enforcement dealt on scene with a domestic violence situation.[29]

It was no mere coincidence that all three of these programs began around the same time. The women's movement in the 1970s and '80s had brought battered women to the attention of a nation just beginning to accept the idea of equality. The focus, in those years, was on shelters—building them, funding them, getting abused women away from perpetrators. But in the 1990s, that began to change. Across the country, advocates, attorneys, police officers, judges, all told me that two primary events caused this. The first was the OJ Simpson trial.

For many, Nicole Brown Simpson became the face of a new kind of victim. She was beautiful, wealthy, famous. If it could happen to her, it could happen to anyone. OJ's history of violence with her had been known to law enforcement. He'd been arrested, then bailed out, then sentenced to "telephone counseling" by a California judge (after which the case was dropped). Nicole's 911 tapes allowed listeners in to a rare scene: a woman under siege by a man who claimed to love her. The threats, the coercion, the terror, it was all right there. Her murder hurled into the forefront a conversation that advocates had been having for years—that it could happen anywhere, to anyone. How to reach victims who didn't reach out to them was one of their biggest problems in those days. But when local papers ran stories about Nicole Brown Simpson and Ron Goldman, for the first time nearly all of them listed sidebars with where to go for help. Victims suddenly began to access resources in unprecedented numbers. Calls to domestic violence hotlines, shelters, and police skyrocketed in the wake of the trial.[30] Domestic violence edged its way into the national conversation.

Simpson's case also became a rallying cry for victims of color who asked, rightfully, why it took a rich, white, beautiful woman to get the story of domestic violence homicide out in the public's view. After all, women of color experienced private violence at the same or even higher levels as white women, except they bore the added weight of racial inequality. That part of our post-Simpson national conversation is today slowly being addressed in Native American, immigrant, and underprivileged communities on a larger scale than ever before thanks in part to the second major event that changed how we treat domestic violence: the Violence Against Women Act.

VAWA put intimate partner violence before lawmakers who had, until then, seen it as a private family matter, a problem for women rather than the criminal justice system. It had first been introduced to Congress by then-senator Joseph Biden in 1990, but it wasn't until the fall of 1994 that the bill passed, just weeks after the OJ trial wrapped up. Finally, for the first time ever, cities and towns all across the country could get federal funding to address domestic violence in their communities. These funds allowed for targeted trainings of first responders, the creation of advocacy positions, shelters, transitional housing, batterer intervention classes, and legal training; VAWA funds meant victims no longer had to pay for their own rape kits and if an abused partner was evicted because of events related to her abuse, she could now receive compensation and assistance; victims with disabilities could find support, as could those in need of legal aid. These and many other systems and services we have to address domestic violence today are a direct result of the passage of VAWA. At the time, then-senator Biden told the Associated Press, "[Domestic violence] is a hate crime. My objective is to give the woman every opportunity under the law to seek redress, not only criminally but civilly. I want to raise the consciousness of this country that women's civil rights—their right to be left alone—is in jeopardy."[31]

VAWA requires reauthorization every five years. The 2013 reauthorization was held up because Republicans didn't want the bill to include same-sex partners, Native Americans living on reservations, or undocumented immigrants who were battered and trying to apply for temporary visas. After heated debates in both the House and Senate, the reauthorization finally passed. The next reauthorization is up for renewal as I write this. Advocates all across the country that I spoke with feel keenly the tenuousness of their positions and their funding in a political climate where our commander in chief displays open hostility and sexism toward women, and has himself been accused by more than a dozen women of groping and assault, as well as sexual assault by his first wife. (She later said she didn't mean this in a criminal sense, but rather in a sense of having been violated.[32]) Trump kept his staff secretary, a known abuser, in the White House, until media and outside pressure—and not a moral imperative—forced Rob Porter out. Indeed, we live in a climate in which the right to own guns seems ever more to supersede the right to life. "The consequence of [Trump's] words and deeds are so profound for women," Kit Gruelle, a survivor and activist, said to me. "We are leaping backwards at an obscene pace."

NOT LONG AGO, I had lunch with a woman named Lynn Rosenthal. Rosenthal was the first White House liaison to the Office of Violence Against Women, a position created by the Obama Administration that remains unfilled two years into the Trump Administration. I asked her if money was not an issue, if she could do whatever she wanted with whatever she needed, how would she solve domestic violence? She said she would take a community, study what worked, and then invest *everywhere*. "You can't look at one little piece of the system and say, 'Oh, that's the magic bullet.' That's what . . . people want to do. If we could invest in one thing, what would it be? Well, the answer is, there's not one thing." And that's the whole point: private violence affects in some way nearly every aspect of modern life, yet our collective failure to treat it publicly demonstrates a stunning lack of understanding about this very pervasiveness.

My goal for *No Visible Bruises*, then, is to shine a flashlight in the darkest corners, to show what domestic violence looks like from the inside out. I've written the book in three sections, each of which tries to tackle one primary question. Section one tries to answer that most dogged of questions: why victims stay. (Kit Gruelle told me once: "We don't say to bank presidents after a bank's been robbed, 'You need to move this bank.'") Michelle Monson Mosure's life and death shows us what we don't know we're seeing, that the question of leaving versus staying disregards the cavalcade of forces at work in an abusive relationship.

Section two, perhaps the most difficult section to report, interrogates violence at its core, with abusers. Too often we've overlooked their important view by speaking only to victims, advocates, and police. In the current climate of toxic masculinity I wanted to know what such a man looked like, how he viewed himself in society and within his own family. Over and over I asked, during the years I was researching this book, whether a violent man could be taught to be nonviolent. The answers almost always fell along these lines: police officers and advocates said no, victims said they hoped so, and violent men said yes. This last response felt to me less like a theory and more like an expression of their willingness. The most common aphorism in the world of domestic violence is "hurt people hurt people." So if a hurt person took his own pain and grappled with it, rather than turning it outward toward the people in his life, how would that happen?

In the third section I shadow the changemakers, people on the front lines of domestic violence and domestic violence homicide, like Suzanne Dubus, Kelly Dunne, and others. I look into what can be done, and who's doing it. Here I delve into advocacy, the judiciary and law enforcement initiatives to explore how they look from street level.

Throughout this book I generally refer to victims as "she" and perpetrators as "he." This is not because I don't recognize that men can be victims and women can be perpetrators, or that I am unaware of the relative lack of resources available for same-sex partners, or the grim statistics of domestic violence in LGBTQ relationships and communities; rather, my reasoning is twofold: first, men remain the overwhelming majority of perpetrators, and women the overwhelming majority of victims by nearly every measure. And I use she/he/they pronouns for consistency in the writing. Please assume that when I write "she" for victims or "he" for perpetrators, I recognize that anyone can find themselves in either of those two roles regardless of gender.

Similarly, while there is a movement afoot to refer to domestic violence victims as "survivors" or in some situations "clients," I often refrained from doing this unless I knew unequivocally that they *were* survivors, that is, that they had managed to escape their abusive relationships and build new lives for themselves and their families. Additionally, I refer to most sources by their full or last names, and those who shared extended narratives with me—who became, in the nonfiction sense of the term, "characters"—by their first names.

Finally, the term "domestic violence" has long been a source of contention among survivors and advocates. "Domesticating" violence implies some kind of softening, that somehow assaults from a family member deserve lesser attention than those of a stranger. There is a trend these days in advocacy circles to use the term "intimate partner violence" or "intimate partner terrorism." This, too, has obvious problems, not least of which is that it leaves out violence by anyone other than a partner. "Spousal abuse" has similar limitations. "Private violence," as a term, has gained usage in the past decade or so. Though all of these terms are euphemistic in the sense that they fail to capture the particular constellation of forces—physical, emotional, and psychological—at play in such relationships. I have, for years, tried myself to coin a better term, and I've yet to conceive of anything, though I believe the word "terrorism" comes as close as any to what such a relationship feels like from the inside. Nevertheless, because we have a collective understanding of the term, I generally refer to "domestic violence" or "private violence" in the book, unless I am quoting someone or there is an obvious contextual redundancy, in which case I have on occasion used the other terms noted above.

AND NOW I RETURN to Paul Monson's house and the waning afternoon. We eventually finish talking about cars and turn at last to that topic he's been avoiding, the source of his most elemental grief: the daughter and grandchildren he used to have.

PART I

The End

Little Lunatics

Paul Monson's house has an open floor plan, living room to dining room, dining room through kitchen. The grandkids run through here, he tells me. Kristy and Kyle, that was the first thing they did when they used to visit. Storm through the house like little lunatics. Kristy and Kyle were Rocky and Michelle's kids.

Paul is from Minot, North Dakota. Came to Montana for work. His father died long ago. His stepfather, Gil, owned Lunder's Kiddyland, a traveling carnival, and before that he was a farmer. Paul calls him an "anything-for-a-buck guy." Michelle loved her grandparents.

"A lot of times people think girls go after guys who are like their dad," Paul says. "But I can't see anything like me in Rocky."

Maybe Rocky's energy attracted Michelle, Paul says. Or maybe it was that she was an adolescent when they met, while Rocky, who looked much younger than his age, twenty-four, had access to an adult world that was new to her. His own place, booze, no authority demanding obedience from him. If she hadn't gotten pregnant at fourteen, hadn't had Kristy at fifteen, if he hadn't been *so much* older, their romance may well have gone the way of most teenage romances. High drama, deep infatuation, and then nothing. Move on to someone else. "I think he was old enough that he wanted to get things nailed down," Paul says. "Get a family going and stuff."

Paul says he and Michelle ate lunch together nearly every day. He worked nearby and took his midday break at her house, and he doubts Rocky ever knew. "I'd take my lunch over there and she'd have *Springer* on the TV and we'd sit there and watch it," he says. "I was closer to her than the other girls. I don't know why. She was close to me, too."

Paul reaches over, then, to a pile of homemade DVDs held together with a rubber band. He says they are for me to take, copies he made in advance of my visit. Home movies. Rocky used to film everything, year after year, particularly the camping trips they took as a family, pretty much every weekend. Rather than special occasions, holidays, birthdays, that sort of thing, the DVDs mostly show the everyday life of Michelle and Kristy and Kyle. Paul says he watched them all. More than once. He was searching for clues, anything that might have suggested what was to come, but there was nothing. They looked like any old family. Kristy, three years old, sitting on the couch watching cartoons. Kyle, child's fishing rod in hand, standing at the edge of a stream trying to catch a fish. Multiple videos of Michelle asleep in bed, woken up by a camera, and her husband calling to her from behind the lens. There were no clues, Paul says. It will be several years before I bring myself to watch them.

PAUL'S EX-WIFE, SALLY SJAASTAD, didn't know Rocky much better than Paul did, even in all the years he was around. The couple's two older daughters, Alyssa and Michelle, had gone to live with Paul when they were fifteen and fourteen, respectively. Sally and Paul had divorced years earlier—when Michelle was eight—and mostly the girls had lived with Sally. But when their teenage years hit, the girls discovered a freedom at their dad's house that simply didn't exist with their mom.

Sometimes Sally would call Paul and he'd have no idea where the girls were, or he'd say, "They're at so-and-so's house," and she'd drive by and they wouldn't be there. Once, Paul gave her an address that turned out to be the halfway house for boys coming out of Pine Hills and transitioning back to the real world. Boys with addiction problems or behavioral issues. Boys too young for jail, but too dangerous—to themselves, to others—to stay at home. Pine Hills was a live-in facility for troubled boys. A place well known to Sally because she did vocational rehabilitation for the state of Montana; she helped people who had disabilities, tried to find them work.

She pulled up that night in front of the transitional house, furious, searching for Michelle, who was just thirteen or fourteen at the time. The man who answered confirmed that Michelle had been there, but had gone off with a boy named Cody. Sally fumed. *My daughter*, she told the man, *is not allowed to come here again. Ever.* Michelle turned up three hours later.

Another time Sally pulled up in front of Paul's house and saw a green hatchback parked out front. A car she didn't know. She knocked on the door and no one answered. But she could see movement in the house, so she knocked harder. Again, no answer. She left, and came back a little while later. Same thing. She hollered through the crack in the door that if they didn't answer, she'd call the cops. That worked. Michelle opened the door. There was a young man there, with shaggy, layered hair, in jeans and a T-shirt. He had a strong jaw, like he'd spent his life clenching it. Full lips, and acne scars on his cheeks. It was the first time Sally met Rocky. He seemed shy, wouldn't make eye contact with her. She told him he needed to go, that he couldn't be there when Michelle's dad wasn't home. He mumbled something to her about how he'd been just about to leave.

Later, Sally told Paul that the boy was too old for Michelle. She didn't know how old he was, but any boy old enough to have his own car was a boy too old for fourteen-year-old Michelle. She thought they'd solved the problem then, she and Paul. Thought Rocky was out of Michelle's life. She never imagined Michelle would disobey her; in Sally's mind, Michelle was still her little girl, the one who did chores without asking and never skipped school. Michelle had never been the rebellious type. When it came time to grow up, which happened far sooner than any of them would have wanted, she did. Grew straight up into an adult. Missed most of her teen years entirely.

ROCKY WAS A WIRY guy, five foot five, and high-strung, jittery. Energetic. (His family describes him slightly differently, as quiet and sometimes devious, also on the shy side.) Before he shot himself, he took the videos, packed them in a bag, and put them in the garage. He wanted to be sure they'd be saved. Homage to a happy American family. If it'd all gone as planned, that might have been the story that survived. A Great American Tragedy. He'd written a message on his arms. No one was meant to see it, and no one can exactly remember what it said. Something like *I deserve to go to hell.*

The dents in Paul's front door, he says, are from a time Rocky tried to beat it down to get to Michelle. But at the time that didn't really register to him as violent, not dangerously so. It's the kind of violence that seems so difficult to evaluate in the moment, but crystal-clear in hindsight—which is to say that this is precisely what domestic violence looks like. Paul is hardly alone in his failure to register the portent of it. But imagine it's not Rocky at Paul's front door, beating at it, kicking it, screaming for a woman inside. Imagine it's a stranger. Who wouldn't call the police? Who wouldn't try to intervene to stop the violence? And yet when it comes to people we know, people we see in other contexts—as fathers, brothers, sons, cousins, mothers, whatever—we have trouble registering the violence. Now Paul says he'd intervene, he'd do something. Take the law into his own hands somehow. It's a Montana thing, the libertarian, individualist culture of the place. He doesn't trust the system. Doesn't think the police really did much to save his daughter. Or the prosecutor. "One thing I want to tell you that'll give you insight into Montana," Paul says. When he asked for the autopsies of the family, the coroner said he could release only those related to Paul by blood. Michelle, Kristy, Kyle. But not Rocky. But when Rocky's father, Gordon Mosure, asked, he got them. All four of them. "The point is the view that the man owns it," he told me. The patriarchy sets the rules. Paul shakes his head. "The more you think about it, the more it'll piss you off," he says. He pulls out a brown accordion file and shows me the three autopsy reports he managed to get. Kyle's report begins, "This young boy is received . . . with blood . . . saturating the clothes." The coroner noted that the decedent had recently eaten gummy candy. Kristy's report said her gunshot wound followed a "pattern of metallic snow." Her heart weighed 180 grams.

I POINT TO A plaque in Paul's living room. It's slightly off-kilter, hanging by itself on a large white wall. Engraved with Michelle's high school graduation. Billings Senior High School class of 1997. By then she was already living with Rocky and had two kids under the age of three, and she still graduated on time. She gave birth to Kyle a year after Kristy. She'd transferred to a high school for—as Paul puts it—"the kids who had kids," about six blocks past her old school. She'd have a stroller, both kids in it, and she'd have to push it uphill in Montana's harsh winters. "I remember seeing her do that and I think that was pretty remarkable." This is the moment Paul's been dreading. Bows his head. He's holding the plaque now. He's gotten up, taken it down from his wall, and is cradling it. He takes one hand and gently wipes across the top, cleaning the dust off. Then his hand trails down the front, eyes spilling over. He sucks in his breath, trying to gather himself together. This is why parents like him don't talk to me, men in particular. They'll do anything to avoid this moment.

Sally Sjaastad is different. I have spent hours with her, over the course of several years. She preserves her daughter's life in some measure by talking about her, by recounting and remembering all she can. She keeps everything of Michelle and the children, letters and art the kids made for her on holidays, notes from Michelle when she was young, stories about the murders from the local press. She drives me past the school Kristy and Kyle attended, where a rock and a bench with their names are a permanent marker to their memory. Sally says she aged overnight after the murders, gained seventeen pounds in four months, looked worn down and crumpled. When she shows me a picture of herself from when Michelle was alive, I don't recognize her even after she points herself out. I've found, in the face of overwhelming tragedy, that women often talk and talk, and men fall silent. Sally carries a swirl of memories like a nest around her; Paul holds those memories like stones inside him.

Michelle had always seemed to Sally to have a sense of responsibility beyond her years. She'd mow the lawn, wash the dishes, vacuum the carpet, all without being asked. One year she and her sisters worked the cotton candy machine and some of the games at Lunder's Kiddyland, and Michelle took the twenty dollars she'd made and stuck it in an envelope with a card that said it was to help her mom with groceries and other expenses. When Sally opened it, she broke down crying.

"It would have been very easy for [Michelle] to quit [school]," Paul tells me. His voice is quiet, a little ragged. He wipes at his eyes with the back of his hand. "I wasn't proud of her for getting pregnant, but I was pretty proud of that. She didn't give up."

Women like Michelle Monson Mosure share this steadfastness. A determination and resoluteness to keep themselves and their children alive by any means possible. They don't quit. They stay in abusive marriages because they understand something that most of us do not, something from the inside out, something that seems to defy logic: as dangerous as it is in their homes, it is almost always far more dangerous to leave. Many of them plan, like Michelle did. They stay. They bide their time. They keep their children safe. They balance, poised, on the front lines. Hypervigilant, and patient, in a constant scan for when they can slip away intact. They do it for as long as they possibly can.

Barnacle Siblings

Michelle and Rocky met that first time on a weekday after school at a house where a bunch of teenagers were hanging out. Alyssa had a best friend at the time named Jessica and Jessica had gotten together with Rocky first. The two of them were together for just a few weeks, maybe a month. Alyssa didn't even note his presence as remarkable, this bushy-haired stranger. It was only later, when Michelle confessed her feelings, that Alyssa could even recall Rocky. He had a muscly build and small pockmarks on his face. His hair was shoulder-length and layered. He was good looking, girls said. Funny.

Alyssa said Michelle had been taken immediately with Rocky. He seemed approachable, solid. He was a decade older and had spent a year in jail in Texas on a drug charge, but that didn't bother her. He had a job and his own place. There was something kinetic about an older guy showing interest in her. About not being under the wing of her parents. About having freedom.

That desire for freedom is why they'd moved in with Paul in the first place, of course. Paul was quiet, kept his thoughts and feelings to himself. His brain always calculating, fitting things together so they made sense. Maybe drank a little too much. But that's the way of most men. Especially in a place like Montana, where the term "good ole boy" is as ubiquitous as a May snowstorm and can mean anything from a cowboy to a lawyer, so long as they toss back a couple of cold ones and know how to work a gun and tie a decent fly. Rocky was a good ole boy. Most of the boys Alyssa and Michelle and Melanie knew back then were good ole boys.

The day Rocky and Michelle met, they were all at the house of a couple who Jessica babysat for. The relations and friendships overlap in Billings like geographical strata. Everyone knows everyone or knows of everyone. The house had a pool table and a garage, where teenagers would sometimes just gather. When Rocky drove up and Michelle saw him she must have felt the pull way down in her abdomen, because they were, almost instantly, a couple. Two or three days and that was that, Alyssa says. Rocky and Michelle were flat-out in love by the end of that first week.

WHEN MICHELLE CONFESSED TO Sally about her pregnancy, Sally wanted to press statutory rape charges against Rocky. She couldn't believe a man of his age would go for a teenager like Michelle. What was wrong with him? But Michelle swore she'd run away with Rocky and the baby if her mom so much as walked in the door of the police station. It gutted Sally. Would Michelle really run away? Forever? How could she protect her if she couldn't even find her? If she was out there in the world with a little tiny baby and not even old enough to drive a car?

Eventually, Sally sought the advice of a counselor, who advised her to wait it out, accept it as best she could, and try to stay supportive of her daughter. Rocky would get sick of Michelle. Sally remembers the counselor telling her, "He's not going to like having a girlfriend who can't go out and do anything." By the time of her death, Michelle had been to a bar one single time in her life. She never went on vacation with a friend. Never had friends over. She wasn't a part of a book group or a yoga circle or a young mothers' club. She wasn't a part of anything, really. Rocky was her world.

ALYSSA WONDERS IF THE older guy she was seeing back when Michelle and Rocky met might have contributed to why Michelle was so hell-bent on being with Rocky. Alyssa and Michelle were best friends. Always. Even as toddlers. In family videos they are always right there beside each other. Barnacle siblings. Giggling, crumpling together in a heap in front of the striped couch in their living room. The day Alyssa learned to ride a bike without training wheels, Michelle was right there on the grass watching her wobble her way down the sidewalk on her pink bike with the white basket in front. Alyssa disappears from the camera's view and then returns, slightly steadier, a proud smile on her face. She stops, doesn't get her feet planted in time, and over she falls, her rear end thwacking on a peddle. Sally scoops her up as she bawls.

And then the next scene it's Michelle's turn, red banana seat on her silver bike. She jets down the same sidewalk on two wheels, then returns, and when she returns, she's waving. Waving high to her father behind the camera, steering one-handed, grin as wide and confident as a moon sliver.

All the sisters were close. Melanie, the youngest, had ADHD, and after the divorce she had the hardest time. She'd scream, kick things, rage. Sally's focus was so much on Melanie that Michelle and Alyssa were left to themselves. They ratted up their bangs, put on lipstick and mascara, and listened to Aerosmith and AC/DC. Michelle had a teenage crush on Steven Tyler. They hung around Pioneer Park or North Park. Sometimes they'd go up to the Rims, a sandstone formation eighty million years old that rings the city of Billings. The Rims draws hikers, backpackers, dog walkers, and errant teenagers. At sunrise and sunset it beams with a fiery beauty reminiscent of the red rocks of Sedona. You can stand on the Rims and see the whole of the Billings valley and beyond. Millions of years in that view, the dispassionate waves of time passing.

But the Rims has another association. Every year, it seems, there'll be a body found up there, someone committing suicide, or someone running from the police who winds up injured or killed, falling from Sacrifice Cliff, a sandstone outcrop that juts into the Yellowstone River and has a five-hundred-foot drop at its highest peak. The story behind the name is that two Crow warriors returned to find their entire tribe wiped out by smallpox and they subsequently threw themselves off the cliff.[1]

The Rims is Billings's most well-known landmark, home to marmots, mule deer, falcons, bats, hawks, and several different snake species, including the western rattlesnake. Diamond-backed and laced with venom. Eventually, Rocky would acquire such a snake, bring it to the house where he lived with Michelle and their two children.

Whatever He's Holding Inside

Rocky was quiet in many of the same ways that Michelle was quiet. In crowds or around new people. He was troubled, rebellious, but he loved the outdoors. Fishing, camping. It's something he had in common with his dad. All of it, in fact: the outdoor stuff, the quiet, even his real name, Gordon, he shared with his father. The nickname had come from his dad when Rocky was a baby, a tribute to the boxer Rocky Marciano.

Gordon and his first wife, Linda, had three kids, of whom Rocky was the eldest. They lived, then, in Columbus, Ohio. Rocky had a younger brother named Mike and a younger sister named Kelly. The kids were close, but not overly. They fought, they hung out, they ignored one another, they protected one another. Mike and Kelly looked up to Rocky, their big brother.

If it'd been another time, another age, Gordon says he probably would have never married Linda. He'd spent four years in the Air Force and returned to find the sexual revolution in full swing in America. "I thought I'd died and gone to heaven," he told me. He says this with a stony face, devoid of pleasure or nostalgia. He found a girl, she got pregnant, and he forgot all about the sexual revolution. Went right back to his sense of being duty- and honor-bound, and figured the right thing to do was to marry the girl you got pregnant. "Her mother and father are saying, well, 'The baby's got to have a father.' Which, now you'd say, 'The baby's got a father, big deal.' [But] I went ahead and married her." Not that he didn't want the kids. He loved the kids, all three of them. Loved Rocky even after he became a handful.

When they divorced, Linda gave him full custody of all three kids. He had met someone at work pretty quickly after he and Linda separated. Sarah. (Linda did not want to go on the record with me, but she did claim Gordon and Sarah began dating while she and Gordon were still together.) His three kids would become Sarah's. She'd raise them.

29

She'd love them. She'd discipline them, too. Once, she remembers, back when they were still in Columbus, Rocky and Mike got into a fight in the living room. She says Rocky was picking at his brother relentlessly, until Mike finally blew up. "Mike got in trouble, and I said Gordon, it's not Mike, it's Rocky," Sarah tells me. Mike was boisterous. Mike would yell, but Rocky was the real agitator. "He was always setting up the others to get in trouble," she says.

Gordon and Sarah married in Ohio and two days later they moved with the three kids to Montana, where Gordon had a new job waiting for him. They didn't give the kids any warning. Or Linda. They think now they should have talked to the kids about it, should have eased the way. Given them some time to get used to the idea, maybe even visit once. "It was probably not the smartest thing to do," Sarah says. Linda said she had to hire a private investigator to find them. Gordon says she found them pretty much right away—his new boss was friends with his old coworkers. Yet still, her letters and cards were sporadic and it was five years before the kids saw Linda again.

"All the thinking, all the stuff that comes into your mind because you know—partly the *Men Are From Mars* thing—but I've always felt like there was something I could do to fix it and save the grandchildren," Gordon says. "I keep coming back to the divorce. How can it not affect kids? But how many millions of kids are involved in divorces every year?"

Although the kids had always had some trouble with school, after the move Gordon and Sarah discovered the kids were further behind than they'd realized, and though they hired tutors, the kids remained behind. None of them wound up graduating. Gordon claims that Linda planted the kids in front of the television or dragged them around with her wherever she went during the day, shopping or whatever. "Instead of teaching them ABCs and all this, they hadn't gotten any of that," Gordon says. When I spoke with Linda she remembered things differently, of course. Gordon admits he was the kind of father who tended to avoid conflicts, rather than confront them. Even Sarah says Gordon never shows any emotion at all, until "something political comes on TV. And oh, man, the roof blows off the house. Anything that doesn't directly impact our home, he'll react to. But if it's our home, our kids, whatever. No reaction," she says. "Part of it is the era in which he grew up."

"I have a master's in avoidance," Gordon says.

Rocky was in trouble after the move almost immediately. At twelve years old he was drinking excessively, engaging in petty thievery. He stole cassette tapes of bands he liked—Aerosmith, Black Sabbath. Once, he stole a bike. Sarah would find Mad Dog 20/20 bottles thrown over the fence into the weeds behind their backyard, and she'd know they'd come from Rocky. He was passive where Mike was aggressive. By seventh grade, Sarah and Gordon knew Rocky needed help.

They sent him to Pine Hills, the home for troubled boys.

They sent him to counseling.

Everyone zeroed in on the divorce, Gordon says. The therapists, the teachers at his school. Like it was the answer to everything: what went wrong, where Rocky went off the rails, why he started to drink so much that Sarah said his eyes would roll back in his head, tongue hanging out. But Gordon would think, *How could this be? Once we were divorced the fighting was over. Wasn't* that *something?* In a family counseling session once, the therapist asked Rocky if he was sad his mother had left, and he said, "No. It was better." Sarah turned to him and asked if he really believed that, and he said, "Yeah, it was better after she was gone because then we got to hang out with [Dad] more, but not have the big fighting between them."

Even if it was the divorce and the sudden move, even if these were the places you could point to where things went wrong with Rocky, what about fixing whatever was broken inside him? The therapy. The live-in treatment. Wasn't that Pine Hills's entire mission? To fix their son? What did it matter where his pain and anger originated? What was it that made him drink at thirteen, fourteen years old until he was incoherent? Made him shoplift whatever he could get his hands on? Made him agree to rules they'd set out about curfews and alcohol, and then just flout them again and again, like he answered to no one? Sometimes Sarah thought Rocky'd been born without a conscience. He could be charming or manipulative, devious or adorable, funny or quiet. Gordon remembers one of the counselors for alcohol treatment saying to him, once, of Rocky, "Whatever he's holding inside, he's not giving up."

Sarah tells me Rocky didn't have a lot of trust for women. Didn't really like them much. "I think when Linda did leave, they didn't all really talk about it. Gordon and the kids. Linda and the kids. I think that had to have affected him, because he was the firstborn and he was the favorite," Sarah says. Then she mentions their move, their sudden departure from Ohio to Montana. "When we all left, why didn't [we] all talk about it?" It seems so ridiculous to her now. What were they afraid of? "Ridiculous" is not the right word. There is no word for it. Why did they not discuss it? All of it? As a family? In the blinding glare of hindsight, the horror they now live with, how could they have once believed that an open, honest conversation about something as common in this world as divorce or remarriage or moving to a new state was so bad it could not be addressed aloud? Would it have explained something to Rocky that he needed an explanation for? Would it have reset his pain somehow?

BOTH SARAH AND GORDON say that Rocky never quite matured. When Michelle came into his life, she was so young, but then she became a mother, and she outgrew him. "That was never going to be understandable to him," Gordon says. "She had grown so much and he hadn't. And basically, the more you learn . . ." He stops. He wonders if the early drug and alcohol use impaired Rocky's emotional development.

This is how they exist in the world today, Sarah and Gordon. Locked in a constant search for what they could have done. It's the legacy of domestic violence homicide, a trauma embedded into entire swaths of families. *What did we miss?* They can't even quite mourn Michelle and Kristy and Kyle, because their minds flip instantly to the fact that they should still be here. Kristy graduating from college; Kyle maybe declaring his major. Or out fishing with his aging dad. Michelle in nurse's scrubs, leaning over some tiny newborn. They can't escape the fact of what Rocky did. That final act eclipsing entirely who he was, whatever good he had in him.

Sarah told me once that on a camping trip about a year before the end, she had a moment where she just felt this unbelievable relief and gratitude that they'd survived as a family. All those terrible, chaotic teenage years, with Rocky in Pine Hills, and then later in jail in Texas, and Mike rebelling and all the fighting. Finally, finally, she thought, they were a normal family. But the memory now no longer holds. She can't think back to that time without the magnetic pull of regret. What they might have missed, what might have been right under their noses.

They're not responsible.

They know this intellectually

But they do not feel it emotionally.

"You just don't want to go on," Gordon tells me. "But you don't have a choice."

They live in this suspended state of grief. A kind of emotional purgatory. They know they are not alone in their sadness, in their rage, but they believe they are alone in their guilt. Michelle's family carries all this, too. The rage, the sadness, but most of all the unbelievable, massive burden of guilt. *What did we miss?*

But you can't miss what you don't know to look for.

WHEN ROCKY BROUGHT MICHELLE home that first time, she was as quiet as he was, Sarah remembers. "She turned out to be really different," she says. Different from Rocky's quiet. "She talked a lot about how she knew people always thought quiet people were dumb. She knew that was what people thought of her, but unless she felt it was worth discussing something, she was quiet and took it all in."

Michelle didn't come around too much in those early days because Rocky had that trailer out in Lockwood. But right away Sarah and Gordon could see he was serious about this girl. When she got pregnant, they found out her real age and they were livid. If Michelle's parents pressed charges, Sarah remembers telling him, "We won't turn you in, but we won't save you either."

Michelle learned she was pregnant on her fifteenth birthday, in September 1993. The baby, Kristy, was due in April. Sally was outraged. She wanted to blame Paul for not watching closely enough. She wanted to blame Rocky for being with a fourteen-year-old. She wanted to blame Rocky's parents. She wanted to blame herself. But none of that would solve this problem. Michelle said Rocky was a great guy. A great guy. They just had to give him a chance. They just had to know him like she knew him.

In December of 1993, Sally took her three girls to Minot, North Dakota, for the holidays. Michelle had a backache that they all believed came from the eight-hour car ride. But then Michelle couldn't eat, she felt nauseated, and seemed to develop a fever. Sally got scared. Michelle was only six months along.

When they returned from Minot, Sally took Michelle to the hospital and told the nurses in the ward that her daughter was in labor. "I'd had three children. I knew what it meant, Michelle being in labor this early," she tells me. But it was hours and hours before anyone came in to look at Michelle. Sally felt like the doctors didn't take Michelle seriously because they saw her as just another throwaway teenage mother. It infuriated her. Michelle was in and out of the emergency room for the next two weeks.

When the hospital staff finally realized Michelle truly was in labor it was too late to stop it. The baby was coming. No one knew if it would be born alive or not. Sally was terrified. For her daughter, for her grand-child. When the baby eventually came, it was a girl with lungs so tiny and undeveloped she was put into the NICU and no one knew if she'd make it through the night, let alone the week, the month, her life. They named her Kristy Lynn. She had Rocky's last name, Mosure. She was a genetic mirror of her young mother, sharply defined upper lip, pale, searching eyes.

Kristy was practically the size of a teacup. And Michelle watched hour after hour, day after day, as the nurses tended to her tiny daughter, pumping air into her lungs, monitoring her, talking to her. To Michelle, it wasn't the machines keeping her daughter alive or the doctors or even her, really. It was the nurses. They were miracle workers. Kristy stayed in the hospital for months. Stayed, in fact, until Michelle's actual due date, when she was released still on oxygen and still being monitored by a machine to the care of Michelle and Sally. Michelle and her new daughter moved into Michelle's childhood bedroom upstairs in Sally's house. Every day, Rocky would be over there with them. Sally had to give him this. He came around; he called. She wouldn't let him live there, but she let him come every day, all day. Devoted, worried, trying to help in whatever way he could. Sally didn't like him much still, but she respected his dedication. And Michelle and Rocky did seem to be in love—with each other and with their new child.

Daddy Always Lives

In July of 1994, when Kristy was six months old, Sally returned home from work one day to find a note from Michelle. She'd written to her mother that she and Rocky and Kristy had to try to be a "real family." She said she owed it to her daughter to give her new young family a chance. She'd moved to Rocky's tiny trailer and would be living there, she told her mother. Devastated, Sally told Paul. They couldn't compel Michelle to return, of course. All they could do was try to be as supportive as possible, let Michelle know they'd be there for her.

Paul couldn't abide them all living in that tiny trailer. "I could reach out my arms and touch both walls," he said. So he bought a plot of land on the outskirts of Billings and began to build a new house for himself—the house where I would someday meet him. The house with the dented front door. He would rent his current house to Rocky and Michelle once he moved into the new one, and they could escape the dismal trailer.

Michelle had kept her word. She dropped Kristy at Young Families Early Head Start, a day care for high school kids who'd had children, and she returned to high school. To her family's surprise, she got pregnant again and had Kyle, just a little over a year after Kristy's birth. Not yet eighteen years old with two kids under two, but Michelle managed. Those were the days that Paul would sometimes see her pushing Kristy in the stroller, Kyle in the baby carrier, Michelle walking two miles in the harsh Billings winter to get to Young Families. She never asked for help. Eventually, Paul bought her a beat-up car so she could drive herself to school. She graduated on time.

MONEY WAS TIGHT. WHEN they'd first met, Rocky'd been working all over the western states on a seismic crew. The job sometimes required as many as twenty hours a day, seven days a week in locations far from

35

Billings, and so Rocky quit because he didn't want to be away from the family for long stretches. He'd work for a while, and then lose his job for one reason or another. He worked construction, or he was a roofer. Mainly jobs where the physical labor was demanding and pay never quite enough. Michelle told him she wanted to contribute; she had ideas about working as a maid at a motel behind their house, less than half a mile away. She'd be close enough that she could dash home if the kids needed her and she wouldn't even need a car to get there. But he blew up, said he wasn't going to have the mother of his children at a motel sleeping with all the guests. He got so angry about it that Michelle called Alyssa to come over, to be a presence in the house, in solidarity with Michelle. He was completely irrational and worked up, Alyssa said, pacing back and forth, outraged that Michelle would even entertain such a thought. It was the last time anyone can remember Michelle suggesting that she work outside the home.

Rocky's was the kind of control that evolves slowly, beginning with little things—most of which aren't illegal (though stalking, which Rocky eventually did to Michelle, often becomes part of the controlling behavior. Stalking is a crime in all fifty states, but can be charged as a felony in more than two-thirds only if it is not a first offense.[1]). Within the first couple of years, it became clear that it wasn't just Michelle's employment that he controlled, according to Sally and Alyssa. He wouldn't let her wear makeup. He didn't allow her to have friends over. He insisted they go camping nearly every weekend when the weather allowed. She never went out without him. Evan Stark, author of the book *Coercive Control: How Men Entrap Women in Personal Life*, coined the phrase "coercive control" to describe the ways an abuser might dominate and control every aspect of a victim's life without ever laying a hand on her. Stark's research shows that in as many as 20% of relationships where domestic violence is present there might be no physical abuse at all. A 2016 *New York Times* article by Abby Ellin put it this way: "To a victim of coercive control, a threat might be misinterpreted as love, especially in the early stages of a relationship, or when one is feeling especially vulnerable."[2] Especially vulnerable like a teenage girl being seduced by a grown man. Especially vulnerable like a young mother with no means to support herself.

In 2012 Stark wrote a paper in which he argued for laws protecting victims from such behavior: "Most tactics used in coercive control have no legal standing, are rarely identified with abuse and are almost never targeted by intervention." He cited, specifically, tactics such as monitoring or controlling the regular activities of life, particularly those traditionally associated with women—like parenting, homemaking, and sex. The control runs "the gamut," Stark wrote, "from their access to money, food and transport to how they dress, clean, cook or perform sexually."[3] Our current body of jurisprudence in the United States misses entirely the real devastation to someone in such a situation, the loss of liberty that eventually and inevitably leads to a loss of self. Kit Gruelle, an activist in North Carolina, calls such victims "passive hostages" in their own homes. Stark insists we look beyond just physical injury as a sign of extreme domestic violence; in his view, women like Michelle are prisoners. It's not at all unusual for people in such situations to talk about how their partners controlled how they looked, what they ate, what they wore, and who they communicated with. The abuser has, over the years, slowly cut off whatever escape routes—family, friends, community—may have once existed for them. And ultimately, coercive control is about stealing someone's freedom entirely.

Stark was instrumental in shaping a coercive control law that passed in 2015 in the United Kingdom that makes such actions punishable by up to five years in prison.[4] France, too, has a separate criminal statute for what it terms "psychological abuse." But in the United States, we have no such law.

ALYSSA REMEMBERS DRIVING WITH Michelle one afternoon. It was after Kristy's birth, but before Michelle was pregnant with Kyle. Alyssa thinks maybe Michelle was sixteen. Suddenly, from behind her, Rocky came flying up in his car, swerving around so he was on her driver's side, and hurtling into oncoming traffic. He began screaming through his open window at Michelle.

"Why didn't he die?" Alyssa asks now. "He did so many crazy things like that, daredevil things, but he never even got hurt." He jumped from cliffs into a natural lake, scaled across skinny trees bridging twenty-foot gaps, got wasted on meth, and never even had so much as an infection or a broken bone. Like some outside force kept him out of harm's way. Like he was stronger than anything that would dare threaten him. He was showing Michelle in every way he could that he would risk his own life before he would risk losing control over her.

Another crucial element of coercive control is isolation of a victim from her own family. It's an isolation that often has nothing to do with geography. After Kristy's first birthday, when Gordon gifted Rocky a video camera, members of Michelle's family almost never appear on the DVDs. Rocky filmed the kids in the backyard playing around, or maybe on Christmas, opening their gifts at Sarah and Gordon's. Or it'd be just the four of them camping. Occasionally, the tapes might show Mike's daughter—the eldest cousin to Kristy and Kyle. But Michelle's family? If one judged by the videos, one might think Michelle had come from nowhere, from no one. Sally rarely saw Michelle on holidays, though they lived just minutes from each other. Rocky would get mad when Sally visited, she told me, and he didn't often let Kristy and Kyle sleep over at their grandma's house. (They called her "Bugga.") Once, when Sally stopped by, Michelle said, "Mom, you need to get a life and stop coming over here so much."

Something made Sally uncomfortable after that. At the time, she was too taken aback by the comment to figure out just what it was that so unsettled her. She understood that Michelle had her own life, her own family to think about, but they'd always been close. Even in that tumultuous year of Michelle's first pregnancy, it was Sally she had turned to. It never occurred to Sally at the time that it wasn't really Michelle telling her to stop coming over so often—the words, yes, came from Michelle's mouth. But the spirit of the thing? "That wasn't Michelle speaking," Sally said. Not the Michelle she'd raised, anyway. Sally knows what it means now: that victims often side with their abusers publicly, to family, to police, to prosecutors. Because long after the police leave, even after charges are filed and a sentence meted out, it is with the abuser that a victim must continually negotiate her life. And the life of her children. Victims who side with their abusers during police calls do so not out of instability, as many law enforcement officers assume, but out of a measured calculation toward their future safety. Sally eventually saw this up close with her own daughter, though she didn't know at the time what she was really seeing.

WHEN PEOPLE TALK OF Michelle today, they refer to her unflappability, her calm in the face of stress, her absolute devotion to her children. But to her family she was also obstinate. And proud. She didn't want to have to go back to her parents and admit they were right. She wanted to be the other, more rare statistic: the one who made it. She was determined that her children would not grow up in what she called a "broken home." And this is one of those impossible equations that every parent tries to calculate in some measure: is it worse for the kids to have an imperfect parent—in Rocky's case abusive, addicted to meth—than to have no parent at all? In the endless constellation of ways we feel we can mess up our kids, which are those that will inflict the least damage?

And Michelle loved Rocky, at least in the beginning. He made her laugh. He was full of life. He taught the kids how to put up a tent, how to fish, how to hang a hammock. He taught them how to shoot a BB gun at a target. He zoomed them through the air as babies and changed their diapers. He pushed them on the swing set in their backyard and bundled them up to go sledding in winter. He was controlling, abusive, addicted to meth; he was also shy, insecure, loving. For a long time, it seemed a balance she could live with.

SALLY DOESN'T KNOW WHY Michelle didn't confide in her over the years; she supposes it has something to do with Michelle's pride—not wanting to admit she'd been wrong—and something to do with trying to save Sally's feelings, to not make her feel guilty for divorcing Michelle's dad. So rather than confide in Sally, Michelle occasionally talked to Sarah. She'd maybe mention Rocky's continuing drug use or how separate their lives seemed—Rocky out there all night in the garage working on his car, smoking whatever he could get his hands on, turning into a meth head, and Michelle in the house with the kids. Even people who spent time with Michelle, like Paul, who had those *Jerry Springer* lunches with her, didn't know what her life was really like because he was never there when Rocky was around. Melanie didn't have long, deep talks with Michelle; she was mostly in the garage, doing drugs with Rocky. And so it was Sarah, but even with Sarah, Michelle was private. "She talked in later years about her family and why she thought she was the way she was," Sarah says. "Through child development classes she had at school, she became very insightful about how people's minds work and why they do the things they do and behavior patterns and so forth . . . I wound up with so much respect for how smart she was and gentle."

And she *was* smart. Smart enough to know that getting away from Rocky wasn't something she'd be able to do overnight. It would require meticulous planning and preparation. Leaving is never an event; it's a process.

AFTER EVERYTHING HAPPENED, AFTER Michelle was killed, Sally was horrified to learn not simply that Michelle had been struggling with Rocky for her very life, but that she'd not said a word to her own mother—not until just weeks before she'd died, and even then, there was so, so much she left out. So much Sally would learn later.

Sarah had, in ways both subtle and overt, tried a few things to get Michelle out of the house in the months before the murders. She once left Michelle a brochure on local domestic violence services, including the Gateway House—Billings's local domestic violence shelter. She tried to talk to Michelle about it, but Michelle wouldn't hear of it. She suggested Michelle take the kids to her sister's place in Arizona for a while, but Michelle refused. She made these suggestions out of concern, and yet Sarah also worried she was overstepping her bounds, nosing into Michelle's life uninvited. She often felt this way around Michelle, even about small things. One of the home videos shows her sitting with Kristy in Michelle's backyard. Kyle is swinging on the swing set and Rocky is filming them all. Kyle isn't yet two years old and his hair is shaggy and feral. Sarah asks if he's had a trim and Rocky says no, he doesn't think so.

"I could trim it just a little in the back," she says. Her voice full of trepidation. It's a summer day, the kids' faces sticky with leftover snacks. "If she'd want me to. I wouldn't want to butt in."

She says it twice, three times. She could do it, but she doesn't want to upset Michelle, doesn't want to go where she's unwanted. The moment is telling. Should Sarah, as the mother-in-law, take charge of something that is simultaneously benign and intimate?

"It grows back," Rocky tells her. "It's just hair."

IT IS 2017, AND I am sitting on the back porch of Gordon and Sarah Mosure's house, at a table underneath a sunshade on a bright spring day in an outer suburb of Billings. Sarah has served us iced tea and crackers and cheese. It is Mother's Day. The two of them do not have plans. Like Paul, Gordon has never spoken with anyone about the murders.

The couple's two dogs sniff around us in search of fallen cheese. The backyard, at least by urban standards—which are my standards—is sprawling, with bright green grass that appears tended with great care. At the far end of the yard in a rectangular cutout is a garden with lavender and bleeding hearts. A boulder sits in the middle of the garden with a bronze plaque embedded into it.

Rocky's father, like his son, is a small man, maybe five foot six or five foot seven, and so very quiet. When he speaks, I often have to lean in to hear him. He wears a baseball hat, Rainbow Run Fly Shop, a gray Eddie Bauer shirt, and a cloth belt with fish on it. The man belongs in the river, in waders with a fly fishing pole in hand. "I believed him, stupidly," Gordon says to me. He's recounting the time he took Rocky's gun—an heirloom from Michelle's grandfather—and thought that would be the end of it. It takes an enormous amount of imagination to believe—before the moment it happens—that a person you raise from a baby to an adult could ever be capable of murder. And after it happens, Gordon asks, "How do you ever get past that? Whenever you think about it, you can't put an end to it because it's 'why, why, why?' and of course you never know why."

He tells me of one night when Michelle called in a panic. Rocky had threatened to kill them, she said. He was carrying her grandfather's hunting rifle. Gordon rushed over to pick up Michelle and the kids. Rocky had already fled the house. After a while, Michelle convinced Gordon that she knew how to talk to Rocky and the four of them returned. "I took him in the other room," Gordon said, "and asked, 'Son? What are you doing? You can't do this.'" Rocky said he knew, he knew. Of course he knew. Gordon emptied the gun, then collected whatever ammunition he could find in the garage and elsewhere, took it all home to his place. Crisis averted.

It was crazy, Gordon told me. "I got in his face. I told him, 'You just don't do things like that.' [Rocky] said he'd never do anything to harm them. I believed him, stupidly." *I believed him, stupidly.*

Gordon begins to cry, silently. Sarah reaches for him. Reminds him that it wasn't his fault. I feel something utterly crushing inside him. Guilt, self-blame. "It's just," he starts, sucks his breath, "you think you should have been able to fix it, or protect the grandchildren, 'cause that's what we men do, right? And I feel like, 'Why wasn't I smart enough to see what was going on? Figure it out? Anything?'" He tells me Rocky was quiet and could also be very gentle. "You'd never imagine he'd do anything like that." Gordon's voice is a broken whisper. I think of Paul Monson; how much these men strain to keep such colossal pain inside them. How unfair it is that we live in a world in which they're made to believe their tears are shameful.

AS THE YEARS WENT by, Michelle grew up, grew out of Rocky, Sarah says. In their many camping videos, Michelle has a near constant expression of tolerance. She smirks, but rarely smiles. She rolls her eyes. She looks away from the camera, puts her head in the crook of her elbow, curled up sitting on a rock. She doesn't perform for the camera like Rocky does, doesn't ham it up. She doesn't pretend to be happy if she isn't. She makes no secret of her dislike of being filmed, or having her picture taken. Hours and hours of videos where she's planted on a boulder watching the kids fish at the shoreline or dip their toes in the icy river, the crackling sounds of the forest—birds singing, water gurgling over stone, the snap of a tree branch—an infinite orchestra. It begins to sound like isolation itself, this music of nature, the sadness of a single hammering woodpecker.

Rocky is behind the camera lens. He pans across the rocks and birch trees till the lens settles on his young wife. Long brown hair, straight as a nail file, she carries their daughter, Kristy, down over the rocks. Kristy wears pink sweats and a too-big camouflage hoodie. 49ers knit cap. She seems unhappy. Quiet. Thoughtful for a child, like she's working out a complicated problem. How to get over the rocks, maybe. Kyle's not in the frame. He's off somewhere. He's the goofball, the giggler. Rocky's voice from behind the camera says "Smile" to his wife. She looks into the lens. Half-smirk, half-smile. Then a video of Michelle perched on an enormous boulder with the kids sitting crisscrossed around her. Kristy leans on her mom. They look identical, genetics coded in their willowy limbs and toothy smiles. The camera jitters from here to there, from pine tree to the Canadian thistle underfoot, and then suddenly we're in the camper where Michelle and Kristy sit across from each other at the linoleum table. Rolls of toilet paper sit on the windowsill behind Kristy. She's got one arm across the table, lying on it, coughing. "Sick girl," says Rocky. "You don't look happy." No one answers him. Bandit the pit bull is outside in their tent, lounging atop sleeping bags. Kyle sits on a log in a Mickey Mouse shirt. In the distance, the rush of the waterfalls, the spring birds. The quiet of their campsite is jarring after the scenes at home; heavy metal music pounding in the background eternally. When the kids are watching TV, when they're playing in the yard, when they're sitting at the table or on the couch, the music is ubiquitous, constant as a toothache.

The next view is behind a boulder. Waterfalls ribbon around a stack of rocks that surround Rocky. He calls Bandit. The dog stays. Calls him again. No luck. He reaches out, grabs the dog's forepaws, and tries to pull him forward. But the dog ripples with muscle and rebellion and fear. Rocky tries again, then gives up. Bandit backs away cowering, unaware of his own power. "That's right, Bandit," Michelle says. "Too dangerous." The video cuts off.

A top bunk in the tiny camper, body prone. "There's Big Mama sleeping up in her bed," Kristy says.

Michelle mumbles, "Big Mama."

Kristy's got the camera. Rocky searches for clean socks in their camper's cabinet; Kyle asks if he can "camcorder." Both kids use the word as a verb. The view jiggles as Kristy hands it to him without complaint. Kyle pans up his dad's body. Jeans, maroon T-shirt, white baseball cap with black rim. "Big Daddy," he says.

"What's my name?" Big Daddy asks.

"Rocky Mosure."

"Rocky what?" Big Daddy asks.

The kids aren't sure.

"Rocky Edward Mosure."

It's Gordon Edward Mosure.

From Kyle's vantage, his father looms like a streetlamp, so tall his head could have rested in a cloud.

"Why am I never Michelle?" Big Mama says to Rocky. "I'm Mama."

Why am I never Michelle?

In a video from the spring of 2001, Michelle's behind the camera. A rare event. Kristy wears a blue-and-yellow sleeveless vest, Kyle a fishing vest. Rocky's off a little ways in the distance, wading thigh deep in the river with the arabesque of a fly fishing line careening back and forth, and Bandit sniffs the sand nearby. Michelle moves the camera across the landscape. Lodgepole pine, juniper tree, fir tree. They fish into the creek. Morris Creek, maybe. Antelope Creek. No one quite knows anymore. Igneous rock formations piled behind Rocky. Michelle asks if the kids know what month it is.

"No," Kyle says.

"No?"

They're quiet for a long stretch. Then Kristy says, "April."

"April. May," Michelle says. "What day?"

But the kids don't answer. They sit on the sand. Kyle fishes. Kristy watches the water. Bandit runs across the view, light brown fur with a large white splotch across his neck. The camera pans quickly across the landscape, across the family, and down, down, down to her own hand. Left hand, wedding band. She holds it there for a moment. Just long enough to understand it's deliberate. Her fingers are thin and long, her wedding ring a small square-cut diamond on a diamond band. The wedding band itself matching diamonds. The camera holds, sees this, notes this, pans away. It moves back up and cuts out.

In the next frame, we see Rocky tiptoeing across a fallen tree that bridges across huge boulders and a series of waterfalls. He smirks for the camera, grins, holds up one knee and his arms like the Karate Kid. The children laugh. *Daddy is crazy!* Rocky makes it to the end, springs up to a rock, looks around, then makes his way back, holding out both arms for balance. When he gets to the other side, safely among the leafy spurge, Kyle says, "Daddy always lives!"

Michelle has a hunting rifle aimed at a target on a tree. She misses. Then it's Rocky's turn. Then Kristy has a turn in her green bathing suit. Then Kyle; the rifle is taller than the children. Alyssa and her boyfriend, Ivan Arne, are with them this time. Ivan's hair runs all the way down his back in a scraggly blond ponytail. Rocky calls himself the family photographer.

"Alyssa, you can have my job," Michelle says, meaning Alyssa can take over for those few times she's expected to film. Ivan takes a hatchet to some firewood.

Rocky ties a fly onto a fishing pole, and then he and Ivan go the shoreline and throw in their lines. The river moves fast, ridges of white foam popping up over the rocks. "Hon," Rocky tells her, "you don't have a job."

A Bear Is Coming at You

I meet Ivan one night at his house, which he shares with several large dogs who sniff around continually for the meat he's just smoked himself and served me on a paper plate. It is the most delicious meat I have ever encountered. In Montana, people have smokers in their yards with the same ubiquity that the rest of America has backyard grills. To me they're a cultural oddity; something I didn't even know an individual person could own until I came here and saw how everyone owns one. Alyssa is also at Ivan's with her daughter. Though they've long since broken up, Alyssa and Ivan remain close friends. People wander in and out. Leather-jacketed motorcycle-driving type of tough guys who shake my hand, graze at Ivan's meat, wander outside to smoke and drink beer. Ivan's hair is shorter now, and his face is rounder than in the videos, but he looks like a solid Viking descendent.

Ivan was Rocky's best friend growing up. As kids, they played Pong and Atari, rode bikes around the neighborhood. Ivan says Rocky was always in trouble—stealing, drinking—but he kept quiet about his problems at home. One day, Ivan says Rocky just vanished and it turned out he'd gone into Pine Hills for the better part of a year, and after that, Rocky moved to Florida for a while to live with his real mom, who had relocated there, and Ivan didn't hear anything about him.

Ivan and Rocky reconnected after Rocky and Michelle got together and the kids were born. Then Ivan and Alyssa started dating, and they moved in together, and Rocky would sometimes come by the house to hang out with Ivan, but Michelle almost never came. "Her age is something he never talked about," Ivan told me. "I knew he was controlling, but I never knew he was abusive."

In the early days, Rocky and Ivan partied together, snorting coke, drinking to oblivion. But after a while, Ivan said he'd had enough. He slowed down, stopped partying, went to school, and became a designer at a consulting firm for electrical transmissions. "He didn't want to quit," Ivan says. "He had no intention of quitting . . . I'd be like, 'Dude, you're going to kill yourself. What're you doing? Enough's enough.' And he'd say, 'I'll be fine.'"

The two would go weeks, sometimes longer, without talking. Rocky wasn't open to confrontation when it came to what he considered his personal life—which was anything to do with Michelle and the kids. Ivan had started dating Alyssa when he was in his early twenties, and slowly, as he heard stories from Alyssa of what was going on in Michelle's house, he'd try to broach the subject with Rocky. "[Rocky would] say things like, 'Dude, it's none of your business.' He was dealing with it; it was his family and don't worry about it," Ivan told me.

Ivan knew things were bad, but he didn't know just how bad, and he didn't know what to do. On several occasions, when Michelle managed to get away for a few hours to Alyssa and Ivan's place, she'd wonder aloud what Rocky was capable of. She'd talk vaguely about how he'd threatened her or threatened the kids. Ivan said he didn't realize what she was really asking him, how he was the only friend she knew who'd grown up with Rocky, and she wanted to know, needed to know, whether her husband would ever follow through on his threats to kill her, to kill their children. Ivan didn't understand that she was speaking this kind of code, using the words most victims of domestic violence use—weighed under by shame, by fear, by economics. Ivan would say to her, "I couldn't see him hurting you, especially not the kids." Never the kids.

What Ivan didn't know and Michelle didn't share was that Rocky would sometimes take the kids away from Michelle if he was angry at her. He'd disappear with them for hours, take them to the movies, camping, or wherever, and Michelle would be stuck there at home, worried, frantic that maybe this time he wouldn't come back, and the kids became pawns, a way for him to keep her obedient, conciliatory. A way for him to make sure she didn't leave. By the time he'd return, she'd just be thankful they were okay. He didn't need to hit her. He had all the control he required.

ALYSSA AND MELANIE SPENT more time at Michelle's house than anyone in those years. Melanie, by now, had developed a full-blown drug habit herself. Rocky had offered her a hit of meth when she was in high school and for the first time ever she'd felt like she could focus. It was a kind of self-medication for her, kept her alert for days on end so that she could do her schoolwork and hang with her friends and still have time to do whatever came her way. She didn't like Rocky, didn't like to be around him, but he provided her with drugs and so she tolerated his mania. They'd be out there in the garage, away from the house, and Rocky would have one or the other of his Mustangs in there, hood up, wheels off, and he'd talk and talk and talk, a completely different human being from the silent man with downcast eyes who'd sit at their holiday table. Melanie says he dabbled in dealing, earning a little extra cash on the side. As a construction worker, he was often unemployed through the winter, and since he refused to allow Michelle to work, money was always tight.

Once, Melanie said, he took her with him on a drug deal across state lines, to North Dakota. Crossing state lines drew a bigger charge if he got caught, Rocky told her, so he was bringing her along, and all she had to do was say the drugs were hers if they got caught. She was a minor and she'd hardly be in trouble at all, he'd promised. Melanie was young and stupid and wanted drugs, so she went along with it. They did these occasional drug runs, leaving after Michelle went to bed, and getting back home before she'd wake. He'd give Melanie an ounce of weed for going with him. Those moments sometimes haunt her now, especially since she has children of her own. She's been clean for a while now, a few years, but the pull toward drugs is always there, and the terrible knowledge of all she's skirted is like a deep-bellied tug that just never quite goes away.

As the years went by, Melanie says, Rocky grew more and more paranoid, the drugs took over logic and reason. He told her once that the FBI was watching him, watching both of them. That they couldn't be too careful. He thought they had cameras set up in the alley behind his house. Melanie knew it was the drugs talking, but she kept quiet and tried to ignore his ranting. After he started shooting up, Melanie says she stopped coming around. She was in her late teens by then, and one night Rocky told her the Feds were coming out of the garbage cans in the alleyway, and she says she just couldn't be around him anymore. It was exhausting. In the year before the murders, Rocky had gotten clean, in fact. But Melanie says it was too late, his mind already far too compromised.

Alyssa says Rocky tried to entice her with drugs, too, early on, but she refused him. Alyssa says she never trusted him after the day he drove into oncoming traffic to scream at Michelle. It was a glimpse into his madness, how he'd put his own and others' lives in danger to avenge the perception he had of being wronged. There were times he'd yell at Michelle for how often Alyssa came over, for how much time they spent together, but Alyssa seemed to be the one person he couldn't force Michelle to avoid.

Still, Michelle didn't confess to Alyssa just how much she put up with from Rocky. And their marriage wasn't without the normal pressures of most marriages: finances, young children, expectations and responsibilities in and out of the home.

Sally says Michelle always wanted to go to college, but felt she had to wait until her kids were in school. Once Kyle started kindergarten, she enrolled immediately at Montana State University in Billings and applied for financial aid. The school told her she had to show her parents' tax returns in order to qualify for any kind of aid and she was aghast. She'd been on her own for years by then; they hadn't claimed her since she was maybe fifteen, and she told the school she wouldn't do it, there had to be some other way to qualify for financial aid. As an adult, with no income of her own outside of her boyfriend, and no savings, she thought she'd just automatically qualify for aid.

Get married, they told her, and you'll qualify.

Sally got a call that very afternoon from Michelle. She said she and Rocky were going to get married at a justice of the peace the following Wednesday afternoon and could Sally attend. It was both sudden and anticlimactic. She and Rocky had been together for nearly eight years by that point. For Michelle, it was the biggest irony of her life, a system that forced her to marry a man she was working so hard to leave.

In their wedding photos, Michelle is painfully thin and wears a pastel tea-length dress. Kristy and Kyle crawl on the grass underneath the table where Michelle and Rocky cut their cake. Both families are there, a couple of other guests, and the reception is held under a picnic awning at the park. The day is sunny, everything a verdant green. Michelle isn't smiling.

At MSU that fall, she began taking her required general education courses. Her plan was to be a nurse. She'd never forgotten how the nurses had cared for Kristy when she was in the NICU, how much she credited them with keeping her daughter alive. The campus was close enough to her house that she could walk. So she'd drop off the kids at their school, and then she'd go to school herself, and always, always, there was Rocky, following her on the days he could, making sure she was going where she said she was going, doing what she said she was doing. He made no attempt to hide the fact that he was following her, as if he wanted her to know, wanted her to get the message that she was his to control, that he was allowing her this luxury of school, but one misstep, and it would all be taken away from her.

She found it difficult to study in the afternoons or evenings, with the kids always in need of something—food, entertainment, bedtime routines—and Rocky always interrupting, so she told him she needed to study in the library or she had no hope of passing her classes. But Rocky refused. She told him she had a study group, other students from her classes. They were all meeting in the library. But still Rocky refused. She could study at home, or she could forget college. So she lied. Told him she'd signed up for another class, and then snuck to the library to study in peace and quiet. She had to track it, the schedule, to make sure she didn't screw up and miss a study session or Rocky would know. Until her death, she managed to keep this lie from him.

IN THE FALL OF 2001, Michelle began to suspect Rocky was having an affair. She claimed to have evidence of this affair, but Rocky denied it. Alyssa remembers talking to her about it, hearing her say she'd put up with so much from Rocky already, that she wasn't going to put up with this. Sally thinks of it with a slightly different shading: "Michelle needed a reason to leave him. She had too much pride to just go, and she knew he'd come find her." The affair provided a kind of cover for Michelle, a rationalization to end a marriage that anyone would understand. Michelle said she was afraid she'd catch a disease, so Sally took her to see a doctor at the Riverstone Clinic. She said she couldn't study; she was so consumed by fear and anger. She had always been a bit of a hypochondriac, Sally said. And she needed to be able to do her homework. The doctor gave her a prescription for antidepressants. Later, Michelle confessed to Sally that Rocky found them, said he wasn't going to have a "psycho-wife" on meds, and threw them away.

One afternoon in late September, Michelle showed up at Sally's house with the kids and asked her mom to watch them. She said she was going home to confront Rocky about the affair. Whatever you do, Sally remembers Michelle saying to her, don't let Rocky take them. And then she left.

An hour and a half later, Rocky showed up at Sally's house. She saw his white Subaru pull up to the curb and she ran to the front door to lock it, following Michelle's instructions. He had a look in his eye that scared her, she later said. To Sally, Rocky had always been just a silent presence at the dinner table, or a shadow sitting in a car. To see him now, his face twisted with rage, was shocking. He stormed through her yard, arrived at the back door just as she clicked the dead bolt. He threw his body against the door and she heard a crack. She told Kristy and Kyle to go to the living room. Melanie was there, too, six months pregnant. Sally heard another crack as Rocky continued to pound the door with his small frame. She yelled to Melanie to call 911. Kristy and Kyle were on her couch, and when she looked at them she saw something that chills her to this day. They didn't show terror or hysterics. They weren't screaming. They weren't crying. They had gone still, their eyes in a kind of catatonia. *My god*, Sally thought, *they've seen this before. They've seen their father like this.*

She heard the crack of glass as Rocky broke the back door window, and then his pounding footsteps across the kitchen. She threw her body on top of Kristy and Kyle, grabbed hold of the couch, and tried to shield them from their father. Rocky grabbed Sally by her neck and one arm, and threw her off them. He grabbed Kristy, held her around the waist. Kristy didn't make a sound, except to say to Sally, "It's okay, Bugga. I'll go." By now, Melanie had called 911. Sally was still partially atop Kyle. Rocky's arm was dripping blood all over. He stormed past Melanie, who tried to block him from leaving through the front door. With one hand, he yanked her away violently. And then he was at the door of his car, tossing in Kristy like an oversized stuffed animal he'd won from a county fair. He peeled out from Sally's house.

It was over in minutes.

THE POLICE, WHEN THEY came, were uninterested, Sally said. They asked her what she wanted them to charge Rocky with. "I mean, isn't that your job?" she remembers thinking. A year after the murders, the chief of police at the time, Ron Tussing, would acknowledge to a local reporter that they could have acted slightly more "sympathetic," adding, however, "it's obviously more routine for us than it is for the victim in these cases."

Rocky was eventually charged with misdemeanor criminal mischief for breaking in to Sally's house. The police report filed from that day downplayed, in Sally's opinion, the violence of the moment . . . the breaking glass, the screaming, the volcanic rage in Rocky's body. It said only that Rocky "broke out the rear window at his mother-in-law's residence while gaining entry into her home to remove his nine-year-old daughter." (She was seven.) But Sally has photographs from that night showing the broken glass, the blood on her wall, the injuries to Melanie, whose arm bruised from elbow to wrist, scrapes and scabs where he had drawn blood. And Sally has her own memory of the children's eyes—so vacant, so nonplussed—and Rocky's eyes, so terrifyingly cold. A look she would come to describe as sheer evil.

Michelle and Kyle slept at her mom's house that night. It was the end of September 2001, and for the first time since she had gotten together with Rocky, Michelle began to tell Sally of her years with him, of how he controlled her movements and who she socialized with, of how he tried to keep her from seeing Alyssa, of how he'd take the kids for leverage, of how he'd threaten the three of them. Stories of being beaten in front of the children. Many people told me they didn't think Rocky was physically abusive. Gordon and Sarah, Paul, Melanie. None of them saw outright evidence, they told me. Sarah says she'd have seen bruises on Michelle at some point and never did. But Sally and Alyssa both say Rocky's abuse was physical, and Michelle herself wrote of his physical abuse in an affidavit that she later recanted. Sally tells me this as we sit on her couch, a large framed photo of Michelle and the two children looming in the corner. Sally's house is just a mile from where Michelle lived and died with her children, in a quiet corner of Billings near the airport and Montana State University, where Michelle took her classes. Directly behind Michelle's house is a parking lot for the emergency room of St. Vincent's Hospital, literally steps away from where she died.

That night was the first time Sally heard about a rattlesnake Rocky had recently acquired from somewhere and kept in a cage in their living room. Michelle was terrified. He told her he would put it in her bed while she slept or sneak it into the shower with her. A murder that would look like a freak accident. Sally understood immediately that her daughter's situation was far beyond her own casual acquaintance with domestic violence. She sat and listened, but felt ill-equipped about what, exactly, to do. She called Paul and asked him to get rid of the snake. She begged Michelle to take out a restraining order against Rocky. Michelle promised her mother that she would.

"I urged her to write it down, all of it," Sally said. And Michelle did. In her affidavit, she wrote: "He beat me in front of my kids. One of the times was Tuesday night on the back porch in front of my son—Kyle. He made death threats in front of my children, sisters and his parents. The death threats were that he would kill me, himself and my kids if I ever leave him."[1]

Rocky and Kristy, meanwhile, had spent the night in his car. Later, Kristy would say they'd gone "camping." In the morning, he was arrested when he returned home to get items to stock the family's camper; presumably he'd been planning to take Kristy camping in the woods for the weekend. Instead, he went to jail.

Michelle filed for a restraining order. The charge was called partner and family misdemeanor assault (PFMA), and the attorney general's office filed it—in the same court docket—alongside Sally's earlier complaint, linking the two in an administrative hiccup that would have far-reaching consequences. In Montana, it takes three PFMA charges before a domestic violence misdemeanor assault can be charged as a felony.[2]

That Saturday night, with Rocky in a holding cell at the local jail, Alyssa took Michelle to a bar for her birthday. It was Michelle's first time in a bar. The first time the sisters went out, alone, without fear of Rocky. Michelle just couldn't quite relax, Alyssa said. She worried about the kids, about whether she was doing the right thing with Rocky. She didn't want to keep her kids from their father; she just wanted their father to change.

"She had one drink," Alyssa said. And then she just wanted to go home, be with the kids. She was twenty-three years old.

"He tried to convince Michelle that the outside world was where the danger was," Melanie told me. "His influence was huge. He didn't want her to see that [the danger] was him. He wasn't safe."

ON MONDAY, SARAH AND Gordon bailed Rocky out of jail for $500. Sarah says it was the only time they'd ever bailed him out, that she was against it but decided not to stand in Gordon's way, and that she called Michelle to tell her. She says that Rocky had called over the weekend, crying, upset, saying he didn't do anything wrong, he was just a father trying to get his child. And then Gordon called a bail bondsman who happened to be a woman, and he remembers her telling him how a lot of "these women" just make all this stuff up about violence. They called Michelle and said they were going to get him. This was back when Sarah and Gordon believed that a restraining order mattered.

Michelle, in Sally's words, "freaked out." She started yelling on the phone, and they promised her they were taking him to his brother's house and he would stay there until things were sorted out, whatever that meant. Sarah thought if he stayed with Mike they could account for him better. And they thought he had maybe changed. He'd been clean for the better part of six months by then. Michelle still had her order of protection. Sarah said she was "wound up. She was not the Michelle I knew." She was irrational, angry one minute and scared the next. She said she wouldn't go to a shelter—why should she? The house was hers, her father's. And Rocky would find them anyway. She said she'd become an exotic dancer to support the kids. Then she said she'd be fine, they'd all be fine, because her father had given her Mace. The Mace would protect her. The Mace would keep her safe.

"There was no reasoning with her," Sarah said.

Michelle's response was the response of most victims.

She thought of the children.

She did not think of the criminal justice system, or whatever domestic violence resources were available to her. She did not calculate what areas of Billings would be off-limits to Rocky with her order of protection. Her response was autonomic: fight or flight? What do you do if a bear is coming at you? Do you rear up and scream to make yourself big or do you play dead? You certainly don't sit and consider the wildlife protection services that might be available to you if the bear would only give you a little time to gather yourself together.

And then there's this: the bear isn't just coming at you. It's coming at your children, too. What do you do?

Would the district attorney be there, in her house, when Rocky was released? Ready to protect her? Would a police officer be there, gun drawn, convincing Rocky that Michelle and the children hadn't meant to piss him off? Would her family members be there? Would anyone, anywhere, in any system be there to stop whatever he might do? To stop the rattlesnake from slithering into her bed at three a.m.? To deflect the bullet that might fly from a grandfather's heirloom rifle? Melanie said the minute she got that call from Gordon and Sarah, Michelle's demeanor changed. "Her confidence about the restraining order, everything changed," Melanie said.

Michelle recanted.

This is one of the most profoundly misunderstood moments in any domestic violence situation.

Michelle did not recant because she was a coward, or because she believed she had overreacted, or because she believed Rocky to be any less dangerous. She did not recant because she was crazy, or because she was a drama queen, or because any of this was anything less than a matter of life and death. She did not recant because she had lied. She recanted to stay alive. She recanted to keep her children alive.

Victims stay because they know that any sudden move will provoke the bear.

They stay because they have developed tools, over the years, that have sometimes worked to calm down an angry partner: pleading, begging, cajoling, promising, and public displays of solidarity, including against the very people—police, advocates, judges, lawyers, family—who might be the only ones capable of saving their lives.

They stay because they see the bear coming for them. And they want to live.

Why victims stay isn't the question we need to be asking. Rather, I think a better question is: how do we protect this person? No qualifiers. No musing about why she stayed or what she might appear to be doing or not doing. Just one simple question: how do we protect her?

WITHIN MINUTES OF ROCKY'S arrival at his brother's house, Michelle was on the phone with him, making plans, making promises, negotiating—though she wouldn't have put it this way—for her very life. "She needed more time to figure out what she was going to do," Melanie said. "And now I know it was all out of fear, her changing instantly as soon as she knew Rocky was out of jail."

Michelle stormed into the Billings district attorney's office, hysterical, as the former district attorney, Stacy Farmer (now Tenney) described it to me later. Michelle recanted everything. *He'd never made a threat,* she said. *There was no snake. She was the one who was to blame. He was a wonderful husband. A wonderful father.* It was the two of them, her and Rocky, against the world. The system was doing this to her family. Stacey Tenney said she knew Michelle was lying. Of course she was lying. But what can a prosecutor do with a hostile witness? There was no evidence; there was no witness.

Years later, I would think of Michelle, this moment, as I'd listen to a domestic violence advocate tell me: "We now know it's the ones who don't show up in court, who don't renew the restraining orders, who are in the most danger."[3]

Stacy Tenney said the snake thing got them all. It was just so specific a detail, such an obvious fact in the shape of the overall story, but at the house, when the police supposedly checked, there was no snake. If there'd been a snake, they might have had material evidence. But they never found a snake. (It is also unclear if they looked. Did they check the garage? Police reports in Montana are not public record.) It was her word against his, and now she was going back on her word, siding with him. What could they do? In court documents, the affidavit filed in support of Sally's claim said just two sentences about the violent incident at her house: "Def broke out the rear door window at his mother in laws [sic] residence while gaining entry into her home to remove his nine year old [sic] daughter. The def was upset that his wife had dropped her off there while the two of them were involved in a domestic dispute." Nothing about assaulting Sally or Melanie, nothing about the blood on Sally's wall, her account of the glazed look of the children, the terror and sheer strength of Rocky in that moment.

"The criminal justice system," Tenney told me, "isn't set up for uncooperative witnesses." And Tenney had enormous gaps in her knowledge, just as they all did then about Rocky and Michelle's history. I'll hear this same thing from prosecutors around the country over the years.

But I'll also hear this: murder trials happen every day in this country without victim cooperation.

UPON BAILING OUT OF jail, Rocky broke the restraining order immediately by accepting the call from Michelle. She later said he had a right to talk to his kids. They met the following afternoon, at North Park, where she and Alyssa used to hang out and smoke cigarettes after school. It must have seemed like another lifetime to Michelle. No one knows exactly what Rocky said to her, but he convinced her to let him return home. Perhaps he found a way to remind her that it was his work that paid the bills, kept food on the table, clothes on the kids' backs. He did provide for her; he also kept her from providing for herself. And where could Michelle hide in the small city of Billings, where everyone knows everyone? Was she going to pull the kids out of school and sequester all three of them at the top of a glacier?

And now she'd gone and invited bureaucracy into the privacy of their home, their life. "It broke so many boundaries between them, her telling on him," Alyssa said. "She was exposing him for who he really was in the eyes of others—something she hadn't done before. It was taking some of his control from him, and she had to give it back to him in order to not die."

Earlier that year, Michelle had received a small inheritance from her grandfather in North Dakota. With the money, she bought a camper for their weekend trips, and then gave the rest to her father, in secret, as a down payment on the house she and Rocky had been renting from him ever since they'd left Rocky's tiny trailer. It was part of her long-term strategy. Her dad would act as the bank since she had no credit and no employment history, and only her name would appear on the deed, so that legally she could someday get Rocky out. Rocky, of course, knew none of this.

But even if all that worked out, how would they survive in the short term? She had no income and no work experience. The day he busted through Sally's door, Rocky had proven that moving in with one of Michelle's parents wouldn't stop him. Maybe she should have fled the state, risked going to prison on a kidnapping charge, or left her kids to be raised by a father who was teaching them to swim one day and threatening them with a gun the next. Alyssa suggested every crazy idea she could conjure. Maybe Michelle could move to California. How about getting a wig, covering her body in tattoos, changing her name, escaping the whole place? Canada, maybe? Sarah offered to give Michelle money to go to her sister's house in Arizona. An old friend of Michelle's offered a cabin in the woods out of state. But Michelle said to Alyssa, " 'Where am I even going to go in this world?' That man would have spent every bit of energy, every penny tracking her down."

Alyssa says her mind went to every possible scenario it could in those days. Change Michelle's identity, squirrel her away, get rid of Rocky somehow. "Your mind goes that far with it, you know?" she says. "I was going, 'Somebody needs to kill him because he's going to kill her.' "

Michelle recanted for the same reasons victims everywhere recant: they believe they have no other viable choice. Rocky moved back in that day.

When Sarah found out, she immediately called Sally. Neither of them knew that Michelle had already dropped the restraining order. Both women called the police. Sarah told them that Rocky was dangerous, but when Sally called to say she'd pressed charges against him for assaulting her and breaking in to her home, she learned her charges had been dropped. It was that administrative hiccup. Her charges filed in the same docket as Michelle's and when Michelle recanted, the entire case was dismissed. Today, Sally believes this paperwork error may well have doomed her daughter. How it kept Sally from going ahead and pressing charges herself.

Soon after, Michelle called both women, furious, saying that the police had tried to arrest Rocky in front of the kids and now they were upset. Until Michelle called them, neither woman had known that Michelle had recanted. Michelle told them they needn't worry about her. She had the Mace, after all.

So Michelle and Rocky cut them off, all of them, both families. October dragged on. Sarah and Gordon, so used to seeing the grandkids a couple of times a week, felt a palpable emptiness. Once, when Rocky drove up to pay back the bail money they'd used to free him, Michelle was in the car with the kids and Gordon went outside. Sarah was still too angry to join him, but she watched through the window as the kids grinned at Gordon. Later, Gordon told her Michelle wouldn't let the kids get out of the car to hug him. "I could not believe she did that," Sarah told me. "That was the last time we saw the kids," she pauses a moment, looks upward, then says, "or any of them."

As she recounts this moment to me, sitting in their backyard, Gordon silently sobs into his hands.

THE TUESDAY BEFORE THANKSGIVING, Alyssa got off work and drove by Michelle's house. She'd been calling her sister since the night before, and then on and off throughout the day, but Michelle hadn't answered or called her back; the house was dark and silent, and something immediately felt off to Alyssa, though she could not—not then and not later—pinpoint exactly what. She wanted to stop to check, but she was physically unable to stop her car. Her body willed her forward. She drove on.

She called Sarah asking if she'd spoken to Michelle. Sarah said they'd been cut off since October. When Sarah hung up, she looked at Gordon and said, "Alyssa can't find Michelle."

Alyssa made one last call, to her father. "Dad," she said, "I think something's wrong."

This Person You Love Will Take Your Life

It is a frigid morning in February on the outskirts of Detroit and Jacquelyn Campbell stands on the vast floor of a lecture room dwarfed by three massive screens behind her. She has flown in from her home in Baltimore just for the morning to teach the hundred or so assembled here about something she created three decades ago called the Danger Assessment. Originally written to help healthcare workers identify potential victims of domestic violence in emergency rooms, the Danger Assessment is probably the single most important tool used in intimate partner assault, treatment, and awareness today. How a victim answers the questions on any given Danger Assessment will determine what comes next: whether a perpetrator is arrested, tried, found guilty, and whether a victim will press charges, be taken to a shelter, walked through the court system. Often it will determine a much starker outcome: whether someone will live or die. The Danger Assessment has changed the course of how we understand and treat intimate partner violence in America and beyond. It has broken through cultural and political barriers, been adapted for use by police, attorneys, judges, advocates, and healthcare workers, among others. It has informed research and policy and saved countless lives.

Campbell is tall and elegant, with a tweed jacket and a black blouse, a thick head of deep auburn curls, and a chunky necklace. Her voice contains a perpetual smile, like a public radio host who has to deliver terrible news to an audience, but still sounds soothing. It's the kind of voice you'd want if you were being told your mother was gravely ill or your family dog had passed on. She is talking about family violence, about the worst things people can do to each other, but Campbell's voice has the assurance of a therapist promising that you're in good hands. In Michigan alone in a single month—January of 2017—eighty-six women and five children were killed, she tells the audience. Many of those victims were known by those in this room.

The attendees gathered in this lecture hall to talk about family violence, everyone from uniformed and plain-clothed police officers to district attorneys and prosecutors, along with domestic violence advocates, mental health counselors, healthcare workers, and shelter volunteers. Campbell's slideshow lists grim domestic violence statistic after statistic: *second leading cause of death for African American women, third leading cause of death for native women, seventh leading cause of death for Caucasian women.*

Campbell says twelve hundred abused women are killed every year in the United States.[1]

That figure does not count children. And it does not count the abusers who kill themselves after killing their partners, murder-suicides we see daily in the newspaper. And it does not count same-sex relationships where one or the other partner might not be "out." And it does not count other family members, like sisters, aunts, grandmothers, who are often killed alongside the primary victim. And it does not count innocent bystanders: the twenty-six churchgoers in Texas, say, after a son in law has gone to a service to target his mother-in-law, or the two spa employees in Wisconsin killed alongside their client by her ex. The list is endless. And it does not count the jurisdictions who do not report their homicides, since homicide reporting is voluntary through the FBI's Supplemental Homicide Reporting Data. So how many people are killed as a result of domestic violence each year? The bystanders, the other family members, the perpetrators' suicides? The victims who just can't take it anymore and kill themselves? The accidents that turn out not to be accidents at all, victims pushed out of cars and from cliffs or driven into trees. Tragedies forever uncategorized.

In this room, Campbell is among the believers, those who understand the underpinnings of how domestic violence operates. Many of them know the statistics intimately, in that they don't see statistics, they see faces—of women, of men, of children caught up in this seemingly intractable cycle of violence. Campbell tells the story of a twenty-six-year-old woman killed in Maryland recently by her seventeen-year-old boyfriend. In Maryland, homicide is the leading cause of maternal mortality. Same with New York City and Chicago, Campbell says. Foreign armies and international terrorists and drunk drivers don't have to kill us, because we are very efficient at killing ourselves.

This Maryland couple, the twenty-six-year-old and the seventeen-year-old, also had a two-month-old child, and the woman had three other children by three other men. Her five-year-old watched, screaming, as she was shot and killed. The two other toddlers came running out and so saw their mother dead, too. Three young children, traumatized, and a newborn. One of the toddlers had been abused by her biological father. The mother's own father had abused her when she was a child. The seventeen-year-old boyfriend's abuse as a child was so horrific that he'd been removed from his family home for five years. Layers, years, generations of abuse.

When Campbell and others looked into what happened in the aftermath of these four kids, they learned the newborn was being raised by the deceased mother's parents—including her own abusive father. The other three are all also being raised by abusers. When the seventeen-year-old boyfriend gets out of jail after his twelve-year term for murder, he'll likely take over raising the newborn, who will be an adolescent by then. And on it goes, the cycle of abuse, laid out right there in a single, complicated family. Campbell says they told Maryland state officials, "We'll be looking at another case involving these kids [in twenty years] . . ." The state representatives balked, told Campbell they weren't interested in what might happen in the future. In how kids who witness abuse perpetuate the cycle as adults. They wanted the immediate answer. What could they do right now? But the future *was* her point.

"This is about the long view of prevention," she says. How to teach people to raise a child without abusing him, how to create a system that reaches out to children and parents and provides high-level, intensive counseling. Even after the murder of a parent, children often are lucky to have just *one* mental health counseling appointment.

There is good news, Campbell says, and several in the room laugh, because, really, up until now it's been pretty grim. Campbell says that states where "we have good domestic violence laws and resources" are states where both men and women, though especially men, are less likely to be killed by their partners. Yes, men. The gender distinction is where they find the causal relationship. The states with fewer *men's* deaths, Campbell tells the audience, are the states with good police responses, with good laws of protection, with decent resources for victims. In other words, Campbell says, "Abused women feel less like there's no way out except to kill him." In fact, since 1976 rates of men killed by women have dropped by nearly three-quarters.[2]

What she means is that there are states where abused women don't have to resort to murdering their abusers to return to freedom. While there are no national statistics, some states collect this data. In New York, for example, two-thirds of incarcerated women in 2005 had been abused beforehand by the person they killed.[3] Though in many states today, still, victims are barred from using their long histories of enduring violence at the hands of their partners in their own defense. One woman I spoke with who is incarcerated in North Carolina for first degree murder, Latina Ray, says she endured over a decade of abuse. Her partner beat her so badly that she lost the sight in her right eye entirely, yet her long history of victimization with him was never used in her case.[4] Prior to taking his gun and shooting him, she hadn't so much as had a traffic ticket on her record. In her mugshot, she is a beautiful woman with tawny skin and a mangled eye.

Listening to Campbell, I think back on the question most commonly asked by victims' families. What could we have done? What could we have seen that we missed?

But it's not really about the families. They can be made more aware, certainly, and Campbell says victims do sometimes confide in friends or family members. But there's another group to consider; more than half of all homicide victims were seen by healthcare professionals at some point. It's up to people like Campbell, in other words. Not just the emergency room, but primary care physicians, OB-GYN docs, and a host of other specialists. These people are often the first or only individuals to interact with a potential homicide victim. I think of the clinic Sally took Michelle to when she thought Rocky had given her a sexually transmitted disease. Though HIPAA law bars them from releasing any information on Michelle, they saw enough to prescribe her antidepressants. What else did they see? What may they have missed? Had the violence in Michelle's life come up? A young, twenty-three-year-old married mother of two being checked for an STD and presenting herself—however that looked—as in need of antidepressants. Surely that's enough red flags to probe a little deeper into her life.

Campbell remembers reading the file of one woman who had a cast on her arm at the time of her death, when she was shot through the temple and killed. Not a word about domestic violence appeared in the police report or in the notes from the emergency room where she'd been seen. A cast! Where had it come from? According to the report, no one had even bothered to ask about it. Another woman Campbell met had been shot and paralyzed by her abuser, but then went back to him after her release from the hospital. Campbell asked the woman if she'd been referred to domestic violence services, and she said she had not, but would have liked to have been. She'd returned to her abuser because she said she had no one else to help take care of her. Campbell was so incensed she marched down to the trauma unit where the woman had first been taken and they allegedly told Campbell they didn't have time to assess for domestic violence. Campbell waved the intake sheet that their unit had filled out on the paralyzed woman and pointed right to where it said *shot by husband*.

On a short break, attendees check their phones, refill their coffees. I ask one of the police officers how he's come to be here and he tells me the mayor of their town, Auburn Hills, recently put out a call to address domestic violence more effectively. They'd been getting trainings like this on the Danger Assessment. A week earlier they'd had some training in how to recognize strangulation. Later, Campbell will take a moment during her talk to stop, look up at the two uniformed officers in attendance and say, "Thank you for your role in keeping women safe."

When her talk is finished, a line forms up the center aisle of people who want to thank her, who want to tell her their stories from the field, of how her work has saved not just "lives" in general, but this specific person or that one. How she helped this woman she'll never meet, this child who will not grow up motherless after all. If there is such a thing as celebrity status in this world, Campbell has it.

CAMPBELL BEGAN HER PROFESSIONAL career as a school nurse in inner-city Dayton. She knew most of the students in the school, boys and girls, though it was the girls who stayed with her. The girls who wound up pregnant, in her office, talking about their lives. How they lacked choices and agency. How they didn't seem to believe they had any control over how their lives turned out. In her position, she got to know the social service agencies around the city, and sometimes she'd call this counselor or that and talk about some of the problems the girls had. One young woman, Annie, came to her as a teenager and said she was pregnant and her parents were making her life miserable. Campbell felt a particular closeness to Annie, a spark she seemed to recognize, but didn't quite know how to help. The teenager father, Tyrone, was also one of the kids Campbell knew, though until the pregnancy she hadn't known Tyrone and Annie were a couple. "He was charming, delightful," Campbell said of Tyrone. "Such a lovely guy." Tyrone wasn't ready to make a lifelong commitment, of course, and Annie was miserable at home, so she managed to get welfare assistance and move into an apartment on her own. She left school, but stayed in touch with

Campbell, letting her know how she was doing. Campbell would sometimes check in with another counselor who knew Annie through an at-risk young mothers program. She prayed Annie could find her way toward a rewarding life.

Then, one day in 1979, Annie's counselor called Campbell, said she had some news. Annie had been stabbed more than a dozen times by Tyrone. Campbell was horrified, distraught. She did what everyone does in the immediate aftermath of such a thing: tried to figure out what she had missed, how she might have intervened to stop it, what had gone so terribly wrong. She went to the funeral and tried to hold herself together. Then later, when she reflected on it, she remembered seeing Annie with a black eye several times, remembered her speaking in generalities, dancing around the edges of the topic by saying things like, "We're not getting along." Or "We're having trouble." Annie didn't have the words, and Campbell didn't know the language of violence yet. Annie had spoken, but Campbell hadn't gotten it. It felt like a gut punch. She thought listening and just being there were the things she could offer Annie. "If I had been smart enough to ask . . ." she says. Smart enough to ask the follow-up questions, to press a little harder, to not be afraid to pry.

And so the entirety of her professional life has been learning what to ask.

Campbell had always been interested in public health but had no larger career goal beyond a vague tugging. The feeling that nursing was fine, but she could do more. She wanted to do more. She'd followed her then-husband's career to Dayton, to Detroit, to Rochester. Interested in public health, she began a master's degree program at Wayne State University. Campbell's thesis committee tasked her with the fuzzy directive to go "into a community and prevent something." She pictured some kind of campaign, like getting people to wear seatbelts.

Their directive would change the course of her life.

There was very little literature on domestic violence homicide when Campbell began her graduate work. She thought of her nursing days, those young women who spoke about their futures with such resignation, and she decided maybe she'd look into the leading causes of death for young African American women. "I envisioned myself teaching them how to do breast exams," she said. Instead, she was shocked to find the leading cause of death for young African American women was homicide. Murder? How could young Black women be dying in such numbers from *murder*?[5]

Campbell had stayed in touch with a number of her former inner-city students in Dayton, so she chose as her "community" these now twenty-something African American women. The place you start in public health, she told me in her office at Johns Hopkins School of Nursing, is the mortality tables. Outside her office, graduate students camped out to meet with her next to filing cabinets called the "Violence Drawers." She remembered trying to explain to her thesis committee how homicides offered little clinical data, so they told her to create it herself. For her master's, and later her PhD from the University of Rochester, she pored through police homicide files in Dayton and Detroit and Rochester, and at the same time interviewed abused women in multiple cities. She began to see patterns emerging, patterns that today may seem obvious, but that no one had measured.

Suddenly, Campbell could quantify what had been largely theory until then: that the single biggest risk for domestic homicide, for example, is the prior incidence of domestic violence. (Her initial research from Dayton's police files showed that 50% of domestic homicide victims had been visited by the police for domestic abuse at least once previously.) Levels of dangerousness operated on a specific timeline. Dangerousness spiked when a victim attempted to leave an abuser, and it stayed very high for three months, then dipped only slightly for the next nine months. After a year, the dangerousness dropped off precipitously. So maybe Rocky Mosure didn't need to be held forever; he just needed to be held long enough. Just as Michelle needed time to get her life together so she could provide for herself and her kids, Rocky needed time to understand that his life could go on without her. It seemed to Campbell that something that appeared random, like it happened in a snap, could actually be quantified and cataloged. At least half the women Campbell interviewed were unaware of the severity of their situations—a fact she says remains true today.

And even for those who do know, or have a sense, like Michelle Monson Mosure, it's an absolute leap of cognition to imagine that this person you love, or once loved, this person you made a child with, this person you made a commitment to and vice versa, this person who shares every big and small detail of your life, would actually, truly take that life from you. Love is what makes domestic violence different from any other crime. That the people involved have said to each other and to the world, *You are the most important person to me.* And then, in an instant, for that relationship to become lethal? It requires us to mentally, intellectually, and emotionally hurdle beyond what we can imagine. "That trauma of knowing someone you love is willing to take your last breath?" asks Gael Strack, a leading domestic violence advocate in San Diego. "How do you live with that?"

OVER THE YEARS, CAMPBELL eventually identified twenty-two high risk factors that, when put together in an almost endless series of combinations, portended a potential homicide. Some of the risk factors were broad: substance abuse, gun ownership, extreme jealousy. Others were more specific: threats to kill, strangulation, and forced sex. Isolation from friends and family, a child from a different biological parent in the home, an abuser's threat of suicide or violence during pregnancy, and stalking all added lethality. Access to a gun, drug or alcohol abuse, and controlling daily activities are among the risk factors, as are threats to children, destruction of property, and a victim's attempt to leave anytime within the prior year. The sole economic factor Campbell identified was chronic unemployment. Many of these latter indicators don't cause violence, she is quick to point out, but they can make a volatile situation deadly. It's not the presence of a single factor that matters; it's the particular combination of factors, each of which carries a different weighted measurement. She had women fill out a timeline of incidents, a kind of catalog of abuse, so that they would be able to see for themselves if there was escalation. (Campbell says many people do the Danger Assessment without the timeline, which misses crucial information about escalation and keeps victims from really being empowered with the knowledge that comes from being able to see their own situations as a collective whole. Indeed, I have seen multiple Danger Assessments done across the entire country, from police to advocates, and I rarely saw anyone do a timeline.)

STRANGULATION IS ONE OF those danger signs that Campbell pointed out in her early research, but it turns out that it is a much more significant marker than, say, a punch or a kick. Sixty percent of domestic violence victims are strangled[6] at some point during the course of an abusive relationship—often repeatedly, over years—and the overwhelming majority of strangulation perpetrators are men (99%).[7] Those strangled to the point of losing consciousness are at their highest risk of dying in the first twenty-four to forty-eight hours after the incident from strokes, blood clots, or aspiration (choking on their own vomit). Such incidents can cause brain injury—mild or traumatic—not only by cutting off oxygen to the brain, but because they are often accompanied by blunt force trauma to the head. Still, domestic violence victims are not routinely screened for strangulation or brain injury in emergency rooms, and the victims themselves, who tend to have poor recall of the incident, are often not even aware that they've lost consciousness. This means that diagnoses are rarely formalized, the assaults and injuries are downplayed and abusers are prosecuted under lesser charges.[8]

Gael Strack, chief executive officer of the Training Institute on Strangulation Prevention, is one of the most prominent voices in the domestic violence community today when it comes to strangulation and its attendant issues. In 1995, she was the assistant district attorney for the city of San Diego when two teenage girls were killed "on her watch," as she puts it. In the weeks before one of the girls' deaths—she was stabbed in front of her girlfriends—she had been strangled and the police summoned. But when they showed up, she recanted and no charges were filed. The other girl was strangled and set on fire. Both girls had sought domestic violence services and had made safety plans. Strack believed San Diego was at the forefront of aggressive domestic violence intervention. They even had a dedicated domestic violence council and court. "We had specializations everywhere," Strack says.

Strack and Casey Gwinn, the cofounder of the Training Institute and her boss at the time, felt responsible for the girls' deaths in some way. Like so many others in the field, they asked themselves what they'd missed. So often a community has a high-profile homicide—such as a Michelle Monson Mosure, or two teenage girls—and it's the event that finally spurs change. Funds are suddenly found. Trainings and implementation of new programs emerge. Dunne or Strack or Campbell get a call for help.

Strack went back and studied the case files of three hundred nonfatal domestic violence strangulation cases.[9] Strangulation turned out to dramatically increase the chances of domestic violence homicide. But only 15% of the victims in the study turned out to have injuries visible enough to photograph for the police reports. As a result, the officers often downplayed the incidents, listing injuries like "redness, cuts, scratches or abrasions to the neck."[10] And emergency rooms tended to discharge victims without CT scans and MRIs. What Strack and the domestic violence community believe today is that most strangulation injuries are internal and that the very act of strangulation often turns out to be the penultimate abuse by a perpetrator before a homicide.[11]

"Statistically we know now that once the hands are on the neck, the very next step is homicide," says Sylvia Vella, a clinician and a detective with the San Diego Police Department in the domestic violence unit at the San Diego Family Justice Center. "They don't go backwards."[12]

There are researchers who take issue with this.[13] Whatever the research and data, human behavior is unpredictable, even sometimes inexplicable, and numbers are not an infallible solution. There are offenders who kill without any history of strangulation, just as there are those who strangle but never kill.

In many of Strack's three hundred strangulation cases, she also saw that the victims had urinated or defecated—an act she chalked up to their fear. She spoke to an emergency room physician named George McClane who offered her a very different view. Urination and defecation are physical functions, like sweating and digestion, that happen below our level of consciousness, and are controlled by the autonomic nervous system. Sacral nerves in the brain stem—which happens to be the final part of the brain to expire—control the sphincter muscles. So urination and defecation weren't a sign of fear, McClane showed Strack, but rather evidence that each of those victims had been very near death. And each one of those cases had been prosecuted as a misdemeanor.[14]

Strack embarked on a mission to train those in the domestic violence field—from police to dispatchers to shelter workers to attorneys—on the signs of strangulation. Since the mid-1990s, she and Gwinn have traveled the country holding training sessions that cover anatomy, investigation, prosecution, and victim safety in strangulation cases; Gwinn estimates that they've trained over fifty thousand people. In 2011, Strack and Gwinn helped launch the Training Institute on Strangulation Prevention with a grant from the Office of Violence Against Women.[15] Based in San Diego, the institute conducts four-day sessions there and nationally to "train the trainers" with the help of an advisory group that includes doctors, nurses, judges, survivors, police officers, and prosecutors. What I've found, anecdotally, in police departments across the country is far, far less training—just a couple of hours at most—and often none at all.

In 2013, Gwinn, Strack, and several other leading voices in the domestic violence community submitted briefs to the Supreme Court sentencing commission that outlined the particular danger of strangulation and suffocation. Subsequently, the Supreme Court added language to its sentencing commission report that specifically addressed strangulation and suffocation,[16] recommending increased prison time for those found guilty. Today, forty-five states[17] prosecute strangulation as a felony, and "every jurisdiction that has prosecuted strangulation as a felony with a multidisciplinary team has seen a drop in homicides," according to Gwinn. Between 2012 and 2014, for example, Maricopa County in Arizona saw their domestic violence homicide rate drop by 30%.[18] Gwinn and his colleague, Daniel Rincon, a Scottsdale detective sergeant and a national faculty member at the strangulation institute, claim this is a result, first, of the training undergone by their entire county-wide team—from dispatch to first responders to detectives to crime scene technicians—and, second, of the use of forensic nurses in examining strangulation victims. The county also purchased high-definition digital cameras that can highlight physical evidence, like broken blood vessels, fingerprints, and other markers. Prior to the training and forensic exams, only 14% of strangulation cases were prosecuted; that number is now closer to 62%.[19] Though the program is too new to draw a direct causation, Maricopa County attorney Bill Montgomery did tell me, "When you look at the objective data, you could say where we have focused on domestic violence strangulation cases and improved our ability to investigate, charge and prosecute, we have also seen a significant corollary drop in domestic violence homicides." At the time of this writing, in 2016, Kentucky, New Jersey, South Carolina, and North Dakota did not have legislation making strangulation a felony. Neither did Ohio or Washington, D.C.[20]

STILL, FOR ANY KIND of prosecution, both strangulation and brain injury need to be recognized and diagnosed. Sylvia Vella, who wrote her dissertation on strangulation, remembers a woman from her research who was in her late twenties and who'd had such severe bruising around her neck and ear that Vella sent the woman immediately to the emergency room, where they discovered a dissected carotid artery. The woman called Vella from the hospital and said she'd been put in a secure room under a pseudonym. "No one knows why she didn't have a stroke," Vella told me. "The physicians were like, I can't believe she survived."

While strangulation has been fairly well documented in medical literature, traumatic brain injury is only now being addressed in the larger domestic violence community. The vast majority of domestic violence victims who show signs of TBI never receive a formal diagnosis, in part because they rarely have visible injuries, and so emergency rooms don't generally screen them for it.[21] "We're really good now in our [emergency rooms], if a kid comes in with an athletic injury or someone's been in a car accident, about working people up for post-concussive syndrome," said Campbell, who is the lead author on a study that examines the effect of brain injuries from domestic violence on the victims' central nervous systems. Such symptoms include vision and hearing problems, seizures, ringing ears, memory loss, headaches, and blacking out. "But somehow we're not as good with [domestic violence] victims," she said. "We're not saying, 'Okay, did you lose consciousness for those bruises? Have you had prior strangulations and/or head injuries?' So we need to do a better job of applying that protocol to abused women."

While there is an emergency room screening tool, called HELPS, that aims to identify domestic violence victims with a potential TBI, its use is neither widespread nor standardized. Audrey Bergin, the director of a domestic violence advocacy group called the DOVE program out of Northwest Hospital in Maryland, says that while the HELPS tool isn't used in their emergency room, their program has a nurse who reviews medical records for their domestic violence cases and looks for possible TBI events. Such clients would have been labeled "difficult" in the recent past, even by her staff members, she wrote in an e-mail.[22] "The police may dismiss them as being drunk, the state's attorney may think they have mental illness . . . Even the medical profession may dismiss them as being overdramatic. We have been able to intervene on their behalf to help other agencies understand that it is the TBI that is causing some of these behaviors and symptoms."

The barriers to diagnosis and treatment are sometimes even more basic. Not every hospital is equipped with an MRI machine, and even those that are may not have personnel available twenty-four hours a day, seven days a week. Victims in more rural or low-income areas would almost certainly have to be transported to trauma centers, which is prohibitively expensive. Add to this the lack of training and awareness among first responders and emergency personnel, and many victims spend their lives grappling with the consequences of an unseen, undiagnosed, untreated, unsupported injury in which the narrative almost inevitably turns hostile—that they are crazy, or somehow they are to blame.[23] Advocates talk of women who've lost jobs and custody of their children. They talk of women with little or no support medically, emotionally, or financially. Vella recalls one woman from her research whose "life was completely ruined" by brain injuries caused by strangulation. She'd lost her job, moved back in with her parents, and had to be escorted wherever she went. "She gets to the porch and can't remember where she was going," Vella says. She tells of another woman she studied who lost the ability to read and write, and child protective services took her children because they felt she couldn't care for them. (Vella said this woman learned how to read again and has since regained custody of her children.)

It is not uncommon for victims of domestic violence to have poor recall of the incidents that landed their partners in trouble. They were in one part of the house and then suddenly another, and they can't remember the sequence of events. Their explanation of what happened is cloudy, and law enforcement and courtrooms put the burden of proof on them. To the untrained, they sound like liars. Often, they also sound hysterical, which can be part of the symptomology. What researchers have learned from combat soldiers and football players and car accident victims is only now making its way into the domestic violence community: that the poor recall, the recanting, the changing details, along with other markers, like anxiety, hypervigilance, and headaches, can all be signs of TBI.

Campbell called these risk factors the Danger Assessment tool. She'd intended it to be used in emergency rooms by nurses, envisioning some version of her former self. In fact, the Danger Assessment would go far beyond emergency rooms to crisis centers, shelters, police departments, law offices, and courtrooms. It would be used from coast to coast in America, and then eventually in many countries around the world. It would change the course of how we view and treat domestic violence victims.

WHEN CAMPBELL'S RESEARCH TELLS her that women often don't know their own level of danger, what she means is that they may not know how to situate their danger in a larger context. They may not realize it is escalating. They may not know the specific predictors of intimate partner homicide. They may assume the children will be safe and even offer a kind of vague canopy of protection. As in, "He wouldn't harm me so long as the children are around."

Michelle's family knows, now, that Rocky's keeping her away from them was a sign of his coercive control. They didn't know then. Another thing they didn't know back then: access to a gun by an abuser is one of the three highest risk indicators for domestic violence homicide. Paul Monson had never thought to wonder if Rocky had access to a gun. Everyone in Montana has guns or at least can get guns pretty easily.

A police officer in Billings once told me that in Montana, when you came of age, they practically threw guns at you. Sally knows now about the stalking, the addiction problems, the unreliable employment. Sally and Paul learned after it was too late. It's an emotional brume of regret and guilt and how they can't unlearn what they know now, but they wish they'd had a chance to learn it sooner.

BUT MICHELLE DID KNOW Rocky was dangerous, even if she didn't know the full extent. She had inklings. Because she instinctively refused to press charges. She knew because the Sunday before she died, she was at Alyssa and Ivan's house talking about it, about how mean Rocky had become. How scared she was. How determined she was to get out. It was this particular context, these sets of elements, that made the situation so immediately dangerous. "She was just through with it. You could tell," Ivan said to me. Alyssa and Melanie confirmed this. The way she talked about it, all that last weekend of her life? She was done. And if Alyssa and Ivan and Melanie could tell, it stands to reason that Rocky must have, too, and it must have lit something inside him, scared the shit out of him. This time she meant it. She knew because she sent her kids to Sally's house for safety. She knew because she filed a restraining order, dipped her toes into the system to see if it could help her.

What she didn't know was how to piece all these clues together, over the years and in the weeks and months before her murder. Clues that would have helped her cobble together a picture that would have told her how much danger she was truly in. She couldn't see the escalation, though instinctively she knew she had to act as a united front with him.

Instead what Michelle saw was what so many other women before her had seen: that an abuser appears more powerful than the system.

And how, exactly, did Michelle receive this message? Because Rocky broke in to Sally's house, hit Melanie full-on, pulled Sally by the neck from where she was covering Kristy and Kyle with her own body, trying to keep them safe, and then he kidnapped Kristy. The decoding of these actions is critical. Rocky broke in to the house, assaulted two women, tore his child away. One after another, the actions sent a signal to Michelle that the safety measures she was trying to put in place—leaving her kids with her mom, facing him alone, finally vowing to leave for good—were weaker than whatever it was that he wanted. The police acted as if the victims—Sally and Melanie—were overdramatizing the entire event. Some guy taking his own kid. It's his kid after all. The gendered messages are crucial: men are strong; women are weak. Men have the power; women are powerless. Men are rational; women are hysterical. Whether you are a violent abuser or a law-abiding officer, the men on both sides of the Monson equation sent a message to the women.

When Rocky bailed himself out it was an even more crucial message to Michelle. This time, it's *Not only am I stronger than you, but the system prioritizes my freedom over your safety.* Rocky manipulated whoever he could to secure his freedom—in this case, Gordon and Sarah—and thus he maintained his control over Michelle. Except now it wasn't just control; it was control and rage.

And in these small, separate moments, Rocky showed her something even more urgent: that if she tried to contain him, tried to use the system to beat him, he'd win, and in case she didn't get those two messages, he made sure she understood that he'd escalate, that he'd take what she valued most in the world: her children.

And so Michelle did the thing so many victims through the years have done. The thing they might not even realize is a last-ditch effort to keep them all safe in the face of a man who'd always been dangerous, but was now dangerous and angry and scared. A man who was now a bear. Michelle sided with him. She went back into the system and tried to show her loyalty by dropping the restraining order, by refuting her own affidavit. She tried to get herself back in his good graces, buy herself some time so that she could figure out a safe way to leave. Another way to think of it is that Michelle Monson Mosure was most assuredly *not* staying. She was a victim trying to figure out how to become a survivor—not that she'd have thought of herself in this way.

So often, by the time a situation is this critical, it is already too late unless those in a system—police officers, advocates, judiciaries—are aware of the context of these kinds of actions and have appropriate measures to address them. Things like evidence-based prosecution (rather than witness-based, so that victims don't have to testify in court, which I'll address more in a following chapter), or police officers trained to understand the emotional and psychological dynamics, or judges who can gauge lethality and offer containment strategies that offenders can't easily manipulate. I filled out a Danger Assessment on Michelle once. She scored somewhere between a sixteen and an eighteen. (There are two questions that can never be known in her case.) This score put her in the highest risk category for domestic violence homicide.

It is a failure to understand these critical moments in context that makes the "Why didn't she leave?" question so maddening.

Look at Michelle Monson Mosure. Look at any intimate partner homicide anywhere in any given year and it will be the same: she tried every which way she could. She tried and tried, but the equation, or rather, the question, isn't a matter of leaving or staying. It's a matter of living or dying.

They stay because they choose to live.

And they die anyway.

Michelle Mosure stayed for her kids and for herself. She stayed for pride and she stayed for love and she stayed for fear and she stayed for cultural and social forces far beyond her control. And her staying, to anyone trained enough to see the context, looked a lot less like staying and a lot more like someone tiptoeing her way toward freedom.

And Then They'll Pray

Michelle picked up Kristy and Kyle from school on the Monday before Thanksgiving. Kristy's friend was over for a bit, and then she left. Michelle fed them dinner. Maybe she played with them a little while. Maybe they watched some TV. She was supposed to go over and help clean her father's house to prepare for the holiday, and for her grandmother's arrival from North Dakota. She never showed up. A neighbor saw Rocky peering in a window around five p.m.

Alyssa had called and called. Monday night, Tuesday morning, Tuesday afternoon, Tuesday evening.

Like Sarah and Gordon, Sally had been cut off since the incident in September, when Michelle recanted. She'd seen the kids once, on Halloween, when Michelle brought them over to show off their costumes. Sarah saw Rocky just once, the day he was bailed out, when she confronted him about breaking into Sally's house. The story he offered was so very different from how Melanie had described it to her that she said she understood for maybe the very first time what "a pathological liar he was . . . I said, 'You're sick.' " It was one of the last things she would ever say to him.

The snow and cold of Billings swept in. Michelle told Alyssa that she had more evidence about Rocky's supposed affair now, though she didn't say what specifically. On the Friday before Thanksgiving, Michelle had shown up at Paul's house with the kids and a suitcase. She said she was finally leaving Rocky and could they spend the night?

In the morning, Michelle made Paul promise not to let Rocky have the kids, no matter what. Rocky must have been casing Paul's house, because as soon as Michelle left, he was at the door and begging Paul to let him have his kids just for a couple of hours. He promised he wasn't going to do anything. He just wanted to take them to see *Harry Potter*. He'd bring them right back after. And Paul believed him.

Rocky spent that night in a hotel with the kids, Michelle frantic with worry. She talked to Melanie and Alyssa, went over and spent hours at Alyssa and Ivan's—something she'd rarely been allowed to do in the past. They sat in the hot tub talking about how this time Michelle had really had it. She was absolutely and utterly convinced that Rocky was never going to change, and she was going to leave him.

On Sunday, Rocky showed up again at Paul's house, this time kicking and punching the door, screaming for Michelle. He hurled his body against it as he'd done at Sally's house six weeks earlier—the dents I would see years later. This time he couldn't break in, so he switched tactics, told Michelle that Kristy was at home vomiting blood. Surely Michelle was smart enough to recognize the lie, but she went back to her house with him anyway, because what parent wouldn't? Kristy, of course, was fine. Michelle eventually returned to her father's house that night, leaving the kids with Rocky for the night.

On Monday, Kristy and Kyle went to school. They wrote little narratives about the upcoming holiday and Kristy wrote about the fun she'd had over the weekend swimming in a hotel pool, about how at Thanksgiving she'd get to see her aunts (*ants*) and when her grandmother came from North Dakota, they'd sit around a big table together and . . . *pray for god for the good things he has done for us.* Kyle wrote about learning to ride a bike.

As the kids sat in their classrooms for the last time, their father picked up the latest *Thrifty Nickel* and found a guy selling a used .45 caliber Llama pistol. Later, the seller would tell police that Rocky had mentioned buying it for his wife. The guy assumed a gift. Background checks or a three-day waiting period were not mandated by law.

After Michelle collected the kids from school, the three of them went home, to the house in her name. Rocky in the meantime had agreed to stay at Sarah and Gordon's. Michelle fed the kids dinner, and started the nighttime routine. Their toothbrushes had toothpaste on them, unused. At some point, before bedtime, Rocky showed up.

Maybe she thought, *I have to run.*

Maybe she thought, *How do I get him out of here?*

Maybe she thought, *I've had enough; I'm standing my ground.*

No one can know.

Rocky had the gun from the *Thrifty Nickel* ad, and he had a can of gasoline, and his plan was to burn the house down, make it look like they'd died by accident. A terrible tragedy. A house fire. He took a wad of chewing gum and stuck it in the ignition of Michelle's car in case she tried to get away.

WHEN HE CAME INTO the house, Michelle must have panicked, taken the kids to the basement. Her purse was scratched up, the contents scattered. Maybe she was frantically searching for the Mace from her father. Rocky shot her first. Four times. Twice in the chest, once in the head, once in the shoulder. She fell in the far back room of the basement. The children must have watched their father do this. They ran, both of them. Kristy was shot next, in the head, and fell at the base of the stairs. And then Kyle, who nearly made it to the stop of the stairs before his father shot him, too, and he tumbled partway down the stairs and stopped, blood trailing from top to bottom.

Rocky took the family movies, put them in a bag, and put the bag in the garage. He scrawled a note and left it: *I am not a cheeter* [sic]. And then, *I love Michelle with all my heart. Til death do us part.*

Then he sprinkled gas around the house, lit a match, went to the basement, and shot himself. The fire burned hot and slow.

He did not die from the gunshot. He died from smoke inhalation. Maybe he lay there thinking about what he'd done, surrounded by his dead family. Maybe that's when he wrote on his arm: *I am the devil.* Or was it *I deserve to go to hell.*

They died on Monday night, the four of them.

The house smoldered, but never really alighted. It was winter, the windows shut tight, so the flames had no oxygen upon which to feed. Smoke circled and swirled until the fire sizzled out, everything left blackened and damaged. The walls looked as if they'd melted. When the police entered the house, the TV was somehow still on, just a blue screen. Alyssa remembers this, too. The blue screen, and how the black plastic sides of the television were all melted. It defied logic. Soot blanketed everything, walls, floors, windows. Most of the furniture was incinerated.

By Tuesday evening, when Michelle still hadn't picked up her phone, Alyssa made that call to their father. And they called Sally. And the three of them went to the house. And the minute they stepped out of their car in front of the darkened house, they could smell it. The acrid smoke, the gasoline. Paul had a key to the house, and as he made his way toward the door, he had a sudden, terrifying thought. Maybe Rocky had set some sort of booby trap; he told Sally and Alyssa not to touch a thing.

Heart hammering in his chest, he opened the door, gingerly took a step inside. He called Michelle's name. It was an ominous, gut-deep quiet, with crackling sounds here and there, and then that smell that nearly bowled them over. They gagged. "I knew," Alyssa said later. "I knew. I knew right away." Sally saw the children on the basement stairs, and at the bottom, Rocky. His face in a grimace. The face haunts her still today, eyes open and staring. Pure evil, she says. The face of the devil. She had to look for a long time to make sure it was really him. She'll never forget it. Twisted in agony and rage. The face of someone who was also himself once loved. Later she would think his face carried what she called "the turmoil" inside him. "He had a lot of pain," she said. "The walking wounded in a way." Though it took her many years to be able to see this.

Sally did not see Michelle, but she knew. She knew. She urinated right there, standing on the stairs, then ran out of the house to the curb. She went to the neighbor's, where she called the police and borrowed a pair of unsoiled pants.

Alyssa ran to the middle of the front yard, fell to her knees, and vomited.

Paul ran out the back door, looking for Michelle, thinking maybe, maybe she was still alive somehow, somewhere. He ran to the garage where Rocky kept his Mustangs, and there he found videotapes and the note from Rocky.

The police arrived.

And they found Michelle.

I Can't Live Here Anymore

Thanksgiving night, the day after they were all found in the charred house, Sarah went to the grocery store. On a good day, she'd get lost in there, since Gordon primarily did the shopping. Now she was in a daze, all those relatives around for the holiday and life as they knew it over, yet they were all still somehow required to engage in the simple act of being a human: to eat, sleep, bathe, dress. They had Thanksgiving dinner that year at Perkins, in near silence. She figured no one would be at the store on Thanksgiving night, so she ran in and there at the checkout line was a former coworker standing in line with her own daughter. The woman said hello to Sarah, wished her a happy Thanksgiving. Sarah acknowledged the greeting; she does not remember how. The woman introduced her daughter and said how it was so nice to have the grandkids and the whole family in town. She pulled out pictures of her grandchildren and showed them to Sarah. So adorable. And, by the way, did Sarah have grandkids?

Well? Did she?

Just a day before, she'd had four. Now she had two. Did that mean she had four or two? What was the mathematical calculation of a murder plus a murder plus a murder? She didn't know how to answer. *I do . . . I did. Four, now two. I lost them.* She was blurting things; she didn't know what.

Them? Sarah remembers the woman saying. *Both of them?*

And Sarah said the words aloud for the first time: *their father killed them.*

It was a national story already, from Billings to Salt Lake City to Spokane.

And the conveyor belt stopped, and the cashier came out from behind the register and wrapped her arms around Sarah and the four women hung there together in the fluorescence of the store, suspended in a kind of agony that had no words.

IN THE AFTERMATH OF this magnitude of loss, you take a different shape in the world. Michelle's family did exactly what Campbell did when she learned of Annie's death: they asked themselves what they missed, how they could have intervened. The family blamed themselves. Turned their pain inward. Sally, Paul, Alyssa, Melanie, Gordon, Sarah, Ivan . . . all of them carry the specter of these questions like millstones. Sally gained weight and she aged overnight. Alyssa went into a haze, fought with Ivan, tried to capture Michelle in an artwork she tweaked compulsively, drawing and erasing the same lines over and over again for years as if she were imprisoned in the paper. Sarah and Gordon lived in the shallow space between grief and guilt, in that private eternal purgatory. "We lost them all, like they did," Sarah says, referring to Michelle's family, "but we have all the shame."

Sally had dreams. Endless dreams that went on for years. She dreamt of Michelle and the kids and things would happen in her house that she could not explain: a toy that Kyle used to play with would suddenly go off when it hadn't worked in months. And she'd feel his presence. Something would brush her hand and she would know Michelle was there.

Melanie was pregnant and so Sally, who had been a grandmother and was now no longer a grandmother, would be a grandmother again in a matter of months. Mitchell, they'd name him. A nod toward the memory of an aunt he'd never know.

The ripple effect of Michelle Monson Mosure's death is still felt in Montana today. On one of my many trips to Billings to talk to Rocky and Michelle's family, case workers, and police, I went into the Billings district attorney's office. Today, the current district attorney is a baby-faced man with pale blond hair named Ben Halverson. On the phone, when I said I wanted to talk about Michelle's case, he paused a moment, and then he said, his voice choked up, "That's the case that haunts me today." Ben Halverson was a teenager at the time Michelle was killed. He never knew her. Never met anyone from her family. In person, he told me he didn't have any kind of experience with domestic violence in his own background. He grew up going to the country club with his parents, where no one talked about family violence. But her death drives his work.

The day I went to talk to Ben Halverson, Stacy Tenney showed up with a stack of domestic violence files on her lap. She'd gone over them again in preparation to meet with me, showing who they'd prosecuted and how. The progress they'd made, in a sense, since Michelle's death.

In person, she is soft and quiet, the kind of graceful woman you imagine might have once spent years in ballet classes. A silk shirt fluttered over her. She told me how much Michelle's death just sideswiped her. She went over the files again and again, tried—much like Michelle's family—to see what she'd missed. And what she missed was what Michelle didn't tell her. "I'm not sure I would do anything different today," she said. And as she said it, it seemed to almost physically pain her. It was her office that dismissed Sally's charges on the same docket as Michelle's. Though the police were the ones who wrote the initial report, downplaying the severity of the situation and not giving her office much to use in order to charge Rocky in the first place. I thought it was an act of bravery for her to even agree to talk to me.

Sally drove me over to the elementary school Kristy and Kyle had attended. There is a tree there, planted in a corner of the grounds, dedicated to Kristy and Kyle, and a bench for meditation and a plaque with their names engraved in it. Kristy's teacher was so grief-stricken that she took a leave of absence from the school for the remainder of the year. Sally says sometimes she'll come across a library book that one of her living grandchildren has, and it'll have Kristy's or Kyle's name in it from long ago, when they once checked it out, and it'll be like a little electric charge on her skin.

One night, a year or so after their deaths, Sally dreamt of Michelle across a river where she was baptizing herself, and she felt a kind of burning in her ear. "I used to pray all the time after their deaths, 'Please let them come to me,'" and now she felt this burning and this compulsion to go upstairs to Michelle's old room, and there was Kristy, and she said to her Bugga, "We're okay. My daddy killed himself because he wasn't very happy." Sally said it was comforting to her.

Paul had wanted to raze the house after Rocky killed everyone, but Sally said the city of Billings wouldn't allow it, and so he sold it for practically nothing to get it off his hands and out of his life. The new owner called Sally one day, said he'd sandblasted the walls to get the soot off, and there were little tiny footprints in the soot. "I know the spirit world now," Sally told me. "I never believed in all that before."

Alyssa said she had one salvation dream after another about the kids, about rolling them into carpets, hiding them in mattresses or cupboards, anything to keep them from Rocky. She drew a picture of Michelle, but she couldn't get the nose right, and she began to work on it all the time, erasing it, redrawing it over and over until one night she was alone and she heard her name whispered, and she swore the picture smiled at her, and she stopped working on it after that. She drove up to where they used to camp, Michelle and Rocky and the kids, and she took a picture of the woods, and later, when she had the photos developed, she saw Michelle's face in the tree with her arms around the kids, and Rocky and Bandit were there, too.

Michelle was buried with her children in the same casket, oversized, with her arms wrapped around each of them. Alyssa shows me a picture one night, and the three of them lay there with their eyes closed, and it felt for a moment like Michelle was my sister, too, and I had lost her, and I had to look away from the picture. Alyssa had a book called *Life After Trauma* and she read the whole thing and took all the quizzes in the book, and the book told her what she already knew: that she was struck down by grief. That she had post-traumatic stress. That she couldn't stop missing her sister.

Sally said she couldn't live in her house anymore, the one where she'd raised her three daughters. It was too painful. And Alyssa told her she couldn't live anywhere else but that house, and so she bought it from her mother, and it's where she lives still today. Sally is down the street. Melanie, who has been clean and sober for several years now, just bought her first house not far away in Billings, and Sally thinks this is one of her life's greatest reliefs, that Melanie will be okay after all and the drugs won't claim her and she won't lose another of her daughters.

Ivan says he and Alyssa fought and fought, and eventually they broke up. He says the murders made his relationship with Alyssa untenable somehow. She was the love of his life and Rocky's actions destroyed his life, too, at least for a while. "They hated [Rocky]," Ivan said, of Alyssa's family, "understandably. But he was my childhood friend. He wasn't always that way." Ivan gained weight, drank himself into oblivion for a few years, and then found his way out again, back to life. He has his dogs, shared custody of a daughter, his wonderfully delicious smoked meat, his career, and his house, and he's kind of okay now.

Sarah and Gordon retreated. She says for a year almost no one mentioned the murders at her job, even one of her coworkers that she'd thought was one of her closest friends. He told her much later how he never knew what to say, so he said nothing. Every day she'd come home to a silent house and a silent husband. They couldn't talk about it. They couldn't grieve. They couldn't share their pain. They were just stuck there, like someone had frozen them where they stood. They couldn't find any way to heal. Sarah saw a therapist, but Gordon clammed up. "He became more and more withdrawn, and he just shut down," Sarah says. "And finally one day I said to him, 'I just can't take it. Walking in this house at night is like walking into a black cloud.'"

And she packed up and even though she and Gordon had been married for decades by then and she couldn't imagine her life without him, she left. She rented herself a condo in town and told him she wasn't coming back. "These kinds of things break families," she says. "I didn't want to get divorced, but I just could not keep living that way."

It snapped something inside him. Something that maybe said he'd already lost so much, he couldn't lose her, too, and so even though talking and opening up was more or less a tectonic shift for a man like him, he hauled himself to therapy, and he got on antidepressants, and the two of them also got counseling. It was something he thought maybe he should have done a long, long time ago. During the time Sarah was living separately from him, he went to her apartment, and he'd take her out on dates trying to win her back, and for six months she told him she didn't know yet if she'd ever return to him. So he just kept at it, dating his own wife, wooing her. Her friends told her it was the craziest separation they'd ever seen. And the therapy helped. He'd talk a little about it to her. Not much, but given his silent stoicism it was a lot for him, and Sarah recognized it and saw how hard he was trying and how much he was hurting. Eventually, she returned. And they planted a little garden way in the back of their yard with whimsical things the kids would have liked. A colorful tin turtle, a bird feeder made from an old license plate, a metal goat painted white. They planted the Russian sage and bleeding hearts for Michelle. In the middle of it all the small boulder I had seen from far away. *Forever In Our Hearts. Gordon Edward "Rocky" Mosure.* He has no grave site. He was cremated, and they didn't know what else to do. He's far away from anyone, and I thought of Paul Monson and how he described the color white. A color all on its own. The best choice for when you don't know what you're doing. Rocky is hidden from nearly every view except theirs, in that "memory garden," permanently planted at their home.

So they all searched for ways to go on, to stay among the living. Sarah eventually volunteered at the local domestic violence shelter in Billings. She's not religious in any way, but she said sometimes when she sees a rainbow she believes it's the kids. "It's bullshit, but you take what you can get," she says.

And Sally eventually read something in the Billings newspaper that would come to offer her a measure of comfort out of the senseless deaths of Michelle and Kristy and Kyle. Something that would make their deaths mean something to many people beyond their own family members. So she got in her car and drove two hours to Bozeman to find a man named Matthew Dale.

Systems, Accidents, Incidents

Many years ago, Neil Websdale, a criminologist and professor at Northern Arizona University—by way of England—needed eye surgery. He arrived to his surgeon ophthalmologist's office the morning of his operation and was greeted by a nurse who, without ceremony, marked a big X over his bad eye. Websdale, being both a researcher and a naturally curious person, asked why on earth they were drawing on him with marker. She said, "You want them to operate on the right eye, right?"

Indeed, he certainly did. It concerned him though that they had to make this mark on him. Was this the kind of thing a doctor normally got wrong?

The nurse told him he ought to read the research on accidents in medicine. It was amazing how many people were operated on inappropriately in the United States annually, tens of thousands at the time, she said. In particular, she told him to read the *Atlantic* articles on airline crashes and the literature on medical mistakes. Later, he did in fact read her recommendations, but on that day, when Websdale entered the surgical waiting room, he saw all these people on gurneys who had Xs over one eye or the other. "This was a simple remedy," he said years later to a roomful of people at a video conference, "to prevent mistaken surgeries . . . And what we've found exploring errors in the fields of medicine, aviation, nuclear fuels is that we can correct problems fairly easily if we're open to reviewing tragedies and accidents with a keen detailed analysis."

WEBSDALE IS A YOUTHFUL sixty-something who begins most days with a brisk run through the thin Flagstaff air, where he lives. His close-cropped hair is silver-white, his eyes a periwinkle blue. He rattles off statistics, facts, theories like a fast-talking character from an Aaron Sorkin screenplay; he is a born storyteller, with a British accent softened by decades in America. He holds views that he concedes are controversial. Like this: he believes abusers are as stuck as victims. "Everyone asks why the victim doesn't just leave," he said to me. "But no one asks why an abuser stays." Here's another one, the paradox of domestic violence, he calls it: that the literature on intimate partner abuse and advocates all say abusers are about power and control, but to Websdale, abusers are simultaneously powerful and powerless. Both in control and out of control.

Websdale is, in a sense, a connections and systems guy, in constant search of meaning and metaphor. Pre-surgical marking. Genius. Such a simple solution. What other solutions were out there, just waiting to be discovered? Solutions to our gravest mistakes. He went far beyond what the nurse that day suggested he read. He turned to other industries—not just the Federal Aviation Administration, but the nuclear fuel industry and the medical industry. How did they grapple with mistakes inside their industries? How did they build systems where the mistakes could be minimal? He learned about the National Transportation Safety Board and how their investigations increasingly made plane crashes more and more preventable. The NTSB built a timeline of the crash, looking into every single detail that mattered, from the ticket agent all the way to the pilot and flight attendants and mechanics and air traffic control and weather conditions. They looked for gaps in the system, moments the crew overlooked, safety mechanisms not yet in place. They worked not as individual experts, but as a team, sharing knowledge across titles and ranks. He read literature on medical mistakes, on nuclear fuels, on what we learned after Chernobyl and Fukushima. He spoke with a colleague named Michael Durfee, who was the medical coordinator for the Los Angeles County Department of Health Services Child Abuse Prevention team, who'd begun reviewing cases of child fatalities and abuse to try to find solutions. And like a slow churn, an idea began to form in Websdale's mind. A way to take all this information, from all these different professions, and adapt it to domestic violence homicides. If systems were more efficient, people less siloed in their offices and tasks, maybe we could reduce the intimate partner homicide rate in the same way the NTSB had made aviation so much safer.

At the time, Websdale was traveling to Florida, researching what would become his third book, *Understanding Domestic Homicide*. For that book, he was looking at the state's homicide cases, at old police reports, talking to law enforcement, when the ideas of what he'd been reading in other industries finally overlapped with the homicide files he researched.

He received federal funding through the then-governor of Florida, Lawton Chiles, to form the country's first domestic violence fatality review team. The idea was to use the NTSB model and adapt it to domestic violence homicide cases, not to, as he says, "blame and shame" but to hold people and systems accountable to better standards, more efficient programs. Websdale says he learned that planes often tended to crash for multiple reasons: mechanical failure, human error, safety breakdowns, et cetera. A combination of factors. "And that's what we find in domestic homicide cases," he says. There's not any one single factor that can be pointed out and changed; instead, it is a series of small mistakes, missed opportunities, failed communications.

Fatality reviews act, then, in much the same way an NTSB investigation is run. Team members build a timeline of a case, gather as much information as they can about the victim and the perpetrator and gradually try to look for moments where system players could have intervened and didn't or could have intervened differently. Today, the program Websdale began in Florida has spread across the country and even internationally. More than forty states now have fatality review teams—and many have multiple teams—as well as the UK, Australia, New Zealand, and others.[1]

ABOUT A YEAR AFTER Michelle Monson Mosure's murder, an article in the local Billings newspaper caught Sally's attention. The piece reported that a new team was forming in the state, Montana's own Domestic Violence Fatality Review Commission (MDVFRC). Their aim, she learned, would be to investigate domestic violence homicides with an eye toward reducing the number of victims annually in the state. She saw immediately the possibility to get some answers about what happened with Michelle; if she couldn't save her daughter's life, at least maybe she could help out another family in their same situation. Sally could point to the moment her own charges against Rocky were accidentally dropped because they'd been filed in the same docket as Michelle's recanted testimony. But that seemed like a human error, not a systemic one. And no one could really say what the impact might have been had those initial assault charges stuck. Rocky had only ever been facing a criminal mischief charge to begin with.

Sally drove to Bozeman, where a small conference about the new fatality review commission was taking place; after the keynote speaker was done, she made her way to him. His name was Matthew Dale, and he headed the Office of Consumer Protection and the Office of Victim Services, (which is housed at the Office of Consumer Protection) in the Montana Department of Justice. He and Websdale had a years-long friendship. Sally told Dale the story of Michelle and Kristy and Kyle, and he listened. She asked him outright to take on her case. It would be the first case Montana's domestic violence fatality review team took on. How, they would all attempt to answer, might Michelle and her children have survived?

TO GET A SENSE of what a fatality review team did, I headed to a tiny town outside of Missoula and checked in to a hotel where the dominant aesthetic theme was taxidermy. An antler chandelier dangled from the cathedral ceiling. A stuffed deer head on one wall. The place had a warm, homey feel to it, with thick wood beams running across the ceiling. In a far back room, thirty-two people sat at long tables in the kind of carpeted, anonymous conference center ubiquitous to hotels across the nation. Outside, it was preternaturally beautiful. The October mountains were already snow-capped, and autumn leaves skittered across the parking lot in view from a wall of sliding glass doors along one side of the room. The hotel sat adjacent to a small river, and the air had that visible, sharpened-crystal quality seemingly unique to the American West. This could be a gathering for some extreme outdoor adventure—a hunting club, a fly fishing group—were it not for the subject matter that had brought everyone here. (According to the tenets of the team, I have agreed not to identify the victims in the case, and thus information like names, geographies, and specific markers like jobs and ages, has been redacted.)

Ruth was killed by her boyfriend, shot several times in the back and in one hand as she cowered to protect herself, and then once in her head. It was the kind of murder that law enforcement often refers to as an execution. Her crouched position while he towered over her tells them something about the couple's dynamic. About power and control. Bullets zinged all over the room where she died, as if she'd run and tried to get outside before sinking into the position where he eventually killed her at close range. We'll call him Timothy. After Timothy killed Ruth, he walked around the outside of the house several times. It's typical for a lot of time to pass between the murder of one's loved one and one's own suicide. "It's easier to kill someone else than kill yourself," Websdale says. Eventually, Timothy shot himself. Unlike Ruth's death, which was pandemonium, a scene of blood, turmoil, bedlam, Timothy's suicide was tidy: two gunshots and he was done. In a few hours, the team will talk about this image and what it means.

Some years, Montana has as few as three domestic violence homicides, and sometimes there are well over a dozen. The year Ruth was killed, there were eleven statewide.[2]

Matthew Dale leads this two-day meeting. The team has spent months gathering and sharing information, looking up old records, interviewing friends, family, coworkers, community members, neighbors, law enforcement, clergy, therapists, judges, probation and parole officers, former teachers, babysitters, nearly anyone involved in the lives of both victim and perpetrator. Fatality review teams don't go over every intimate partner homicide in their own various states, but they'll review a select few where the information might offer a tweak to procedures or systems that might have kept a victim alive. Perhaps bystanders or children were killed, or perhaps there was something left behind that could offer insights—diaries, letters, social media posts, or e-mail histories. Maybe they were unusual as a couple, very old, very young, wildly rich, or chronically poor. Maybe the families are cooperative, as had been the case with Michelle Monson Mosure. In the case of Timothy and Ruth, they both left written information behind, letters, social media posts, and histories that overlapped with law enforcement records.

Dale is a slight man with thick, bushy hair and a runner's physique. He wears his cell phone on his belt and a tie daily, despite this being a casual affair. He tells the assembled team—who have driven from all corners of the state, some as far as eight hours away—that the crime scene photos are available for viewing on a private computer, but he will refrain from showing them to the group as a whole. The pictures are catastrophic and grotesque, full of blood, as might be expected, and terrifically sad, but they are also telling. Ruth was found in the kitchen, on her knees, slumped forward. Timothy lying in bed, a gun in each hand, his arms crossed over his heart and bullet holes in his chest. The details will emerge later and reveal important elements about both the perpetrator and the relationship itself.

Montana's fatality review team is notable for two reasons. First, they do a deep dive. Dale calls it long and wide. Other teams do less investigating but cover more cases. The Montana team investigates, at most, just two cases a year. And second, it's a state with a population such that lawmakers and judges—those with the power to actually change policy—are accessible. In fact, Montana's attorney general is a member of the team, as is at least one judge. It's arguably easier to change a law in a place like Montana than it is in an area with a much denser population, like New York City.

Teams like this have no regulatory or enforcement function, but rather through individual cases they try to determine if some systemic change could have made a difference. Maybe the judicial system might have played a larger role in locking up that abuser or keeping the victim safe? Might the police have done something different? Or the local church? There is, in fact, an infinite number of possibilities when it comes right down to it, so a team has to examine outcomes to some extent before they are even known. In the case of this particular murder-suicide, several elements drove them to take it on. First, the victim had a premonition of her own death; upon leaving her boyfriend, she knew she was in a dangerous enough situation that she spoke about her own funeral. The perpetrator, too, had enough of a history with local police that they anticipated a violent situation with him someday. "Suicide-by-cop" was how one police officer who knew him put it. That is, when someone compels police to shoot him by not, say, following orders to drop a weapon. Montana, for reasons no one quite knows, has one of the highest suicide-by-cop rates in the country. So, given that he was a known danger, and she feared for her life, why hadn't the system protected her? What more could they have done? What more could they do in the future?

ALONG THE FRONT WALL giant sheets of paper are affixed, and Dale opens the meeting by reminding the team of confidentiality; all files must be destroyed immediately afterward. They spent so many months interviewing families, friends, and coworkers prior to the review who knew the deceased that painful details emerge.

Perhaps the most crucial element to a fatality review is something few team members discuss openly: that is, it forces them to ask how a system they're involved in full of hardworking people with the best intentions failed enough that someone lost her life. Websdale's phrase—"no blame, no shame"—is repeated often during the two days I observe and turns out to matter a great deal. Websdale told me that aviation has gotten considerably safer over the past two decades, whereas medical mistakes still happen far more often than they ought. (In fact, death from medical errors in hospitals is now the third leading cause of death for adults in the United States.)[3] Websdale credits a burgeoning culture of openness in highlighting human error wrought by the NTSB as the primary reason for today's relative flight safety. "If you go into a cockpit today," he said, "and there's a safety issue, that pilot is going to listen to his copilot, his flight attendants, what have you." In medicine, however, there is a pervasive hierarchy that keeps the lines of communication closed. He cited the operating room culture, how the surgeon is god, and god is never second-guessed. But the systems that work best, Websdale says, across the country—whether they are police, advocates, social workers, probation officers, judges, or even just family members—are those that focus on working as a team. In domestic violence, the two main entities poised at the front lines are advocates and police. Two professions with entirely different cultures: the modern feminists and the traditional patriarchy. Indeed, in my near-decade of reporting and researching domestic violence all across America, the most successful cities and towns I encountered that had either lowered their domestic violence homicide rates or increased available services all had this in common: they'd broken down the cultural barriers between their police departments and their domestic violence crisis centers.

Dale begins by asking what we know of the victim's life. One team member, in particular, was responsible for gathering as much biographical information on Ruth as possible. She'd grown up out West, but moved around for much of her life. Her grown children both still lived in the western part of the country. A member of the team named Beki begins writing down these known elements of Ruth's life on the tacked-up sheets of paper with a Magic Marker.

Ruth had worked as an aide in a retirement home and had divorced her children's father many years earlier. She and Timothy met online and began dating immediately. In letters, Timothy professed to finding her the woman of his dreams despite having spent only one week with her at that point. Letters and notes found after the murder give the team unique insight into Ruth's mind-set and even Timothy's at times. Ruth had visited him several times in the Montana trailer park where he lived, and after three months, he asked her to move in with him, which she did. Within a month or two, she'd sold off most of her furniture and household items in Utah, packed up her car, and moved to Montana to live with him. He promised her the trailer was temporary, that they'd find a nice small house soon.

Unable to find work in a retirement home, she took a job with an office cleaning service, though Timothy lived on disability and whatever part-time work he could get as a handyman. It meant she had to work nights and weekends, which seemed to make Timothy insecure in their relationship, even when he knew she was at work. Their volatility was immediate. He got mad when she worked too much, but then complained about never having money. He got mad when she refused to cook or didn't clean up the kitchen and once when she slept in till noon. But Ruth, in a notebook that appeared to be left for her children, said she felt stuck. She'd left a decent job in a neighboring state, sold practically everything she owned, and now felt she had to give this "relationship the best try [she] could." She believed Timothy when he told her he was in pain and his pain caused him to act erratically, to explode over small events, like when she was too tired for sex or when she didn't feel like going fishing with him. Having seen up close what it really meant to be sick, she wrote, she understood how pain could mangle someone, how the wrong drug combination could affect a personality. Indeed, she wondered if she had been sent to Timothy to help him with these very issues, some sort of preordained destiny. Like maybe she alone could save him. Because when he was nice, when he came up behind her as she was pouring a cup of coffee in the morning, when he'd wrap himself around her on the couch in front of the television, he was as warm and comforting a man as she'd known. It had been so long since she'd been in love. Decades, she'd been lonely. And now she was alone no more.

The subtext to this biography, what the assembled team members kept in the back of their minds, was whether or not something or someone in Ruth's life could have intervened enough for her to be alive today. Did her friends know of the violence, and if so, when? Did she attend church? If so, did any of the church members know? Perhaps the minister? Did she ever show up with visible injuries? What about her work history? Had she missed days? Had she been in other romantic relationships that had turned violent? If so, what had been the outcome of those? Was it ever possible to whittle down a murder to just one single moment that could have made it all turn out differently? The fact that the relationship got serious so quickly matters, too. Short courtships— let's call it love at first sight—are a hallmark of private violence. Rocky and Michelle had this, too.

When they finish with her timeline, it fills several pages, and it's midmorning now. With Timothy, they will fill the rest of the wall space, and the enormous sheets of paper wrap around the entire room.

MONTANA'S TEAM INVITES LOCAL players to their fatality reviews to offer context. These are not members of the regular team, but contribute to the discussion of any given homicide. In the case of Timothy and Ruth, several local police officers come and talk about what they knew of Timothy. He was an ex-service member who loved dogs. He had delusions of grandeur and would often boast about exploits with search and rescue, though he was never a member of any search and rescue team. He'd had several accidents—a car accident, an ATV accident—and was on prescription pain medication, and seemingly had several different sources of such medicine, from the VA and various local doctors. Like many Montanans, he had a small arsenal of weapons in his house, though unlike many, every single one of them was fully loaded and ready for Armageddon at every moment. Websdale says that often the rage an abuser feels is highlighted in the particular details of a shooting or a crime scene. One common scenario: multiple bullets in a victim's body, evidence that the perpetrator kept shooting long after what was necessary for death, perhaps even emptying an entire chamber into his or her victim. Such crime scenes point to a level of rage held by the offender. Often the one who will offer the most resistance is killed first in a family (as with Michelle Monson Mosure). Or a stepchild who is the source of tension between a couple will have an inordinate number of bullets. Sometimes police will find a single deadly bullet in one victim and a constellation of bullets in another. These aren't simply gratuitous details, Websdale says. They're clues to the mind-set of an offender, details about the particular psychology of a couple, and often they speak to interventions that could have been made, for example, by mental health professionals.

In Timothy and Ruth's case, the team begins to make connections that they've seen before in other cases. Timothy eventually did find them a house and move them from the trailer, but the house was in the middle of nowhere, completely isolating Ruth. Timothy's tendency to fabricate stories of his own fake heroics spoke to a deep feeling of inadequacy and insecurity, and probably a clinical narcissism. As an ex-service member, he'd been in and out of the VA seeking various services, and he'd had run-ins with the local police, who knew him well. One officer called him a kind of Yosemite Sam. Another said he knew exactly what he could get away with and skirt the law. He had multiple restraining orders against him in other states that Montana's law enforcement did not know about, because systems across states rarely communicate. Nor, presumably, did Ruth. Even today, in this world of hyper-connectivity, where we can get a drone to deliver our toilet paper and a robot to vacuum our carpets, we still seem unable to create a database that speaks across state lines and across civil and criminal courts when it comes to violent people and their histories. One of his ex-girlfriends told a team member that she kept track of him on social media just to keep herself safe and make sure he was nowhere near—this, though she lived over a thousand miles away now with a family of her own and hadn't spoken to him in many years. In a couple of cases, he had temporary restraining orders filed against him, and he'd wait until they expired and a partner wouldn't show up to renew them, and he'd start coming around again. It was one of the ways in which he would abut the law but not break it.

"He had all these temporary restraining orders with other women," says one of the team members. "But not Ruth. He killed the one who didn't leave."

The team learns he was married once before but only briefly. His wife sought help from a pastor, who comes today to talk about his experience with Timothy and his ex-wife. The pastor is tall, with a mustache, and, like nearly everyone in the room with me that day, carries a gun at his belt, because Montana. One team member, a retired forensic nurse, is so outspoken about her hatred for guns that the other members tease her endlessly. Every time she says it, she's holding needles, knitting away, wearing a sweater vest. When it comes time to make recommendations, she will take Beki's giant Sharpie and write *guns, guns, guns* all over the white pages. "You want to get rid of homicide?" she'll ask. "Get rid of guns." She says this on and off for the two days we're there.

The pastor talks about Timothy's ex-wife. He went with her to file for a restraining order, and convinced her to tell the judge how terrified she was. The judge turned down her request. But the pastor knew she was in danger and he stepped in and created a safety plan for her. "We got her a new car," he says, so Timothy couldn't track her. And the church found her a safe place to live, though not before the church itself received threats. "We're pretty sure he was behind them," the pastor says.

Police, even local police familiar with Timothy's odd history, knew none of this. They didn't even know he'd once been married.

It's easy to look at the judge in such a case and lay blame, but the judge knew none of Timothy's history of stalking other women or restraining orders he'd had with former girlfriends, because most of these incidents happened when he was living in another state, not Montana. And, perhaps even more important, restraining orders are generally a matter for civil courts; it's only once those orders are broken that they become a criminal matter. And Timothy, of course, even with a history of restraining orders, albeit largely unknown, had no criminal history. The systemic gaps, across courts, bureaucracies, state lines, are epic.

So here, then, is where the work of the team becomes so crucial. They have the timelines for Ruth's and Timothy's lives. They've listened to local police and local clergy offer what information they had about the two. They've learned a little about the economy and culture where the incident happened, and now they put it all together and look for red flags. Timothy was known to law enforcement; he had unstable employment; he had a history of stalking and stay-away orders; he had significant amounts of pain medication; he had visions of grandiosity, profound narcissism, and a wicked streak of manipulation. He told lies about what he'd done in the military and posted on social media accounts of bravery and heroism that no one could ever find evidence of (local newspaper articles, for example). In the crime scene, his death was tidy; he lay himself comfortably in bed. There was very little blood. But Ruth's spoke to frantic chaos, terror. For Ruth, she wrote of wanting to save him, of how the world had given up on him, but she wouldn't. She, too, had unstable employment, but she also had very little support in the area—no family or friends. Just a minister at a church she sometimes attended. Ruth and Timothy's relationship got very serious very quickly, and Ruth found herself nearly completely isolated. Timothy rarely allowed her to leave the house, citing his need for her. The variety of red flags are things everyone in domestic violence has seen before: the quick courtship, the isolation and control, the unemployment, the medications, the narcissism and lying and stalking.

The question now is where Timothy and Ruth interacted with the system in some way to see where interventions might have been possible. Slowly, they're inching their way toward recommendations they can make in a report they prepare every other year for Montana's legislature. The proverbial X over the eye, you might say.

The VA, where Timothy sought treatment, is the first place they identify. And then there was the court with his ex-wife. The police knew him, and he'd had that history of stalking and protection orders. He also had a home health aide who worked with him several times a week, who tried to warn her supervisor about his instability, and she was told to ignore it and just do her job. And then there was Ruth's minister. "That's five intervention points," Matt Dale says. "The VA, mental health, law enforcement, the judiciary, and the clergy."

One of the advocates raises her hand, says she wasn't sure earlier, so she put in a call to someone in her office, and said that, in fact, Ruth had visited her office once, long ago. She hadn't seen Ruth, but one of her coworkers had. That day, Ruth was driving around with everything she owned in her car. The advocate had no other information, whether this was during her relationship with Timothy or not or if Ruth had actually obtained any services, but it's another possible intervention point for the team. If you count a homeless shelter, it's just one more missed opportunity.

By lunchtime on the second day, the team asks everyone to call out recommendations. The retired nurse says, "Guns, guns, guns. Get rid of the guns." Some of the police officers on the team laugh. "This is Montana," someone else says.

"So what?!" she says. She is charming in that way of a grandmother—the knitting and all—but fierce in her opposition. She knows it's a battle she'll never win in this state, but that doesn't deter her from fighting it.

Recommendations come from all sides of the room, five, ten, fifteen. The goal is to put all ideas on the table, and then they'll whittle down the most realistic ones—those that will cost little or nothing to implement or those where the legislature might not have a big battle on their hands. One of the most significant is the gap between Timothy's history of restraining orders and what local police who dealt with him knew. This becomes one of their primary recommendations: that they have access to a history of such orders in other states. Dale says they also ought to take a page out of the DUI statutes. DUIs now remain on a person's record in Montana. That's a simple fix, keeping the history of temporary restraining orders in the system, even after they've expired.

And there are other recommendations, too, all of them seemingly small tweaks, and some that have come from other fatality reviews: invite clergy to trainings so they know how to deal with domestic violence. ("More women talk to their pastors than police or domestic violence advocates," Websdale told me once.) Talk to the VA about ways in which their medical treatments and prescriptions can be accessible to other doctors electronically. Close the technology gap in the courts. By the end, more than twenty recommendations are listed, but Dale and the team whittle them down, and ultimately only a handful will go on to be included in their report, and though the reports cover at least four reviews done by the team, the recommendations aren't linked to any case specifically for privacy. So that by the time the team issues their report for the period in which I sat in on the review, I recognize only two or three as likely originating from the case of Timothy and Ruth, and they include expanding the use of lethality and Danger Assessments, training judges, law enforcement, and healthcare workers on the complexities and contexts of domestic violence cases.

They seem like such small changes that it's almost disheartening. But Montana and other states have seen profound change with these seemingly small tweaks. One story Matt Dale likes to talk about is the case of the woman who had an active restraining order against her abuser, but when he broke the order and the police were called in, the officer on the scene couldn't read her actual stay-away order for the most trivial of reasons: it was typed on a piece of paper. Paper, which degrades after a time. It had been issued from the court, and in the intervening time in which she'd been granted it, had become illegible. As a result, Montana eventually implemented something called the Hope Card. It is the size of a driver's license and laminated and contains identifying information about the offender, including a picture, the active dates of the protection order, and any other pertinent information. Victims can get multiple Hope Cards and pass them out to coworkers, teachers and administrators at a child's school or anyone else who might need to be made aware of the order of protection. Two other states, Idaho and Indiana, have implemented the Hope Card, and more than a dozen other states have looked into Montana's program.

MICHELLE MONSON MOSURE AND her children were the first case Montana's fatality review team took on. Today, as a result of Michelle's fatality review, Rocky wouldn't have been allowed to bail out first thing in the morning. Meaning, he would have been held longer. It gives domestic violence advocates more time to connect with a client, to go over safety plans, a Danger Assessment and timeline, to offer up services like shelter or other emergency plans, to give a context for what victims and their families might not know they're seeing or experiencing. Michelle had no time. The bear was coming at her. A domestic violence advocate would have met with Michelle and done a Danger Assessment on her. Billings now has a dedicated domestic violence police officer named Katie Nash; Nash would have followed up with Michelle, as she does with all the domestic violence cases that come through the department from street officers. They'd have come up with a safety plan that may have included changing the locks on the house, putting Michelle and Kristy and Kyle in a safe house or hotel for a few days, putting Rocky on a GPS bracelet. He may have also been prosecuted for several felonies: unlawful entry and remaining unlawfully within the home (burglary), vandalism, possible kidnapping, criminal endangerment, and possibly others. The police may have done home checks on Michelle. A judge may have ordered Rocky to abuser intervention classes. The range of possibilities is endless.

The Montana team made other recommendations based on her case as well. They recommended an automatic no-contact order with anyone arrested in conjunction with a partner or family assault; today, Rocky would have been barred from contacting her from jail. They also recommended a systematic method of warning victims when abusers are due to be released—either having served their time or after bailing out. So Michelle would have been warned far in advance of his release. They also recommended that any victim who rescinds his or her testimony, recants as Michelle did, be provided with domestic violence information, including area services. Hopefully they'll be more aggressive in their evidence-based prosecution in years to come.

There are recommendations that appear from year to year in Montana's and other states' reports. They include the ever-increasing use of Danger Assessment and closing technology gaps, such as those that exist so often between civil and criminal courts or between advocates and police officers. More trainings, too, make the recommended list again and again. Gun control, however, at least in Montana, rarely does.

One of the things Sally stressed to me over and over was the moment Michelle learned Rocky had been bailed out of jail. She just instantly changed; all her resolve to leave disappeared, Sally said. "She really thought he'd be in there a while," she told me. Maybe there's no way of knowing if these changes would have kept Michelle Monson Mosure and her children alive. It's like trying to prove a negative. The only sure thing is that doing nothing will ensure that nothing ever changes. And what everyone I ever spoke with in Montana was utterly and absolutely convinced of? That the death of Michelle Monson Mosure had saved many other lives.

And What Happens Next

It took me a long time to finally watch the home movies that Paul Monson had given me. Sally had told me how she'd watched the tapes over and over in the early days just to hear Michelle's voice. And Paul had watched them multiple times, too, but there was nothing he could find, no aha moment that could explain why he'd lost his daughter and his grandchildren.

I held on to them for a long time, partly assuming I, too, wouldn't see anything if Paul hadn't. But also, if I'm honest, I dreaded seeing them. I wondered if maybe I didn't want to see Rocky as a family man. Or I feared I would search them, like Paul has searched them, scanning for clues, and find nothing. Or the texture of their lives would remind me that Rocky and Michelle and her children were just like all of us, as frail, as vulnerable, as scared and angry and needy. And that any one of us, or our family members, friends, neighbors, is as capable as the next of being in the same situation Michelle was in. I've yet to meet any victim anywhere who doesn't say some version of this to me: *I'm not your typical victim.*

But there was another reason, too. A reason writers and journalists like me don't often admit: after all the time I spent with the surviving Monsons and Mosures, I felt the loss of Michelle and Kristy and Kyle and, yes, even Rocky in a way that was already reshaping my world, distorting my view. There was a period of time when it took a force of will for me to not look at every man I met as a possible abuser and every woman as a possible victim. This is not the way one wants to walk through life. I knew that. I know that. So before I watched the videos, I took an entire year off from anything having to do with violence. I worked out, and I read, and I painted, and I went to therapy, and I avoided abuse and homicide and police reports.

And finally, after that year, I returned to it all on a summer day not long ago. I was staying with friends, and I had the videos on my hard drive, and I began to watch. They were all out of order.

In the first one, I saw Kristy in pink sweats and that camo hoodie carried down those large boulders by her mom and then later on her father's shoulders.

To his wife, Rocky says, "Smile, smile," from behind the camera.

In another scene, Michelle is uncharacteristically drunk, wearing tan overall shorts, trying to stand up in their kitchen. Laughing her ass off. Rocky is laughing, too. He tells her to walk a straight line, then walk backward, then say her ABCs backward. She takes a sip of beer, spills some. He says, "We'll check back in later." As if he's a reporter with breaking news. In the next shot she's on the floor of the bathroom, still wasted, this time in her black underwear, which is pulled down to her hips. The scene is uncomfortably intimate. Invasive. He says, "Who did this to you?" He laughs. She grins, but her eyes are closed. "Leave me alone," she says, over and over. Then there's a split second where she's naked on the toilet, and she's been sick and he wants to film her throwing up into the toilet. She's annoyed, but defenseless, her limbs splaying everywhere as she tries to hold herself up. He says, "We'll come back, folks. We'll come back to this."

Every once in a while there is a clip from some Christmas or family event, more or less always at Sarah and Gordon's house, but the vast majority of the videos are just the four of them, and most often camping. Rocky cajoles Kyle into jumping off a rock with him into the frigid water, but Kristy does not. Nor does he ask her. The gender expectations are already established. Later, Rocky sets up the video on a rock and there's a rare shot of the four of them. Michelle and Kyle wear life vests. Kristy walks up to the camera, smiles, and says, "I'm eating an apple." The apple is twice the size of her hand. It's the most animated I've seen her. She was a quiet child. Observant, but not talkative. Kyle was the ham. Kristy walks toward her family. Rocky and Kyle jump off the rock together. Then a second later, Michelle jumps off. In the background, Michelle shrieks from the shock of the icy water, hiding behind the rock. The three of them leave Kristy standing alone on the rock with her apple.

The kids play in the hammock like larvae. Tom Petty bellows in the background, "Good love is hard to find." Later, Rocky retrieves a towel from the bottom of a river. Saves the towel, and says, "It's not cold, it's warm," over and over, mind over matter. "You just gotta psych yourself out." He takes Kyle in the yellow inflatable canoe, down a small rapid, perpendicular to it. "Stupid," Michelle yells to him. He straightens out. Long shots of the distant snow-capped mountains, a waterfall pouring down so far away it's soundless. Kyle walks through the marsh grass in his life vest with the canoe paddle. There are long stretches where Kyle is the videographer and he zigzags with the camcorder as it blurs dizzily across the pebbled, rocky ground. "There's bugs in the water," Kyle says in his little-boy voice.

"Kyle, how much bugs is there in it?" Kristy says. They are beside a road; several cars speed by.

AT HOME, THE KIDS swing on a swing set in the backyard. It's July 2001. Kyle swings so high the chains hiccup. Later on the couch, Kyle sits beside a baby eating green Popsicles. The TV is on. A commercial comes on, and the announcer says, ". . . to embrace life and over on her own terms." The baby is a blond boy named Tyler, a neighbor's baby.

Then Rocky has a garter snake from the backyard in a yellow bucket. "Where's Kristy? I got a snake for her," he says, walking through the house.

She screams from behind the bathroom door. "No, don't, you're scaring me."

He laughs.

He holds up a Popsicle.

"Don't," she says. "It's not funny."

He laughs at her fear, hands her the Popsicle, and walks away with the bucket.

THEN THEY'RE CAMPING AGAIN. Kristy throws branches in the fire. It smokes wildly. Michelle is filming. Rocky's wearing a red T-shirt and jeans, drinking a beer. Kyle's hollering for his dad's attention while he swings on the hammock, "Daddy, watch. Watch. Daddy, watch." AC/DC blares in the background. Sally said she remembers the constant heavy metal when she'd visit them. How it was always on so loud. Rocky frog leaps, one leg up, backward, toward Kyle, but he won't turn around. Kyle leaps from the hammock, falls on all fours. Rocky glances toward him, but keeps up his frog jumping in a wide circle. Kyle climbs back in the hammock. "Daddy, watch. Watch!" Rocky plays air guitar, bangs his head to the drums. Circles back to Michelle, grimaces and arcs his face toward the lens. He looks momentarily menacing, but then he steps backward, smiling. He holds up the beer, gulps the rest of the bottle at once, Adam's apple bobbing.

In between the camping videos, there is one DVD from when Alyssa, Michelle, and Melanie were small. Sometimes Melanie is there; other times it's clear she's not born yet. All three of them look alike and they look like Sally. Dominant upper lip, large round eyes, long faces. As babies and toddlers, Alyssa and Michelle are always in tandem. They dress up as clowns or cowgirls for Halloween. They feed each other cake on their birthdays. In one, Paul puts them both in a pile of leaves in the back of his pickup truck. Paul and Sally are still married back then, and Sally is in the background, thin and smiling, in curlers with a scarf around her head, or a Dorothy Hamill bob. The three girls take baths together, ride bikes and tricycles and Big Wheels, share a tiny grocery cart and push it around the living room. They play ring-around-the-rosy in the living room. *Ashes, ashes, they all fall down.*

Rocky had a tendency to film Michelle in her underwear. Her legs are long and lean. He films close-ups of her ass all through the years, the male gaze at its most sophomoric. She offers up an occasional rebuff, asking him to leave her alone, but for the most part she seems to just simply ignore him, knowing the camera will pan elsewhere eventually. As in cinema, this objectification—woman as an erotic form for the filmmaker or viewer—underscored the power dynamic in their relationship. He does what she does not want him to do. He continues to do it despite her objections. Finally, she concedes to his power and he, as he expected all along, wins. I am tempted, of course, to avoid reading too much into these moments, to throw up my hands and say, "Oh, come now. They're just family movies. He was just *teasing*." I also consider how ceding power to another person does not happen in a vacuum. It's a slow erosion over time. Step by step, moment by moment, whittling away until a person no longer feels like a person. For Michelle, the loss of power was so complete and so obvious to me—from his disallowing her economic opportunity, to filming her body in parts and pieces, and all the way to his eventually taking her life. Why is it not okay that he filmed her over and over and over in her underwear?

Because she asked him to stop.

And he didn't.

And eventually she gave up asking.

This is loss of power at its most elemental.

THERE IS A RARE moment where Michelle is behind the camera. She's filming Kyle on his bike in the woods, zooming through a small clearing. She catches Rocky making his way down the rocks, shirtless, a towel over his shoulders, cigarette dangling from his mouth. His hair is blond-tipped from a summer of camping in the sun. When he reaches her, he asks her something inaudible, something like *what is that?* She says, coyly, "My evidence."

It's a fraction of a second. Still, I don't know how Paul missed it. Rocky comes at her, his lip curled in a grimace. He mouths something like *motherfucker*, and his right arm swings out—toward the camera or toward her, and the tape cuts in that instant. But you see the flash of anger. Instant and raw. There is no lightness in his body, no gesture toward play. His arm, fast as a whip, goes for her and the camera goes black. I watch again, trying to slow the scene. It's unmistakable. His face, in a nanosecond, turns beastly. His arm snaps toward her. And the Pavlovian response to the moment isn't just Rocky's. It's Michelle's, too. Turning off the camera in one practiced movement. Exit viewer. I call a friend into my office, and don't offer him any context. "Watch this," I say to him, "and tell me what you think happens next."

It's only maybe two seconds long in total. A sneeze and you'd miss it. We watch together, my friend Don and I. I've seen it now three, four, five times.

"Holy shit," Don says when he sees it.

THE FINAL DVD FROM Michelle's dad was labeled *Mosure Family 2001 Last Tape*. There is more camping and Kristy and Kyle sitting on the couch watching TV. There's Rocky unhooking a fish from their line, his jaws working as if he's chewing something. And a small blow-up swimming pool in their backyard in which a tiny duck swims. "Ducky," Kristy says to the duck, trying to pet it. "I went underwater and you freaked me out!" Later, I see a turtle walking across their front yard. Rocky's white car is parked diagonally across the lawn, next to a scooter on its side. There's no hood on the car. Then there are silent videos of the Mustang Rocky was forever working on in their garage.

The tape picks up again, but there's no telling how much time has passed. Weeks. Months. It's Kristy in purple, Michelle again behind the camera, watching as her little girl's head is trained toward the ground, standing at the water's edge. Kristy takes a few hesitant steps. She walks up so that just her tippy toes are in the water. And she stays there.

Then they're in a cave. It's September of 2001.

Michelle's wearing cut-off jean shorts. "Even in all this darkness," Rocky says, panning from the cave walls to his wife's ass, "show your mom what she really looks like."

THE LAST SCENE OF the video shows a hexagon-shaped cage. And inside the cage a snake is curled up, with its view trained on the camera, its upper body in an S curve. It has dark brown diamonds on its back, a thick middle body in the foreground. Rattlesnake. It's tight as a ribbon inside its enclosure, far too big for where it's landed. Rocky is filming, the kids' voices in the background. Rocky takes one finger from his left hand, taps on the glass five or six times. The snake doesn't move anything but its eyelids, lazily, slowly, watching that finger tap, tap, tap. Its tongue flickers a few times, but it appears nonplussed by the human trying to catch its attention. Then, all of a sudden . . . *snap!* The snake bangs the glass and reels back so quickly you don't even see the move. All you hear is the thump. "Wooo," Rocky says, saved by the glass barrier. *Daddy always lives.* "Crazy."

It's the final image on the videos. The snake. The tap, tap, tapping, Rocky showing his power over a thing that in another landscape, could kill him in an instant.

Rocky's voice.

"Crazy."

And then nothing.

PART II

The Beginning

Penance

The kinds of girls Jimmy Espinoza hunted were weak. Vulnerability clung to their skin like powder. It was in their eyes and the way they moved, and Jimmy could spot them. If they met his gaze with that searching, hungry look he knew he could get them. They were mostly young, though not always. They were lost. They were controllable. "If a girl didn't have a father," he says, "I knew I could get her." He treated his partners the same way he treated his working girls: as items he owned or discarded at will. He hit them or he didn't. He fucked them or he didn't. It was up to him where and when and how. Their role was in service to him.

Whether what he was doing was right or wrong didn't factor into his thinking. Morality had no part in his internal conversation. Money followed its own cannibalistic logic on the streets. The more you got, the more you had to lose. The more you had to lose, the more you needed. The more you needed, the more you hustled, and on and on. There was a time in the '90s when Jimmy Espinoza was one of the most notorious pimps in San Francisco. He estimated on his best days he'd pull down fifteen grand. It was back when the Mission wasn't a place you went for lattes and designer jeans. It was a place you went when you wanted trouble.

This marked history makes Jimmy an unlikely figure to lead an anti–domestic violence program inside the very jail that once held him captive. His violence—they own it with a possessive pronoun in the world in which he lives now—was against the women who worked for him and the women who had relationships with him, against rival gang members, against just about anyone who looked at him in a way he didn't like. Rape was a weapon in his arsenal; in his own estimation he was a "low-life motherfucker." Where to put his hordes of cash was his biggest worry in those days. Stuffing it in mattresses, in car seats, anywhere he could. You don't put that shit in a bank. Hundred-dollar bills crammed in Nike shoeboxes. He had a BMW, a Mercedes, a crotch rocket. "I want everyone to know what a scavenger I am," he says, speaking always in the present tense. "I'm a bottom-feeder, man."

Jimmy's bald head is covered in tattoos of San Francisco's great sites: the Transamerica building, the Golden Gate Bridge, a streetcar. Chart your tourist journey across his scalp and the back of his head. Tattoos on his knuckles say *tuff enuf* and one on his neck bears the sign *Est. 1969*.

Not long ago, he gave five hundred dollars—an utter fortune to him now—to the Huckleberry House, which serves at-risk youth from the area. Jimmy describes it as a place for "runaway girls who are usually into prostitution." It's penance for him, a way to address the vast numbers of women he once terrorized. Women lost in the wider world, women he wishes he could find again to say he's sorry. He didn't know, he says. He didn't know. He fears that some, maybe even many, are dead.

There are three stories that make up the emotional axis of Jimmy's life. A play in three acts, so powerful to him that they are somatic as much as psychic. They can be summed up in three questions: what is the worst thing that ever happened to you? What is the worst thing you ever did? What is the worst thing to happen to someone you love? Anyone who's lived a life in which these three questions are immediately answerable may have some kind of understanding of what drives Jimmy today. In the first story he's a kid, maybe eight or nine years old. In the second, he's a young adult, midtwenties. In the third, he is all grown up. He tells these three stories again and again, not because the telling is cathartic but because the stories hold so much power among the population he works with. The world blasts you with some unpredictable horror and then what? No one escapes the blast. If you're someone like Jimmy, you get mean. And the meanness means you get blasted again, because you're daring the forces around you to do it again. Go ahead. I can take it. I'm tough. I'm a fucking *man*. And it works. The angrier you get, the more things happen to you. The more things happen to you, the angrier you get. A real-life infinity symbol.

You keep at it until one day you wind up dead or some miracle intervenes to wake you the fuck up. Jimmy got the miracle. If he'd have been born in some other state, spent time in some other jail after what he did, maybe he'd have been the "wound up dead" guy and not just the guy with these three stories. Plenty of guys he's known ended this way. He's still burying some of them today. But he was born in San Francisco's Excelsior district where the "gangster" shit he pulled landed him in a jail called San Bruno at the exact same time that San Bruno became the site of an unusual and audacious experiment.

BEFORE THE STORY OF the San Bruno laboratory, and before Jimmy's three defining episodes can be told, I have to go to another story first. It begins more than sixty years ago in a working class village in Scotland with a curious kid named Hamish Sinclair.

Sinclair's grandfather was a stonemason who died young of silicosis. His father was a furnaceman, an authoritarian, who also died young, when Sinclair was just thirteen. All his life he was aware of the struggles of the working class. He lived inside it, where every family in his village of Kinlochleven depended on work at the local aluminum factory. Kinlochleven was surrounded on three sides by mountains. The village had no other industry, no other options for anyone back when he was growing up, apart from that factory. "The whole thing in that village was to get the hell out of there," Sinclair told me. "If you had one guy working in the plant with four kids, only one kid could take his place. The other three had to go somewhere else."

So Sinclair was an escapee. He'd planned to be a painter, an artist. He attended the Bryanston School in England, which taught the Dalton system, similar to Montessori in its holistic approach to education. Dalton rejected the rote memorization taught in most schools in the early twentieth century and instead advocated that students become their own teachers. Curriculum plans were individualized, and students were tasked with learning to study, learning to learn by themselves. In Sinclair's school, there was always a teacher to ask, to offer some guidance, and tutors were available, but the whole idea was to be an active participant in one's own educational formation. It is a philosophy that threads itself into his life and work still today. As I sat with him one night at a restaurant in the Tenderloin district of San Francisco and he told me about his life, it became clear that his career was made up of projects and that he had created the methodology for each project, whether it was documenting marches against the Vietnam War in New York City or diving into the River Thames to film protests against the nuclear submarines. We talked for hours that night, moving to the bar when the restaurant closed, moving by a fireplace in a nearby lobby hotel when the bar closed, until long after midnight, and long after the rest of the city was fast asleep. And in every new story, in every decade, this fact of creation was central.

Sinclair, who is eighty-five now, has a mop of gray curls and speaks as if he's just walked off the Haight set and it's 1968. He wears Crocs and reminds me of someone's charmingly disheveled eccentric uncle. For years I couldn't place his ever-so-slight accent. Canadian? Irish? Minnesotan? Scottish.

After he graduated from Bryanston, his story is long and convoluted and fascinating, and perhaps it will be fully told by another author in another book someday. It involves a bed and breakfast on the Irish coast, an actual dark and stormy night when he gave up his proprietor's bedroom to an American filmmaker who would eventually bring him to New York as a cameraman and activist, where he would accidentally assault an FBI officer during the Vietnam War protests, leave New York briefly for London, and then return to the United States and become a key figure in the drive for unionization, first among Kentucky coal miners and then later among Michigan auto workers. "I was in a tidal wave of social unrest, and I was right on the cusp of it," he says of his arrival in America, those early years of activism and civil disobedience. He was watching the Black Power movement of Detroit, the burgeoning of 1970s feminism, and as he traveled and organized and learned from Americans all over the country, a single question began to form in Sinclair's mind:

Why did so many of the men he knew beat each other up?

Not all men, of course. But those he'd worked with, those he'd organized, befriended, so often. Working-class men in New York, in Kentucky, in Michigan. Even back home in the UK. Domestic violence wasn't on his radar. He was thinking of radical action. Class politics and labor rights. He was thinking of what the Detroit Black Power movement had in common with those Kentucky miners. He was a social activist, trying to organize them into a unified movement, but he kept butting up against the patriarchy, macho attitudes about who should lead and why and how. After the 1968 riots in Chicago, he headed to Detroit to organize guys in the auto industry. He'd been focused, at least in part, on race relations, on getting more whites to work with their Black brothers. Gender wasn't anywhere in his purview.

After a few years in Detroit, a group of women came to him and said they, too, wanted to organize. Some of them were the wives of men he'd organized in the past. The way he saw it, he'd help anyone who wanted to be helped. If you were ready to fight systemic prejudice or unfair labor conditions, if you were a justice warrior, he didn't care who you were. The more bodies, the bigger the impact. The bigger the impact, the bigger the chances of change. But the men he worked with, it turned out, weren't as egalitarian in their gender views. They were vehemently opposed to women organizing. It was 1975; women's liberation was still in its infancy. As more women began to attend Sinclair's community organizing events, some of the men Sinclair had already helped organize would complain about the women, and say women can't be organized. Organization was for men. "Five years I'd been doing this city-wide organization," Sinclair told me of his time in Detroit, "and that was all destroyed when these men said, 'You can't organize girls.'" It shocked Sinclair.

Sinclair and the men held a series of meetings, each one seeming to escalate in emotional intensity and patriarchal entrenchment until one night, after the third meeting, one of the men who'd been pivotal in Sinclair's organizing of men went home and beat his own wife so badly that several women—"tough as nails women" Sinclair called them—came to him the next day and asked him to call it all off. This guy was serious. A lot of their husbands didn't want them organizing. It had to stop. At the time, Sinclair said his attitude wasn't that the husbands should refrain from beating their wives because it was morally reprehensible, but rather because it split up the community. "I was caught in the middle of this thing and the guys put a price on my head," he said. For six months, he went "underground," rarely leaving his house, and if he did, he brought bodyguards.

After those six months, they declared a truce. The men came to him and wanted to start up the organizing again. Sinclair said all right and then asked if they were ready now to bring in women. The men were aghast. Hadn't they been through this already? they asked him. And he told them, "Well, I'm not going to work for someone who wants to divide the community in half by gender."

His partner convinced him that it was time to leave Detroit. The men and women were at an impossible impasse, and if Sinclair didn't leave, he'd wind up dead.

So he headed west to Berkeley, where he was introduced to Claude Steiner.

Steiner was a giant in the field of gender theory, the father of the so-called "radical psychiatry" movement in Berkeley in the 1970s; he wrote about men and women's "internalized oppression" and advocated for social-justice-based therapies; he helped popularize the idea of emotional literacy. Radical psychiatry criticized standard modes of clinical treatment that often ignored the social context in which patients were living—a world in which war, poverty, racism, and inequality were endemic. Radical psychiatry called for systemic upheaval to the social and political order. It was an antiauthoritarian movement born of a counter culture outspoken in its criticisms of standard medical interventions, like drugs, involuntary hospitalization, or electrotherapy. It aspired to a treatment model that purported that mental illness could often be addressed through social theory and personal change, rather than the medical industry.

Sinclair became a devotee and friend of Steiner until his death in 2017.

For five years, under the mentorship of Steiner, Sinclair worked with schizophrenic patients in a psychiatric facility outside of San Francisco and he read Steiner's works and the works of his contemporaries. He began to understand violence as the result of a belief system men all seemed to share, which told them they were the authority in their lives, that they were to be respected, obeyed. Top of the human hierarchy. It was a belief system that not only distanced them from people around them, but also limited their range, kept them boxed in by their own narrow ideas of what men could be and how men could behave.

But why? Why did men believe this? Sinclair understands, of course, the arguments about human evolution, how we must kill to survive (to eat, he means). He's willing to believe that maybe at some point, far back in human history, men had some kind of predisposition toward violence in order to feed their families. But no longer, not today, and not for many hundreds of years. Beyond this history, he rejects the notion that violence is inherent to the male species, that men are somehow born to fight. For starters, we no longer need such violence to survive; instead, what we need now is to "intimate," as he puts it. And in this, men have no belief system, because men are taught violence, but they are not taught intimacy. "Violence is a skill that we all had to learn just to stay with the pack growing up," he said. "The trouble is, it doesn't work for intimacy. That's a whole different set of skills."[1] Read any news story today about domestic violence homicide and you're likely to see some version of the question *why didn't she leave?* What you almost surely won't see is *why was he violent?* Or better yet, *why couldn't he stop his violence?* Men, Sinclair believes, get one type of training and women get another. In a white paper he sent to me from a conference presentation some years ago, he paraphrased an assistant sheriff from San Francisco who told him, "men learn to be men by defining themselves as superior to each other and to women, and much of the violence in our communities is due to men's ongoing enforcement of this learned belief in their superiority, be it spousal abuse, gang turf wars, street assaults, armed robbery, and all the other crimes that men in the jails had been charged with. Men . . . had learned that it was normal to use force and violence in all of the forms above to enforce their social obligation to be superior."

Sinclair is unapologetically unabashed about the gender specifics here. It is *men* who are violent. It is *men* who perpetrate the majority of the world's violence, whether that violence is domestic abuse or war. Even those relatively few women who are violent, he says, are most often violent in response to men's violence. Indeed, this is the single most effective argument I know for why it doesn't make sense to arm women with guns to protect them against men with guns: because arming a woman with a gun is asking her to behave like a man, to embody the somatic and psychological and cultural experience of a man while simultaneously quelling all that women have been taught. It says to women, if you want to protect yourself from violent men, you need to become violent yourself. To Sinclair, this is exactly the wrong way to the solution. It's not women who need to learn violence; it's men who need to learn nonviolence.

If men are taught not to cry, women are taught crying is acceptable. If men are taught anger is their sole allowable emotion, women are taught never to be angry. Men who yell are being men; women who yell are shrill or they're drama queens or they're hysterical. (Many before me have pointed out that there is no greater "drama" than a mass shooting, but the term "drama kings" hasn't yet captured the popular lexicon, however accurate.) Sinclair calls this "the elephant in the room." That we won't say, simply, that it is men who are violent. It is men who take their violence out on masses of others. School shootings are carried out by young men. Mass murders. Gang warfare, murder-suicides and familicides and matricides and even genocides: all men. Always men. "Every commonly available domestic violence and official general violence statistic, and every anecdotal account about domestic and all other kinds of violence throughout the United States and around the world, point clearly to the fact that men almost monopolize all sectors of violence perpetration," Sinclair wrote. "The generic descriptions of violence seem to be a careful attempt not to see this crucial piece of evidence . . . a careful way of avoiding the gendered source of violence.

This error in analysis will mislead us in our attempts to find solutions to the problem."

In other words, if we can't honestly name who the perpetrators are, how can we find the solutions?

Sinclair suggests that the fear of naming the real perpetrators is, itself, a sort of meta-violence; by refusing to call out men we are aiding and abetting this belief. But the fear of a backlash is justified. We live in a world in which we have leaders who get away, literally, with bragging about this belief system, where sexual assaults on college campuses are at a crisis point, and where casual violence is an accepted and celebrated form of entertainment, where former attorney general Jeff Sessions deemed intimate partner terrorism not enough of a threat to qualify an immigrant for asylum, and where men with histories of abuse like Rob Porter are given illustrious jobs with the commander in chief of our country, despite those violent histories. Indeed, the commander in chief himself has a history of known violence, at least to his first wife, Ivana, as described in her divorce deposition. David Frum, a former speech-writer for President George W. Bush, in a 2018 op-ed for the *Atlantic*, wrote that "Violence at home indicates a dangerous temperament for a high official, including vulnerability to blackmail . . . This president sent a message to the people around him about what is permitted, or at any rate, what is forgivable."[2]

I thought of a field trip to see *Camelot* with my daughter's school that I chaperoned not long ago. Fourth graders from all over the city attended. After the performance the actors came out on stage for a Q&A and the moderator, who worked at the theater, asked the kids two questions: one, do you think Guenevere was wrong to allow her feelings for Lancelot to lead to a betrayal of her husband, King Arthur? And, two, should King Arthur have forgiven Lancelot or executed him? To the first question, the kids hollered, collectively, that yes, she was wrong. She should have ignored her feelings. To the second, the boys' voices erupted in in a massive prepubescent holler, "Yes! Kill him! Kill him!" These were children growing up in the liberal enclave of Washington, D.C., children with two working parents in families that often defy gender norms from the day they're born. And yet, the audience was asked only about the female character's feelings, not the male's—as if Lancelot and Arthur were devoid of human emotion. And when the choice to forgive or avenge arose, the answer fell squarely along gendered lines. The boys said kill, unequivocally. Fourth graders had already gotten the message, even in spite of their liberal surroundings. (It was a great disappointment to me that none of the adults—not the teachers, not the actors, not the chaperones—took the opportunity to address this gendered view.[3] Indeed, I'm not at all sure that anyone but me noticed it.)

To all of this, Sinclair throws his hands up and says, "No kidding." He tells me about an antiviolence conference he attended some years ago where a presenter was asked about a family who encouraged their child to go back to his harasser and beat him up. The target of the fight was a boy. The child of the family in question was a boy. The parent offering the advice was the father. (It is the rare mother who would exhort her son to "go back out there and beat him up.") So here was a father advocating that the solution to his young son's problem of violence was more violence; his solution reinforced the male-role belief system, recycling it to yet another young man. Violence begetting violence begetting violence. But none of the participants at the conference even mentioned the gender dynamics of this scenario, Sinclair said. Instead, the focus was on the anecdote itself, the possible result of the fight, but not the gendered exhortation in the first place. Sinclair points to this as "part of the problem." This refusal to see or acknowledge the gendered source of violence. The whos as much as the whys. Violence, he says, is not a "relationship problem. It is a problem of [a woman's] partner's commitment to violence."

"Violent men are aware that they are violent and even take pride in the manliness of it to their friends," he said. "But, they will often deny that their violence is actually violent when questioned. Their denial allows violent men to minimize the impact of their violence on their victims, blame them for it, and ask their families and friends to collude with them by approving it." What he means is that incidents of violence are downplayed: perpetrators tend to use phrases like "it wasn't that bad." They accuse victims of overreacting. They claim they didn't mean to "hurt" her when they threw that household item in her general direction or slammed that door on her or tossed her against a wall. As if the objects—wall, door—were to blame. These men do everything they can not to own an act as violent.

Five years after he moved to California, Sinclair became restless, yearning to get back to the critical work of organization. One day he was asked by a woman he knew who worked out of the Marin Abused Women's Services in San Rafael if he would consider doing a men's department within their shelter. He thought about it but couldn't quite wrap his mind around the particulars of what it would be. And then he went back to his roots. He wasn't an administrator; he was an organizer. An activist. He put together Dalton and those Detroit union guys not wanting women around and radical psychiatry, which acknowledged the world we all lived in, and his mind started percolating. He told her he didn't want to run a men's department inside a woman's shelter. Instead, he wanted to create a whole new program, an intervention for violent men. "It was based on women's urgency," he said. "The women wanted a program that addressed their experience of *our* violence. They said *your* violence." Men's violence. It is a thread that you can hear still today, running through Jimmy's interventions at San Bruno every day with violent men.

Sinclair's program began in 1980, but wasn't named until 1984 when it became ManAlive, a fifty-two-week program, divided into three parts. The first twenty-week part tries to get men to be accountable for their violence. The second sixteen-week session gives them a skill set of alternative behaviors to violence. And the third part, also sixteen weeks, teaches them strategies for creating intimacy and fulfillment in their lives. For the first decade, there weren't many guys flocking to take part in a program that would upend everything they believed about what a man was supposed to be and do. Then the Violence Against Women Act passed, and suddenly courts were referring guys to them—not just to ManAlive, but to batterer intervention programs all over the country, in Massachusetts and Colorado and Minnesota. A law in California passed that made it mandatory for violent men to do the program or go to jail, and the law specifically said that the intervention had to be gender-based, not therapy-based. They couldn't just be sent to anger management. They couldn't have a few sessions with a therapist and be done. They had to learn about gender roles and expectations as part of their curriculum; they had to study the role of gender in their own acculturation. (Although, Sinclair is the first to say that a lot of what comprises the ManAlive curriculum does, in fact, borrow from therapy.) The inspiration for his curriculum was gender theory and neuro-linguistic training (NLP).[4] In the ManAlive curriculum, it is simply a way of asking men to notice their bodies, their voices, and the responses of those around them during a violent incident in a way that the vast majority of them never have.

The ManAlive program became an area leader among the many batterer intervention programs that arose in the aftermath of VAWA; it emerged at the same time as several other early notable programs: Amend in Denver, Emerge in Boston, and the Domestic Abuse Intervention

Project in Duluth. And all of these did something that no one, up until that point, had really thought to do: address violence not in its aftermath, with victims, but at its core, with the abusers.

The program's reputation grew throughout the region. In the late '90s, it came to the attention of an innovative prison guard named Sunny Schwartz, who had grown frustrated with the system's inability to address violence in the men she was seeing year after year, decade after decade. Schwartz had witnessed firsthand how violence worked in cycles, both within the lives of the men she guarded and also generationally. Men she met in her daily work life did some violent act to land them in prison, then did their time in the culture of violence that is incarceration in America today, and then brought that heightened level of violence right back into their families and communities. Schwartz began to see the children of the men she knew from her early days in corrections. And then the grandchildren. There had to be a better way, she thought. Violence isn't supposed to be genetic. She'd seen the levels of incarceration rise year after year, but she knew crime in the United States wasn't falling accordingly. Locking up men punitively wasn't doing anything to change the reasons they got locked up in the first place.

After years with these men, she began to think that violence was something that could be reduced if prison became a place not to toss away and forget those who broke the law, but a place to reform them. There were two philosophical pillars to her program. The first was the ManAlive curriculum: an intervention in the cycle of violence passed down from man to man, father to son to son to son. But she wanted more. The second pillar was the concept of restorative justice. Restorative justice insists that the perpetrator acknowledge the pain and suffering he has caused and "restore" his victims and community as much as possible. Reconciliation is the primary goal, through offenders meeting with domestic violence victims. Though restorative justice sometimes means an offender is meeting with his or her specific victim, in the context of San Bruno, general victims of domestic violence are brought in weekly to talk about their experiences and about what it means to live with and beyond trauma.

Watching Violence in a Fishbowl

The woman speaking today is named Victoria.[1] She is fifty years old and in the past five years has finally stopped picturing her father's gun pointed at her head. She used to hear her mother's body as it slammed against the wall, but thought her mother was weak and boring. Her father was charismatic, charming. Once, when she rode her bike to a boy's house, Victoria's father followed her in his car, brought her home, and held a gun to her mother's head, saying, "If you ever allow her to do that again I'll kill you." Sometimes, Victoria says, if she or her brother did something wrong, their father would threaten to kill their pets.

I'm in the San Bruno jail today, my first time here, sitting with dozens of men in blue plastic chairs, lined up as they listen to Victoria's story. The men wear matching orange jumpsuits, laceless white shoes. Some have long sleeves under their jumpsuits. Some have tattoos on nearly every visible inch of skin: fingers, necks, faces. For most of them, it's the first time they've ever sat, quietly, and listened for several hours as someone talked about domestic violence in her life.

One day, when she was sixteen, Victoria says, she heard her mother's body once again, thump, thump, thumping against the wall. By now she had stopped calling the police. ("Oh, that little lady is tough," she remembers hearing during one of her many 911 calls.) And then her mother escaped the bedroom and ran to the car. Victoria dashed outside behind her. "He tried to kill me," her mother said, breathlessly. "You have two seconds. You can get in the car or not."

Victoria froze. Stay. Go. Stay.

Her mother started the engine.

Victoria stayed.

"For years I carried the guilt of being the one who stayed," she tells the men. "I became anorexic."

For many of the men here, it's not merely the first time they've ever really listened to a survivor of domestic violence tell her story, it's the first time they ever considered how trauma and violence can have a long-term impact on someone. Many of them wipe away tears. "My dad used to write men in prison who'd killed their whole families and tell them they were brave," Victoria says. "I always had the sense that something bad was going to happen." She says that eventually, as an adult, she realized how bad he was and she cut him out of her life. She found her mother and they reconciled. She had always remembered her mother as loud, as screaming and yelling, but she says she has learned that her mother is actually quiet and keeps to herself. Victoria lives near her now. One Father's Day she decided she'd see her dad at Denny's. It had been years, but she immediately recognized his glassy-eyed look. When she, her brother, and their father walked out of the restaurant after an uncomfortable breakfast, her father put his arm around her and whispered, "I have a gun in my sock. I was going to kill the family, but I took one look at you and I could not."

It was the last time she ever saw him. She keeps her daughter away from him now. "You've heard the saying 'hurt people hurt people,'" she says to the men gathered. "Well, I also think healed people heal people."

The men are allowed to ask questions afterward. They are sheepish, almost reverent when they stand to speak. Some are trembling as they raise their hands. She is asked how her relationship with her daughter is compared to that of her own mother. ("Completely different"; she won't even raise her voice.) She is asked if she forgives her father. ("No.") She is asked where her father is now. ("No idea. Southern California, maybe.") She is asked if she dated men like her dad. ("Narcissists, yes. And players.") And then one guy gets up, a young guy in his early twenties, his hands visibly shaking, holding a ratty notebook, and he half raps/half recites a poem he wrote, just then, for her, about her victimhood, and then her survival, about how brave she was.[2] By the time he's done, Victoria is crying, and a good number of the men have tears in their eyes.

In the afternoon, the men talk through her story in small groups, contextualizing what they recognize from the curriculum and attaching it to their own incidents of violence—Victoria was verbally threatened; her father blamed her and denied wrongdoing thereby refusing to take responsibility for his violence, and he was physically violent toward her mother; Victoria was emotionally violated; she was manipulated by her father; her experience was trivialized by her father, and one guy with short braids in his hair points out that when her mother left it was a resource taken from her. By "resource" he means something that might have kept her safe. The talk about their own incidents of violence, times they also denied any wrongdoing, moments they manipulated or verbally threatened partners, instances of trivializing their own violent events. They begin to see, some of them for the first time ever, the effect their violence may have had on their victims. That is to say, they begin to see the world through someone else's eyes.

"Now imagine," a facilitator named Reggie says to them, "if that was your child up there where Victoria was standing. What would your kid say about you?"

THE SAN BRUNO PROGRAM is called Resolve to Stop the Violence (RSVP). Sunny Schwartz convinced the former San Francisco sheriff, Michael Hennessey, to fund her vision, and it began in the late '90s.[3] ManAlive and Survivor Impact (or restorative justice) are the pillars of this antiviolence experiment, where Jimmy Espinoza's violence would stop and his life would begin again. The program began in the San Bruno jail, just south of San Francisco, and surprisingly, despite its relative success, has not spread much beyond San Bruno. San Quentin had a version of it for a while, but then Sinclair said it lost funding. There was talk of creating a similar program in Westchester, New York. At its inception, RSVP was a year-long program, a six-day-a-week, twelve-hour-a-day immersion aimed at restoring violent men to contributory, nonviolent members of society. Where most batterer intervention programs are once a week for twenty, forty, maybe fifty weeks, RSVP was total immersion, a multimodal approach. The core goal was making them take responsibility for their violent behavior and learn alternatives, but Schwartz's program also addressed substance abuse, child abuse, mental health. It began each day with meditation and ended each day with yoga. Challenging gender norms, specifically how men and women are conditioned by social and cultural standards, and how men are taught violence to solve their problems and women are supposed to be subservient to their men, was at the core of the curriculum. For many of the men, it flipped everything they thought they knew about their world.

Schwartz didn't want to just hope RSVP worked. She wanted to know, unequivocally. So she called in two of the country's foremost violence researchers to study her program, James Gilligan and Bandy Lee. Another wing of the prison was their control group. They tracked multiple data, including violent incidents in both the RSVP and the control wings (or pods), recidivism rates, and violence within communities after offenders were released. The results, by almost any calculation, were stunning: the recidivism rates dropped by 80% and those who did wind up back in jail tended to be for nonviolent misdemeanors, like drugs or motor vehicle offenses. In the year prior to the program's implementation, Gilligan and Lee noted twenty-four violent incidents that could have been charged as felonies had they happened outside of the context of incarceration. Once the RSVP program began, there was a violent incident in the first quarter of the year, and none thereafter in the program wing; the control group, however, cataloged twenty-eight such incidents.[4] And researchers found that once offenders were released back into their communities, if they'd gone through the program in its entirety, they often became voices of nonviolence. People, they mean, like Jimmy Espinoza.

It also saved money. Gilligan and Lee found that although RSVP increased the cost per inmate by $21 a day, for every dollar spent in this kind of violence-reduction program, the community gained four extra dollars.[5]

It's been twenty years now since RSVP began, and despite the success of the program, it's been replicated in fewer than half a dozen jails, most of them overseas. While it retains its basic organization, rather than six days a week, twelve hours a day, RSVP is now more like five days a week, six hours a day. This is partly because funding programs for incarcerated people is often a challenge depending upon who's been elected and what priorities exist inside a world of limited resources, and partly because San Bruno now offers so many different programs to offenders, including GED and community college classes, art therapy, theater, and substance abuse and twelve-step programs. (San Bruno is colloquially referred to as an "all program jail" for this reason.) The current director of programs at San Bruno talked to me informally one evening, and when I asked her why RSVP hadn't migrated to other prisons, she told me that unlike a lot of other prison populations, violent men just don't have their own "champion."[6] A parallel might be incarcerated veterans who have a lot of outside support, and a consensus that we as a country need to be doing more to address their needs, particularly in light of post-traumatic stress. But the most prominent voices around domestic violence are the survivors who, naturally, prioritize their own needs over abusers'.

Sunny Schwartz, who has retired, is happy to see RSVP still ongoing, but disappointed at the lack of replication. "Why isn't [RSVP] the rule rather than the exception?" she asks. "What pisses me off so much is the lack of imagination we tend to have for people who haven't had the same experience we have. As if lives are synonymous." We're sitting in a diner in Noe Valley, Schwartz in jeans and a T-shirt, her dark brown hair threaded with gray. She is a commanding presence in person, tall and powerful.

It frustrates Schwartz that there are so few resources available to those coming out of the RSVP program and back into civil society. Things like job training, meditation, parenting classes, alcoholics and narcotics anonymous, housing support, twelve-step programs, art and humanities therapies, and educational opportunities. These guys go through RSVP, she told me, and they learn all this stuff about gender, about themselves, about culture and society and violence and communication, and then they walk back into a world in which all of that theory is real again, and all of those challenges are real again, plus all of those threats and all of that pain, and they're just more or less on their own.

The United States spends as much as twenty-five times more on researching cancer or heart disease than it does on violence prevention, despite the enormous costs of violence to our communities.[7] A 2018 study published in the *American Journal of Preventive Medicine* put the cost of intimate partner violence at nearly $3.6 trillion (the study examined forty-three million U.S. adults, so it doesn't count costs associated with, for example, dating violence); this equates to $2 trillion in medical costs and $73 billion in criminal justice expenses, among other costs, like lost productivity or property damage. Intimate partner violence costs women $103K and men $23K over the course of a single lifetime.[8] These figures are a steep climb from a 2003 Centers for Disease Control report that put the cost of domestic violence at nearly $6 billion a year to American taxpayers.[9] That report did not include criminal justice costs, incarceration expenses, or anyone under the age of eighteen.

Prison creates more violence in our communities, not less. And so, Schwartz asked me, "What is our alternative?" She told me an anecdote that had stayed with her for years, a story that was equal parts call to action and reason to hope. It was about a Holocaust survivor who, in the midst of being beaten by a guard, never stopped smiling. It infuriated the guard. The guard hit him harder and harder, until finally, he stopped and asked the prisoner why he was smiling. He said, "I am grateful, because I am not like you."

Schwartz and I began our discussion that day not with the advent of RSVP, but instead with a man named Tari Ramirez. Ramirez's tale is the kind of story that derails the work of RSVP, that makes anyone who's involved question whether any of this, all the hours they pour into these men, all the chances they give and then give again, is worth it. Can a violent man learn to be nonviolent?

In his RSVP classes, Ramirez appeared by all accounts to be an active participant. He was quiet, reserved, but he contributed to the class and seemed to take the material seriously. It had taken four separate incidents of violence against his girlfriend, Claire Joyce Tempongko, four different calls to the police, four different attempts at restraining orders (that were issued and then vacated and issued and then vacated) just to finally get a judge to send Ramirez to jail, and even then, he received only a six-month sentence. He had gone through the first stage of RSVP and had just begun the second stage when he was released from San Bruno.

Shortly after his release, Ramirez stabbed Tempongko to death in front of her two young children. Ramirez had had a significant history of violence against Tempongko, who was only twenty-eight when she was killed. An investigation by the deputy city attorney after the murder showed that Ramirez had dragged Tempongko by her hair out of the apartment multiple times, he'd threatened her with a broken beer bottle, told her he'd burn her house down and hurt her children, punched her more than eighteen times, strangled her and shoved his fingers down her throat, and kidnapped her on several occasions.[10] And again, for all this, he was given six months. When the average person who knows little about domestic violence believes a misdemeanor is no big deal, one need only point out the Ramirez case. Misdemeanors, in the world of domestic violence, are like warning shots. And all too often they go unheeded.

Schwartz knew that ignoring what Ramirez did would be intellectually and emotionally disingenuous. More to the point she knew that while the devastation Ramirez's act wrought on the victim and her immediate family and across the entire RSVP program was enormous and profound, to her it wasn't entirely a surprise. "We're dealing with really badly behaving men," she said.

Since Ramirez did not finish out the program in its entirety, as a case study in efficacy, it's not particularly useful. Nevertheless, the murder devastated those in the program, the facilitators and the jail personnel, and even the guys who'd sat in that circle with Ramirez, sharing their worst moments and their deepest vulnerabilities. The day they learned of the murder, Schwartz told me she walked into the jail and everyone was "crying hysterically, uncontrollably." It was a moment of crisis for the entire program, but it didn't shake her belief in the work and in its urgency. "This stuff is too delicate and compelling to pretend that any one thing is the answer," she said. "I think of the cancer analogy. You have people going through chemotherapy and then someone dies. Does that mean you stop your clinical trial?" You keep at it, keep tweaking, keep developing, keep trying new combinations. "That's what this is," she said. "It's a clinical trial."

TO SEE MORE OF RSVP in action, I meet Jimmy Espinoza on a breezy January morning at the entrance to San Bruno nearly a year after my first visit, when Victoria told her story. South of San Francisco, San Bruno sits atop a hill in the suburbs, surrounded by single-family pastel houses. The thick metal doors open for him freely now. He jokes with guards and inmates alike. One guard with a chest the size of a smart car, who happens to be gay, recounts a story from the weekend that involves a recent vacation and an unwanted advance and a self-deprecating joke about being a "flyin' Hawaiian," which has Jimmy crying with laughter. (San Bruno is the only jail I've ever been in with openly gay guards. Prison guards can be stoic, tough, even violent; I just hadn't ever thought of them as also possibly gay, and my surprise was yet another reminder of how deep stereotypes can run, even in someone like me who was actively in that exact moment trying to upend such stereotypes.) Jimmy wears a beige Dickies button-down shirt and matching cargo pants; his clothes are so oversized he could fit both himself and the flyin' Hawaiian in there. Reading glasses are perched on his forehead.

The RSVP wing of the jail maintains a waiting list that sometimes has a dozen men or more on it. The reputation throughout San Bruno is that no one fucks with you in the RSVP pod. So guys want in. Guards, too. It also looks good in court if you can show a judge you're trying to change. But it's also this other thing, so obvious it rarely gets mentioned: people don't want to be in violent situations. When I'm told, as I often am, that violence is simply human nature, I think of San Bruno and wonder, if that is true, then why, given the choice, do people deemed so violent they must be locked away from civil society, try to put themselves first and foremost in a section known for its lack of violence?

The pod is a carpeted fishbowl, with a semicircular guard's desk in the middle. The desk is slightly higher than ground level so that he can see into every cell and every corner of the entire pod at once. There are two floors. A large staircase dominates the middle of the space. In another setting it might be the kind of grand staircase from which royalty descend. Twenty-four cells with glass fronts hold forty-eight guys who range in age from eighteen to seventy. They are white, Black, Latino, Asian, Middle Eastern, all in orange scrubs with laceless white shoes. A bank of pay phones lines one wall. The ceiling soars and it's quiet as a library when we enter. Some of the men are murderers. Some are dealers. Some are burglars. But all of them have domestic violence histories. All of them also have yet to be sentenced, which means they're on their best behavior; the newest guy has been here three days. The longest, two hundred and ten weeks. The length is a signal of the seriousness of his crime. Felonies, unlike misdemeanors, can take years and years to go through the court system. Each of them, though, knows he is lucky to be here. One of the founding tenets of this program is a zero tolerance for violence.

Jimmy is here today with two other facilitators: Reggie Daniels and Leo Bruenn. Some of the men come up and greet Jimmy with a kind of tough-guy handshake, a slap on the back and a half hug, or just simply a nod. They steal glances at me and one or two come and introduce themselves, call me ma'am. Reggie's group goes into a classroom, and Leo's takes up the area in front of the stairs. Jimmy and the fourteen men in his group today (and me) carry blue plastic chairs and form a small circle more or less underneath the arching staircase. The guys sit in a prescribed order: those who are newest to the pod sit to Jimmy's left and they wrap around the circle in order of seniority so that the guy who's been in the group the longest winds up on his immediate right. The order matters because the curriculum is peer-led—one of the elements here that differs from most other batterer intervention programs. Sinclair insists on the peer-led curriculum, pulling from his years in the Dalton system, where students participate in their own advancement, carve out their own education within the framework of the curriculum. I can feel myself being watched with curiosity. One of the agreements I made to be able to be here was that I be part of the process as much as I can and not simply an outsider combing these men for stories of the worst moments of their lives. This contradicts the role of most journalists, but part of the point of the course for these men is that we are all from the same community, and we share the same burdens: the need to be loved, the fear of vulnerability, the suffocating weight of shame. To make myself a viewer is, in some ways, to create the very kind of hierarchy that this program is trying to dismantle. In other batterer intervention groups, I am a silent viewer in the corner, but here I am somewhere between participant and viewer. So when we sit down, Jimmy asks me to start off the group by talking about myself.

I begin with my name and where I live, and tell them about this book and the university at which I am a professor. I tell them that we don't spend nearly as much time talking to offenders as we do their victims. And then I tell them the more important story, the story that probably leads me to write what I write in the first place: that I am a high school dropout, like many of them, and that sometimes violence swirled around me. The particulars of our lives differ in scope and detail, but every one of us in that room knows what a second (or a third, or a fourth) chance means, and the gripping fear of failure that accompanies it. Many of them later thank me for sharing a little of my life, and it leaves me feeling a sense of vulnerability that, despite being a woman in relative touch with her feelings, is unnerving and uncomfortable. Even here, writing it, I feel shame.

I wonder at how difficult public vulnerability must be for these guys. I didn't grow up being told not to cry, being told not to be a sissy, being told that I had to win, and if I didn't win, I had to fight to become the winner. I was told other things, yes. Certainly. Many of the same kinds of things that Michelle Monson Mosure was told. About what girls should be and do, and how girls should act. I was told that men were the head of the house and women subordinate. But sharing some of the most shameful moments? The most embarrassing moments? James Gilligan, the violence researcher who'd evaluated the RSVP program initially, told me that for many of these guys it's not becoming nonviolent that blows their minds about themselves; it's learning that they've been fed a line about what they're supposed to act like and who they're supposed to be, a line about what masculinity means and what being a man means. How as men they can acknowledge anger, rage, and authority. But not empathy, kindness, love, fear, pain, sadness, care, nurture or any of those other "traits" that are deemed feminine. And that they've been manipulated by forces larger than themselves, shaped by a world they had never thought about in this way, which is shocking to them. What a relief to learn they've been coerced into their violence, not born into it.

This morning's group is a kind of check-in for the guys. Later, the entire pod will have a community meeting led by Leo, and Jimmy will lead an addiction group in the afternoon. Jimmy starts off by asking them about emotional abuse. Do they understand what it means? How it's perpetrated? So much of the class is simply helping men identify and experience their feelings: fear, sadness, empathy, shame, even anger. It's not wrong to feel things; it's wrong to feel things and then purposely avoid them, is the point. Jimmy asks them, "Why will drug addiction affect your family?"

"Because we're not there even when we're there," one man says. He's in his midfifties, African American, hair gone gray. "We're manipulating their time and energy. They call us and we don't answer . . . We manipulate the space in their hearts."

The man beside him nods, his braided hair tied up in a massive knot. "I snapped on this bitch, but I came *on* drugs." What he means is that his loyalty was to drugs and not his partner. He sought out a high before he bothered paying any kind of attention to her. He's giving an example of how he *used* to think, before he knew what he knows now.

"I did a lot of emotional abuse without putting my hands on [my partner]," a man named Devon says. (I have changed all the men's names to protect their privacy.) "I used to go drinking and I took myself away from her. I started doing drugs and she'd cry. I'd be gone for days. I minimized her."

In ManAlive, drugs and alcohol aren't excuses for violence, Jimmy says. "I'm a drug addict. I'm a batterer. Me not coming home is violence toward the family. I'm not beating them, but I'm still affecting them. You're self-separating first." In the background, I can hear the guys from Bruenn's group talking, but the fourteen in this circle have their eyes trained on Jimmy. It's calm and quiet; a complete departure from the kind of chaos depicted of most jails in movies.

"We're all grounded in the unresolved shit, the shame of leaving your kids 'cause you're out drinking, or 'cause you're going back to jail," an inmate named Gary says. He's in this program for the second time; he never finished the first time around. A few of the guys murmur their agreement. A number of them tell me that being without their kids is the hardest part of being in jail.

And this brings Jimmy to his first story. The worst thing that ever happened to him. In this story, he's eight, maybe nine. He's got parents who are still married and who don't beat the hell out of each other, so that's something. He's got family all over the neighborhood. His grandmother lives down the street. Cousins are nearby. And then there's this guy, the relative of a friend of his. Buys him alcohol one day. He's this little kid in a neighborhood that's half Italian and half Irish, half cop and half criminal. He drinks the alcohol. The guy wants something from little Jimmy. He gave him alcohol, didn't he? A gift. He's a good guy, right? Little Jimmy can see that, right? Maybe Jimmy could do something for him now. Won't take long. Maybe Jimmy could just let the guy touch him a little bit? And maybe then little Jimmy could touch this grown man back? And little Jimmy does it even though it about makes him retch, because isn't it what he's supposed to do? Obey? Adults make the rules, right? Adults know everything. All the questions you ever have as a kid will have answers when you're an adult. Right? Like, why is this horrible, disgusting thing happening to me? Or maybe, am I making this horrible, disgusting thing happen to me? And eventually, am I a horrible, disgusting thing now?

It happens two, maybe three times. Little Jimmy tells no one. Holds this horror inside him like a fistful of molten asphalt for decades.

"It's my shame," he says when he tells this story today. "Not fighting back." Roughly 12% of male inmates in jails like San Bruno today were sexually assaulted before the age of eighteen. (In state prisons, the number is higher, and for those boys who grew up in foster care, the numbers are shocking, nearly 50%.[11]) I once asked Jimmy what he'd do if he saw the guy today.

"I'd kill him," he says.

And I'm not sure if he means it or not.

Around that same time, first one neighbor girl, and then soon another who took turns babysitting him also began to ask him to touch them. One girl would tell him to use his mouth, which made him want to gag. He was nine, ten years old. Had no earthly idea what he was doing, except that it was sexual. He knew that from movies. In movies people took their clothes off and moved around each other in some way, like snakes. One of the girls was high all the time on something. He was too young to know what it was, but later she became a dusthead. Dust-heads are what they called people who were always on PCP. The moles-tation went on longer with the girls. Two, maybe three years. He didn't know if what he was doing was wrong or right. All he knew was that he didn't like it. He thought it was his fault. He thought he'd done something wrong. He thought all the things that any child who's been violated thinks—boy or girl. When his family found out, they told him there'd been another man they thought had abused him because little Jimmy would cry whenever this guy came around. Jimmy doesn't remember. Maybe. Who can say. But it's the moment he points to. "The molestation from the man was worst," he says. "That right there made me violent. Made me a rageaholic, right? Lying, right? Just all these defects of character started growing at that moment."

I look around the room, fourteen men in jail staring him down as he tells this story. Half of them are nodding, partly from empathy. Partly from experience.

The Fatal Peril Club

When I first met Jimmy, he was supervising an intern named Donte Lewis. Donte had gone through the RSVP program twice (the first time he didn't finish, so he started from scratch again) and had recently been released from San Bruno, after serving just shy of his four-year sentence. Sitting in Yerba Buena Gardens with coffee and cigarettes, he told me how several years earlier, he'd been out of jail for under a week when he and his friend Mooch drove over to Donte's ex-girlfriend's house. Donte wasn't supposed to be there. He had a restraining order out against him—the result of an earlier kidnapping charge after he caught his girlfriend, Kayla Walker,[1] with another man one night and he'd wrapped her in a sheet and dragged her down the stairs to a waiting car. But most of his clothes were at Walker's house since they'd lived together on and off for years, and as far as he was concerned, she was still his girl, restraining order or not. He called her his "bitch."

Mooch gave Donte a lift, and he scaled the deck railings from the first to the second floor and slid open the glass sliding door of Walker's apartment. He remembers hearing Ja Rule blaring from her bedroom. When he stormed into her bedroom, she was there, in SpongeBob SquarePants pajama bottoms, and another guy was in the room with her, clothed, and sitting in the opposite corner. A guy they called Casper. Donte pulled out a Colt .45, aimed at her, and Casper went for the gun. "This ain't for you," Donte remembers shouting. In the melee, Walker ran out of the room. Casper attacked Donte and they tussled on the bed; Donte elbowed Casper in the face, and broke free, still holding the gun. Casper escaped the apartment and ran out into the night. Donte stormed after Walker.

He found her in the living room, phone pressed to her ear. He didn't want dispatch to record his voice, so he mouthed to her, "Is that the cops?" She didn't answer, but her eyes, he remembers, "were hella scared." He hit her over the head with his gun and she started to fall.

He pulled her up by the hair. The phone dropped at some point, though Donte doesn't know if the police were still on the other line or not. He hit her three or four more times, until he thinks she may have passed out; she was foaming at the mouth. "I knew I had to kill her," he says. "No way was I going back to jail."

He stood over her, pointing the gun down. At six foot two with long, blond-tipped dreads and tattoos covering his arms and legs, he was an intimidating figure. He and Walker had known each other more than five years, since he was fourteen and she was thirteen. She'd been his girl the whole time, and now he had to kill her.

But Mooch intervened, pushed him toward the door.

Then the two heard sirens. They fled the apartment and ran round the corner to where Donte's aunt lived. In a small dirt patch at the entrance to her apartment, Donte buried the gun. Then he ran inside, climbed up into a loft, and there began a five-hour stakeout with the police. He had a bottle of Rémy Martin up there with him in the loft and part of a joint, and he smoked it, and then drank from the bottle until he passed out. He woke up with a police light in his face.

AFTER HIS RELEASE FROM San Bruno in November of 2014, Donte moved into a halfway house, where I met him. He spoke of his past with both fear and awe. In East Oakland, where he'd grown up, the culture was "music, big rims, guns, and killin'." If you didn't have a thirty-round clip on a Glock, then you weren't a man, he told me. Violence was a way of life. Even if you didn't want to be part of it, it was impossible to stay neutral. No one had a choice. He called it Baghdad. Said it was war all the time. He saw this now as part of the "male role belief system."

When Donte first met Kayla, he'd rarely used her given name. Everybody called their girlfriends "bitch." As in, "That my bitch." Donte was tall and lanky, with hazel eyes and a tattoo on his neck that said *death over dishonor*. He and Kayla had gotten together so young, long before they knew who they even were in the world. They were practically babies, playing at a relationship. It's true of so many relationships where violence lurks—short courtships and very young people—and sometimes those become the patterns that stick for the rest of someone's life. You could see it in Michelle and Rocky's relationship, too. Donte and Kayla had been together on and off for years, but still he had any woman he wanted on the side. He'd never thought of how he was treating her, never thought of gendered stereotypes or how culture played into his actions. In prison, while he was going through the RSVP program, he'd read the book *Emotional Intelligence* and begun taking classes in psychology and sociology. He had a seven p.m. curfew while he was on probation now, but he said he didn't mind. It kept him off the streets at night when the temptations were great. But it was hard to live. His internship paid him just about $700 a month after taxes, he said. He had a cast on one arm because he'd punched someone about a split second after his release from jail and had nearly lost the Community Works internship. He claimed to be deeply sorry for having done it, and the cast was a visual reminder, he said, of how big the battle was—the violent versus the nonviolent him, past versus present, ignorant versus knowledgeable. He had big dreams. He wanted to finish his community college degree, then maybe his bachelor's. He wondered about becoming a psychologist. What would that be like? Could that even be something that was possible? Could he eventually help other guys like him?

Earlier in the day, I'd asked Jimmy how many interns like Donte he'd supervised over his four years as a group leader. He rolled his eyes, said, "Shiiiiiit. I dunno." Too many to remember them all. On his desk, a paper plate held a steaming enchilada and refried beans. His coworkers and others at the sheriff's office were always giving him a hard time about his weight. Skinny as a swizzle stick, but he ate like a horse. His brown jeans were held up by a black belt on its last hole, bunched up around his waist.

How many had gone on to become group leaders? I asked. Of those interns he'd supervised.

"None," he said. "Only me."

The odds were against Donte, and he knew it. "The old me got a whole lot more ammunition than the new me," he said. The simplicity and the truth of his statement stuck with me. He, too, spoke like he was still in the gang, still working the streets, but then every once in a while, he'd shoot out some unexpected phrase that showed the new him, like this one time when we were sitting in the lobby of a fancy hotel in downtown San Francisco, sharing a basket of organic strawberries while conference goers in lanyards murmured past, heels clicking with intention on the marble floor, and he was in the middle of the story of how he and his homies called women "bitch." Girlfriends, yes, but even sisters and mothers were bitches. Sometimes, "my old lady." No woman had an identity; no woman had a name. "By calling her a 'bitch' all the time," he said, suddenly, "what I was really doing was taking away her humanity."

Both Jimmy and Donte were employed by Community Works, an Oakland-based organization that runs antiviolence and justice reform programs. Community Works also creates various arts and education initiatives to address violence and the impact of incarceration on prisoners and their families. One night I sit in on a group led by Jimmy and Donte together, part of Donte's training. Like all the courses Jimmy teaches that are not in San Bruno, this one is taught at an outpost of the San Francisco sheriff's department. Some of the night's attendees began with RSVP in San Bruno, but they'll finish the class here, in this weekly ManAlive program. Men occasionally come to ManAlive voluntarily, but not many, and those who do attend voluntarily take the course not here in the sheriff's office, but in churches or community centers, at groups facilitated by people like Hamish Sinclair, who still runs multiple meetings every week.[2] Of the night's eight participants, four are Hispanic, two Black, and two white. They are all court-ordered to attend. Most had felony convictions, but a few have misdemeanors. Most have multiple issues, too: weapons or other criminal charges, drug or alcohol abuse, mental health concerns. As ex-cons and ex–gang members, Jimmy and Donte have social capital with this population. They understand the rules and language of the streets, know intimately the struggle of being surrounded by violence and trying to break free from the behavior. They meet here in their groups weekly, and if they make it to the end, they'll have spent a year on what boils down to trying to teach these men self-awareness: of who they become and what they look like when they're violent, of how their violence affects those around them, and of alternative responses to stressful situations.

Many of us on the outside of such a world tend to see something like intimate partner violence in a silo, a problem all its own that needs addressing all its own. Social service interventions have tended to treat such problems singularly, too. But a home with intimate partner violence might also have child abuse, alcoholism, and employment or housing instability. Traumatic brain injury or other serious medical conditions might be present. Education may not be a priority or may not be available or may be compromised. Treating just one of these doesn't mitigate the issues that arise from the others. Treatment programs, not to mention research, are understanding this more and more, that problems are multidimensional and thus treatment must be, too.

The office we're in is within a grimy two-story building tucked away between warehouses with windows overlooking pastures of concrete and asphalt, and the traffic noise of an overpass nearby. The place looks like it hasn't had a face-lift since the postwar years. Paint so old that in the right light, it's turned yellow. A hand drawn picture of Elmo kissing Nemo is taped up on one wall. Another bears a poster: *How do you stop a thirty-year-old from beating his wife?*

Talk to him when he's twelve.

Donte gathers dry-erase markers and wet wipes. Participants wander in, slowly, as if this is a kind of torture for them—which, perhaps, it is. "Who's the scribe tonight?" Donte asks. One man in sunglasses with teeth grills says it's him, writes on the whiteboard, *Separation cycle exercises—Denial, Minimize, Blame, Collude.* Some of the men arrive straight from work, others from wherever they've been hanging around all day. They nod to one another, crack a one-liner here or there. Someone whispers to the scribe. He laughs, says, "Shit, man!" Then he turns to me. "I apologize for my language, ma'am." It's like a play in which the actor suddenly breaks the fourth wall. I want to not be noticed; but I'm a white, middle-class, middle-aged woman with a notebook sitting amid dreadlocks, shaved heads, and goatees, low-slung jeans and sports jerseys, overpriced trainers. I may as well have just walked in from a movie set. Or into one. Unlike at San Bruno, I'm not asked to participate for this night.

Another one laughs, says, "Check it out. Fatal peril club right here." They understand fatal peril as the exact instant when a man's sense of expectation is most threatened. What the world owes him, what his own sense of self demands. Something challenges him— maybe his partner says something, or does something, and he reacts. Maybe a guy in a bar insults him. Maybe some coworker tells him he fucked up. It's a split second that changes everything. Eyes narrow, chests pump, fists clench, muscles tense, blood rushes. The body language is almost universal, running across race and class and culture, sometimes even species. A man, a lion, a bear. The body reacts the same way. Fatal peril. A moment that, Jimmy and Donte hope to eventually show these men, is a decision. Violence as a learned behavior. We don't know it, but we have another word for fatal peril. "Snap." On the news, the mourning neighbor, the crying coworker: *he just snapped.* But the snap is a smoke screen, a cliché, a fiction. The snap doesn't exist.

*   *   *

IT IS WEEK TWELVE of their curriculum. They focus on just one man tonight, named Doug, as he recounts the single primary event that got him in trouble. Sinclair used to call this exercise the Destruction Cycle, but he renamed it the Separation Cycle because the pedagogical point to him was that it's meant to show how a person separates from what Sinclair calls his "authentic self" in a threatening moment, and it's this separation that allows for violence to happen.

Doug sits at the head of the circle. "I'm nervous, man," he says.

"Pretend you're on Sixteenth and Julian talking to your homies," Jimmy tells him. One of Jimmy's many jobs before RSVP was driving a cab. He often relies on the metaphoric value such an experience offers: what it means to sit in traffic, how one's knowledge of routes can help you avoid where traffic jams up. Every time I leave the office, he asks me which way I'll tell the cab to go, then checks his watch—is it rush hour? He eventually offers a series of directions so complicated that I give up after the first four or five turns. That he does this repeatedly is endearing. He never wants anyone to suffer through traffic. And traffic is like violence: there's always another avenue to take to avoid it.

Jimmy addresses the rest of the group. "I need you guys to stay focused right now," he says. "Don't collude if you hear something that to you appears to be funny. He may describe how he assaulted his partner and you laugh and he may shut down. What we did to our partners is not funny, so let's be delicate with that. Let's treat that in a mature manner. This work is serious. It's not funny."

Among the many tattoos on Jimmy is one across his forehead: *saint*. Then in back: *sinner*. Jeans hang from his gaunt figure, and he wears an oversized white T-shirt, his belt hanging like a snake halfway down his thigh. Says he can't keep the weight on. No one knows why. Coworkers tease him. Skinny motherfucker. Jimmy's got a secret, though. Why his ribs show, why his jeans hang low.

"I need, like, ten seconds," Doug says. I can see his hands slightly tremble as he holds them between his legs.

"Just breathe, man," Jimmy says. "Just let yourself know you're alive."

Donte has been told by one of his supervisors to talk more, to intervene if he feels inclined. If he makes it through the yearlong internship, he'll be guaranteed a full-time job with Community Works as a facilitator, like Jimmy. He's six months in now. A lot of people have a lot of hopes on him, not least of all himself. But there is still a staggering amount of work in front of him to accomplish. Getting off probation and turning his internship into a real job with a real paycheck and then finishing up his college degree. So much lost time to make up for. I felt, when I was talking to Donte earlier in the day at the park, that even the ability to envision "psychologist" as a career was something brand new to him, that looking to the future rather than just surviving the present was a whole different way of moving through the world.

"My girl went to another pimp once," Jimmy says. "I raped her. That's terrible. That is *terrible*, bro. You have feelings. This isn't *you*. But it *was* you that day."

"That's me, too," says another.

A third says, "I got forty-two weeks in [to the program] and I re-offended. Went back to jail." Started the program all over again.

"I violated my restraining order and I'm back here," says another. They're like a football team at halftime in the locker room when the outcome of the game is so close it's unpredictable. They're pumping each other up, letting Doug know they've all been where he is now, that no one here is innocent.

"I fed off women who had no dads, women who were sexually assaulted," Jimmy tips back on the legs of his chair for a moment, then slams back down. "And then I stole their souls."

FINALLY, DOUG BEGINS. HIS ex-girlfriend, Ashley, had been in her bedroom and Doug was over. Just hanging out. They'd broken up a week before and were trying out this friend thing. She was texting, drinking Wild Turkey, teasing him a little. She told him she couldn't stop thinking of some other guy. "It makes me feel that fatal peril, when I think about it," Doug says.

"Don't use program words," Jimmy says. Program words are an important context for understanding one's actions, but in a Separation Cycle exercise, where a singular moment is deconstructed, they can also be euphemistic, a way of not taking ownership for one's actions. It's the difference between, say, *I had a moment of fatal peril* and *I punched her in the eye*. So the story comes first, and then the group together contextualizes the story within the pedagogical framework of the program, attaching certain elements from what they learned during the curriculum. *This split second was a threat to your male role belief system*, for example. *And this split second was where you entered fatal peril. And this split second was where you separated from your authentic self.*

Doug apologizes. Another deep breath, eyes fixed on his shoes. He launches into the story again. They'd been going through "issues" for about a week, and it was the last straw, and it "escalated." Jimmy calls out this word, says it's a program word, and Doug restarts. "It went from bad to worse . . . I remember she kept smiling, and a song was playing: 'Friday, I'm in love.' I don't remember the artist, but every time I hear the song nowadays it reminds me of that day and it makes me really angry . . ."

"Stay on track," says one of the guys.

This nudging, the language, the gentle urging to keep with the story is part of the curriculum. It shows how language matters, how much we can lie to ourselves, take ourselves off track to avoid responsibility, how we use words to frame our guilt or innocence, how easy it is to manipulate and how so often that manipulation starts inside our own minds, how we can minimize our impact on someone else. Later, the group will be harder on Doug, but for now, they let him talk.

"She kept smiling and rubbing it in my face that she had some other dude," Doug says. She was buzzed by then and he grabbed the bottle, took six or seven deep swigs. "I felt like I was bein' played, man . . . I invited her violence, told her to hit me and she did. I remember I took my arm and just gave her a hit across the face, and I think that left a mark on her nose . . . Later, she came at me again and at this point I don't remember what happened. I remember being really drunk for like five minutes and I realized I was being violent and I walked out of her room and her grandma got in the way between me and her . . . I was half conscious at this point." He stops for a minute, thinks, then says, "One thing, I hit the door and I pushed right through the door and hit the wall and left a good mark—"

"—pushed or punched?" Jimmy asks.

"Punched. I punched through the door, and I punched a hole or a dent in the drywall." Doug goes on to say that he threatened to "split" the face of the other guy, and then he walked out of her apartment. The story emerges in pieces, only partially linear. He remembers things and backtracks. Her grandmother was there. He held Ashley back with his foot before he hit her. After he left her apartment, he heard sirens in the distance, knew they were for him, and sat on the curb to wait, hunching over to "make myself look as helpless as possible so I wouldn't be restrained in a violent manner." He says when the police came they poked fun at him, asked him if he was gay, if he was helpless, if he was racist.

It takes him maybe ten minutes to tell the story.

"Can I ask you a clarifying question?" asks Donte. They frame it this way, as a "clarifying" question so the participants know the question isn't meant to antagonize.

Doug nods.

"When you say 'held her back with my foot' what was the position? I mean, what was you all doing?"

"I was laying in her bed," he says, "and I tried to keep her away. I used my foot to keep her away."

"When I put my feet on anybody, it's physical violence," Donte says.

Doug nods.

Jimmy thanks him for his honesty, rubs his hands together. When Doug said he'd "split the face" of the other love interest, it was a verbal threat, Jimmy tells the group. "Can I ask you a clarifying question?" he asks Doug. "Did you ever call her any names other than her own?"

"Yes."

"What were they?"

"I remember calling her a slut," Doug says. "I think I called her a ho."

"That's a big component. That verbal."

Donte chimes in about the name-calling. "Listen, man, in order for me to put my hands on her, she's not Ashley anymore. She's a slut. You gotta rename her, see what I'm sayin'?"

Jimmy asks Doug to recognize how his body moved through the room that night. What was he doing with his muscles?

"Clenching them," Doug says.

And what was his heart rate doing?

"Racing."

Jimmy stands up for a minute, asks if Doug's body was lax or stiff?

"Stiff."

And then Jimmy takes on the posture, shows Doug and the group what it looks like. His back curves slightly like a boxer's, his fists are clenched, his face hardens. He's got one shoulder slightly jutting out, his weight on the balls of his feet like he's ready to pounce. In the context of the room, which is relatively relaxed and quiet, it's a startling juxtaposition, a complete epiphany for some of these guys to see how their body communicates a message even if no words are uttered.

"This," Jimmy says, holding the posture, "is what she sees."

He's excavating the body's limbic system response to a threat, like seeing an animal in the wild under siege. And Donte and Jimmy push

Doug to drive home the point. What would this look like to someone else in that room? This fist-clenching, heart-racing, stiff-postured person?

It would look intimidating.

It would look scary.

It would look bad.

That's the beginning: notice your body.

Next comes language. Some of this becomes obvious immediately. Substituting a slur for a partner's name, for example. But language in general is more subtle than this. It works at both the conscious and subconscious levels. Painfully, word by word, second by second they go. Don't say "pussy." Don't swear. Don't say "my old lady." Don't say "ho," "slut," "woman." Use proper names. Use the term "partner." Maintain eye contact with the person you're speaking to or with the group. Sit up straight. No slumping. When describing the incidents that landed them in the place they're in at the moment, they have to use "I" statements, possessive pronouns. It's not "our" violence or "men's" violence or "society's" violence. It's "my" violence. Own your violence. Be accountable for your violence.

When they do this exercise in San Bruno, it may take an entire morning. Hours to deconstruct an event that in real life may have been just a couple of minutes long. The guys don't have to pick the inciting incident that landed them in jail, though most do. They are asked to notice every little detail that they can possibly remember: their body language, their heart rate, their breath, their muscles, their tone of voice, their words, their feelings, the sounds and smells. One day sitting in Jimmy's group at San Bruno, he asked them how long they thought it took them to get from yelling at their partners to being in the back of that cop car? The guys guessed twenty minutes, twenty-five minutes, half an hour, maybe an hour. "No," Jimmy told them. "Ten minutes. Bam! There you go, brother." Minutes to go from a man to a bear to an inmate. But tonight, with Doug, they do the whole exercise in under two hours.

We coerce, Jimmy tells them. They coerce themselves, their victims, their kids. It's taking them away from themselves. Jimmy says they have to be willing to take action. That awareness plus action equals change. I can see him looking around the group, guy to guy. "I'm going to speak on that for one fucking second," Jimmy says, standing up. "I've been aware of shit my whole life. I'm aware of everything that I ever did in my life. Lying, cheating, stealing. I heard 'Don't sell drugs' all my life. 'Don't do drugs, don't put your hands on girls.' I heard that all my life, but I did it anyway." A guy with his elbows on his knees sits back in his chair. "This is important, guys. How do I get the willingness to stop my violence?" He waits a beat, looks around the circle. "If I don't look at the destruction that I caused, then I'm not going to give a fuck."

That moment becomes Jimmy's second story. What is the worst thing you ever did to someone? That was the day he kidnapped the woman he loved. Nearly killed her. The mother of one of his beloved four kids. His ex-partner, Kelly Graff. They were estranged and Jimmy was pissed. She was his woman. He'd get her back. He called her, said he had $500 for her, and could she come pick it up? She made him promise he wasn't up to anything, and he promised. That's the coercion. Then he says he went and rented a U-Haul truck, after which he got himself very, very high, and he waited. Waited till he saw her car come from down the block, and when she was just there, a breath away from the U-Haul, he put it in reverse and slammed on the gas, rammed into her car as hard and as fast as he could. Could have fucking killed her. Then like a panther he was at her car door and pulling her out while she was screaming. He threw her in the back of the U-Haul and shut the gate, then drove to her house. Power and control. *He was wasted; he hadn't slept in a couple of days. He was a dumbass.* His current self shakes his head in disbelief at his former self. They got to her house—the house he used to share with her—and he got her out of the truck and pulled her inside, and that's where he says his memory stops. Maybe they fought a little. Maybe he slapped her around. He's pretty sure he walloped her a couple of times. He can't remember, but he says he went to sleep. He slept and when he woke up, she was gone, and he knew he was fucked. Dumb fuck. How could he have gone to sleep? He ran out of the house to a taco place on the corner that they all frequented, and a guy at the taco place said Kelly had been in there earlier with a girlfriend, freaking out, scared out of her mind, and that she was going to the police. And Jimmy ran and ran. Right into hiding.

Kelly remembers it very differently. Jimmy showed up at her work one day claiming his grandmother had died. Kelly knew how close he was to his grandmother, so she thought he was telling the truth. But the minute she stepped outside with him, she could tell he was lying. They'd been together since she was sixteen and he was twenty-six. Now they had a young daughter, and Kelly was twenty-one.

When she saw that he'd coerced her to come out, she fled back into her office, where there was security. Jimmy, she told me over the phone, found her car in the parking lot and lit it on fire. The car had been brand new, and the San Francisco fire department called to give her the news. It was she who'd rented the U-Haul to move out of their apartment, she said. After Jimmy burned her car, she borrowed a car from a friend of her mom's, but Jimmy stalked her, jumped in the passenger seat when she left work. He had a knife and she remembered him saying, "You're leaving me, bitch." She'd spent years as his punching bag. He manipulated her, coerced her, scared the shit out of her. He stalked her constantly, wouldn't let her socialize, accused her of cheating. "I'm not leaving you," she lied to him. "We just need a break." She was "trying to calm him down, because I didn't know what he was capable of." They picked up the U-Haul together, she said, and drove to their shared apartment, a basement apartment she described as a "dungeon." She managed to convince him that she was hungry, and he let her go and she told me she "ran like it was the last second of my life."

She went straight to the police station with her cousin, where she says they initially asked her to go back to her house and get the knife and bring it in. "I said, 'Are you crazy?'" She said they weren't interested in helping her at all, but they did eventually put a warrant out for his arrest. In the meantime, Kelly had lost her car, her home, and eventually her job (she was laid off after 9/11). It was the lowest point in her life.

One morning, just days after the U-Haul incident, she went to drop off their daughter at preschool and Jimmy was hiding out near the school. She says he made her take their daughter out of school and for eight days he held the two of them in a hotel room at gunpoint. What happened in those eight days is off the record, per both of their requests.

She says she was finally able to manipulate him and get away.

He says he turned himself in.

Memory is fickle in the midst of trauma.

When he described this moment in his life to me, he remembers being on the run, in hiding, spooked by every siren he heard, keeping his gaze averted. He was so high he was hallucinating half the time, Kelly told me. And so maybe he truly doesn't remember all that much.

But eventually he was caught, and they both said the prosecutor wanted to charge him with kidnapping and assault with a deadly weapon, but Kelly says she felt bad for him and recanted a lot of her statement. When she tells me this, over the phone, it's clear she can't believe she was once that woman, the woman who recanted. In the end, he pled out. He said he was sentenced to four years; she said he served just over one.

Regardless, this is when he found RSVP and he learned about what he'd done, to himself, to Kelly and their daughter, to his community, to the rest of his family. He tells the guys in his group how violence has a ripple effect, how he hurt Kelly, which hurt his children, his parents, her circle of friends, and on and on. Violence is a darkness that migrates into a community, infects it so that it multiplies. When Donte talks about East Oakland as Baghdad, I think this is what he means, exactly what Jimmy is talking about. How one violent act by one person begets another. How violence matched with more violence never really solves any kind of problem. I have an ex-husband who spent his entire career in the military and he used to say to me that the problem with having a gun, no matter who you are, is that its presence automatically puts you on a side. You are no longer neutral. Violence, it seems to me, does the same thing. It splinters individual people, yes, but it also splinters families, communities, cities, countries. This is what Jimmy is trying to get at with his own story.

The names Jimmy has for himself—"bottom-feeder," "low-life motherfucker"—are street lingo, a kind of gritty poetry, cred with the homies in the classes. But here, let's call him what he really was in that moment and on that day. He was a domestic terrorist. That's what terrorists do. They terrorize. All the men in the RSVP wing of San Bruno and beyond. They're the terrorists in our midst, purveyors of a horror that many people today, including some of our country's leaders, feel is simply a "private" matter.

Jimmy served his time and just before his release, he says he got a letter from Kelly. She hadn't written him the entire time he was locked up. And he remembers her letter ending with this sentence: *Please don't kill me.* (She says her letter was in response to one from him in which he allegedly refused to pay her child support.)

He tells this story with a shake of his head, the remorse threading itself through his body language. *How many women across time?* I think. How many have pled this same sentence? Women around the world, in a thousand languages, across the centuries, the span of human existence. *Please don't kill me.* See how polite we women are? We say "please" when we're begging for our lives.

"That poor girl," Jimmy tells the class, with Doug still at the head of the circle. His voice is practically a whisper now. "That poor, poor girl. She went around asking my friends if they thought I was going to kill her when I got out." The room vibrates with his story, this terrible thing he did, and how he crawled his way back to his own humanity.

"And that girl is my best friend today," he says. "She totally has my back."

Kelly refuted this characterization. She believed he had changed, believed he had "learned to accept what he's done, and he knows it was wrong." She said he was more humble today. Probably at the best place in his life. But still. "I will never allow myself to be alone with Jimmy again in my life," she said.

JIMMY WAITS A BEAT. Every guy in here has a similar story, and every guy in here will be where Doug is tonight. Jimmy looks at Doug. "When you started drinking Wild Turkey, brother, you were doing violence to yourself. That's where it started, right?"

Doug nods, picks at calluses on the palms of his hands.

"Pushing her away is violence to her, right? Hitting her in the face three times, too. And punching through the wall. You told the guy you'd split his face, right? That's verbal violence right there, that threat."

Doug is nodding, acknowledging the contextualization of these actions.

Behind Doug, the guy with teeth grills is writing it all down on a whiteboard, circling what the moments mean. Drinking is "self-violence." Calling names is "verbal violence." Punching walls is "physical violence."

"Can I ask you a clarifying question?" Jimmy says. "What was your first fatal peril?" The first time, in other words, he can identify his male role belief system being challenged.

In the pedagogy of ManAlive, the male role belief system is what society tells men to expect. In group, Jimmy or Sinclair or whoever is leading will often stop and ask the participants to offer some examples of the male role belief system: *man does not get disrespected. Man does not get lied to. Man's sexuality does not get questioned. Man is the authority. Man does not get dismissed. Woman should be submissive, obedient, supportive to man.* When a man's belief system is challenged, he goes into fatal peril and that is the moment where violence is a choice. ManAlive uses a kind of hokey phrase for this moment: when a man's "inner hit man" comes out and his "authentic self" disappears. A hit man operates in silence, alone. A hit man blends into a crowd, destroys people in stealth, then disappears. A hit man takes no responsibility.

A hit man has no moral center. Jimmy points out to Doug that when he is in a moment of fatal peril, Doug is not only not noticing his partner, he is also no longer noticing himself, his own feelings, his own needs, his own body. He is simply reacting to the challenge that's been made to his belief system, and it's in this kernel of conflict where a decision to become violent or not resides. One man who'd gone through the program said he had learned to literally take a step backward to try to recalibrate his mind and his body in such a moment. Sometimes an adjustment this small is all they need to remind themselves to stop, take a breath, don't escalate.

Jimmy asks again when Doug first went into fatal peril.

"When she told me she couldn't stop thinking about the other guy," he answers.

"I been that right there," one of the guys says.

Donte chimes in. "When you said you had decided you all were going to be like friends, that to me sounds like denial." Doug nods. He wanted her back. He was denying his own feelings. "When you say 'I've never been so drunk in my life' that kinda sounds to me like blame. And you said she came at you—that's kinda like blame again." Blaming the liquor. Blaming her. Blaming everything and everyone but himself. Doug acknowledges that Donte is right.

They go on in this way for another twenty minutes. One of the guys points out his body language when the police showed up, how Doug was sitting there on the curb waiting for them, trying, as he said, "to make myself look as harmless as possible." That sounded like "minimizing," the guy told Doug. So Doug was in denial about his own feelings, and his own part in the violence. He blamed her and he blamed the other guy, and he threatened them verbally and physically, and he minimized his role in all of it, and it's all right there in what his body did and what his words were.

PERHAPS THE MOST SIGNIFICANT challenge to this entire program is that men who've gone through it—either RSVP or ManAlive—are still operating in the same world as before they went through the program. The guys in San Bruno? They have it so much easier than the guys who are in the outside world, trying to live a nonviolent life where everything and everyone around them hasn't changed. Donte talked to me about this earlier in the day, how his mother and grandmother saw the change in him, but also didn't trust it. How even he himself didn't trust it. And he didn't have any kind of equation for how to even out the imbalance of his life, except time.

Before they leave for the night, Jimmy asks the group about intimating. About how to be intimate. It's something they'll learn more in another stage of the curriculum. Doug says, "Listen and disclose." The "listen" means listening to their partners, but also listening to themselves, their feelings, their own bodies.

"There's no judgments here, man," Jimmy reminds them. "No advice, no judgments, no opinions."

Donte thanks Doug for his courage, sitting up there at the head of the circle for hours, having one of his worst moments laid bare for a group of strangers. "Seeing the expressions on your face. Them was the same expressions on my face 'cause I really hurt somebody that I loved—you feel me? So I want to say thank you for doing the work. I really want you to see the violence that you did to the person you supposed to love. Thanks, bro."

Doug nods, takes a deep breath and lets it out, then laughs, because he noticed his body in the moment and recognized the relief it was expressing.

TWO MONTHS AFTER THE group's meeting with Doug, Donte disappeared. He didn't return my texts or e-mails. I tried calling the two mobile numbers I had for him, and left message after message. Nothing.

Finally, after several months of trying, I got hold of someone at Community Works. Donte had been caught riding in a car with a gun owned by the driver of the car and the police rearrested him. As a term of his probation, Donte had been required to stay away from all firearms—his own, those belonging to others, just anyone's. He also had a nugget of crack in his pocket at the time and he was back in prison, awaiting trial. He'd been assigned a public defender. I called the public defender multiple times, and wrote him several e-mails, but he did not respond to requests for an interview. Donte faced up to fourteen years in prison, if convicted. If he was very lucky, he'd get one.

All the time he'd wanted to make up, the college degree, the job at Community Works, the chance to rebuild his life? I wondered what he was thinking of it all now. Donte was a young Black man facing a system that did not give lucky breaks to young Black men very often, if ever. He had a serious criminal history. He had no money for a decent lawyer. His chances, as I saw them, were nil. He'd wind up just another violent man fated to the life he'd always known, carried along by forces he couldn't fight alone. As far as I could tell, Donte had been honest with me. He didn't pretend to be a good guy. He knew he'd fucked up. And he'd told me, too, how impossible it was to live on an intern's paycheck in San Francisco. When his time at the halfway house was over, he'd planned to move back to his mother's house, smack in the middle of the neighborhood that set him on his troublesome road so many years earlier, not because he wanted to, but because he had no choice. *Of course*, I thought. Of course he had a rock of crack in his pocket. What else is he going to do? He's got a job, and a seven p.m. curfew. Community Works, Jimmy Espinoza, RSVP, they were all doing everything they could for Donte Lewis, but they were all also fighting the same systems with their other priorities, and with racism and classism embedded into their architecture, with limited resources and limitless need.

I wanted to talk to Donte, but I didn't have his mother's or his grandmother's phone numbers, and there was no way to get hold of him by phone, of course. And then one night my cell rang. The Atwater Correctional Facility. An inmate was on the line, asking me to accept the charge. In fifteen-minute increments, I got Donte's story.

It had been around midnight, and he was looking for a ride home. He'd moved out of the halfway house and lived with his mom and grandmother back in East Oakland. His sister's "baby daddy" picked him up. The dude was drunk, but Donte didn't consider not going with him. He'd recently been getting pressure from his new girlfriend about living with his mom, but what could he do? His take-home pay was not enough to live on under almost any conditions in the San Francisco area. But he had been trying to stay clean, stay on program, keep his head above water and stay focused. His boss had warned him not to hang out with anyone who'd get him in trouble, but he said he was fine. He had it taken care of.

He thought he'd just do a couple of little cash deals with some crack and get a small jump start on his finances. Nothing big. Nothing that was going to take him off his antiviolence program. That night, he had a little baggie in his pocket. Way he saw it, there was no other way he could ever hope to get out of his mother's house for a long, long time. He was twenty-eight already, pretty old to be living at home.

The driver also had some weed on him. Shortly after Donte got in the car, sirens went off behind them, but instead of pulling over, the driver turned sharply, drove two blocks, and rammed into a wall. Donte claims he doesn't remember anything after that. He woke up in the hospital, his lip and face all banged up. He's pretty sure the airbag didn't deploy. The cops found a Glock in the airbag compartment, hidden away. It wasn't Donte's. He claimed he didn't even know about it. The floor of the car had a Glock magazine and some spent casings that had rolled around when they crashed into the wall. Donte's blood splattered. He didn't know where, but he knew it must have gone all over the car, because it was dripped down the front of his shirt, he later saw.

The accident hardly mattered. The drugs mattered a little, but not nearly as much as the gun. By being around a gun, he'd violated his probation—a charge that brought an automatic two years in prison. Add to that that if his DNA was found on the gun, on the magazine, on any of the spent casings—from, say, splattered blood—he was looking at a best-case scenario of four years, and a worst-case of many, many more, depending on the jury at trial. His boss from Community Works wrote him a character reference. He wanted to reach out to some of the guys from his group for character references. But his lawyer said not to bother; it would only anger the judge.

"The thing is," Donte told me on the phone that night, "they already know me. They *all* already know me." The judge knew him, the probation and parole folks, maybe even the police. Even if they didn't know him, his record preceded him. "They know me from before, who I used to be. Nothing going to change their mind now."

Donte's case never went to trial. He pled out, like so many others in his position. Young. Black. Broke. Criminal histories. He got six more years, and this time it wasn't a cushy little county jail, with community college programs and restorative justice and art therapy. This time it was federal, first at Atwater, and then, halfway through his sentence, they shipped him all the way across the country to a federal penitentiary on the border of Pennsylvania and New York, thousands and thousands of miles from anyone he knew or anywhere he'd ever been.

Then I tried Jimmy, but he, too, had seemed to vanish.

Clustered at the Top

Around the same time that Hamish Sinclair was asking his seminal question on why men beat each other up, a community organizer in Boston named David Adams ran a monthly gathering that he refers to as "very '70s"—by which he means consciousness raising, hand-holding, and kumbaya—out of the Boston Men's Center. One day, Adams was approached by a group of women, friends of his in the community, who'd begun a battered women's group. The women asked Adams for help. It was one thing, they said, to help victims after they'd been abused, give them support through the community, but what about the men who'd done the abuse? Why couldn't that be stopped in the first place? The women didn't feel it was in their purview to help abusers, so they asked Adams to step in. The formation of Sinclair's ManAlive was still a few years away. There was no real research on how to address men's battering. Adams and the women were far ahead of the rest of the country; VAWA was still decades away.

The first meetings were held at Adams's apartment, and they'd invite battered women in to discuss what abuse did to them and their children. Adams didn't know to categorize it as batterer intervention at the time, but what he was really doing was a kind of restorative justice. But there was no plan to follow, no protocol, no best practices guidelines. Adams and his colleagues were learning as they went along. "We were so naive," he said. "We just thought we'd tell them we think it's wrong [and they'd stop]."

HIS WORK IN THOSE early days led Adams to write a dissertation that tried to dissect what happened in abusive households that didn't happen in households where there was no abuse. Adams had grown up with a violent father, had seen and felt firsthand how such hidden violence could devastate a family. In his PhD dissertation, he'd looked at childcare and housework in houses where there was abuse versus those where abuse was not present. He assumed the research would support his theory that abusers did far less of the housework and childcare. But Adams was shocked to find that both men did about the same amount in each home, 21%.[1] Where the two groups tended to differ was that the non-abusers knew they were getting a good deal and appreciated and acknowledged their wives' double shifts, whereas the abusers would say things like, "I do a lot more than most men, but does she appreciate that?" Adams's research showed that the abuser's perspective was that they "weren't being appreciated for what they did, rather than what their wives were doing." Non-abusers, on the other hand, "would say things like 'I'm lucky. My wife does a lot.' And that acknowledgment meant a lot to the wives." Abusers also tended to be more critical of their wives' housekeeping.

What Adams realized, then, was that the clinical narcissism of these men kept them from being able to really see how their behavior impacted their victims. "Narcissism filters how they see everything," Adams told me.

David Adams, like Hamish Sinclair, seems to embody the geography and culture in which he resides. He holds himself more rigidly, speaks more carefully. He is serious, less cheerily confrontational with the men in his groups, on the quiet side. He has graying curly hair, a mustache, and, like many who work in the social services field, his own story of childhood violence. An abusive, emotionally stunted father. A mother who looked away. His oldest memory is one from when he was four years old, his maternal grandmother taking him to the granite quarry where his father worked. He said his grandmother hated his father and vice versa. He stood at the edge that day with her as she pointed to one of the tiny dots—men working deep in the hole—and she said, "That's your daddy, there." Adams told her no, his daddy was much bigger. It was impossible, that tiny little speck of a person, no bigger than an ant from his vantage at the edge. But then eventually he got the point. How very small his father was, how he could be a different man than his father had been. It was one of the most lasting and profound lessons of his life, something that today he calls his greatest gift from his grandmother. As he grew up, he made it his mission to be as different as possible from his father, who belittled education and thought boys should be tough. Adams kept his face in a book for two decades, until that education so despised by his father could offer him an escape. "Kids are quite literal," Adams said to me, "and it was a revelation that I didn't have to be like him."

Adams eventually formed what is widely recognized as the country's first batterer intervention program: Emerge, a program for controlling and abusive behavior. Along with the Duluth program, Emerge is perhaps the nation's most widely emulated. The program is forty weeks long and covers topics ranging from effects of abuse on family members to jealousy and healthy communication. A few years ago, Emerge also began offering classes on parenting as well. No one wants to identify as being a "batterer," Adams says, so Emerge reframed how they talk about what they do. About 30% of their participants come voluntarily now, and the rest are court-ordered. (Nationally, most batterer intervention programs are 5% voluntary.)

Hamish and Adams share an essential origin story in that it was women who compelled them both to act, feminists who pointed out the need for male allies. They wanted men to join in their fight.

One day, early on, Adams told me the story of a woman who brought in a recording of her abusive husband to his group. On the tape, the husband said things like, *"I wouldn't have such anger and rage if I weren't so crazy in love with you."* It was the first time he really heard and understood how manipulative abusers could be. How they romanticized both their abuse and their jealousy. The "I love you so much you make me this way" excuse. The "I wouldn't do X if you didn't do Y" rationalization. Blame and denial. Adams and other researchers point out the framework of these kinds of sentiments. They minimize the violence, rationalizing abusive behavior and blaming the victim. And it works. The trifecta is cyclical: minimizing, rationalizing, blaming. And then comes the remorse. The deep, tearful apology, the promises of better behavior, the adoration and claims of love. The script is strikingly similar no matter who's saying it.

One morning, I sat in on a series of domestic violence cases in a Cleveland courtroom and in one case, an offender had broken his no-contact order by calling the victim repeatedly. In fact, he called her more than four hundred times in a three-week period. She accepted the calls about 20% of the time. The prosecutor, Joan Bascone, played for the court just a small collection of the recorded calls, while the offender, with a shaved head, in a forest green prison uniform stood smirking in front of the judge, Michelle Earley. Here is a small sampling of things he said to her:

"Give me one more chance. One more. Jail's not worth it. This shit ain't worth it."

"You're blowing it out of proportion. I was just fucking with you. I wasn't trying to kill you . . . Why you keep fighting me instead of helping me get outta here? Why ain't you apologizing, too, for staying out all night?"

"I am in love with you, bitch, and I wish I wasn't, 'cause you're putting me through fucking misery. Why you doing this to me?"

"I don't owe you no explanation . . . You done nothing but put me in jail. You ain't sent no letters or pictures. I don't care if you come to court on me. I ain't calling you no more."

"You don't got to come to court. They talk about me, you tell them to shut the fuck up. They lying to you. Just tell them you're going to file for a dismissal. Don't let the prosecutor give you another chance to come to court."

"You ain't gotta sign. Don't answer the door . . . I trust you. I don't think you're doing anything. You're not dumb enough."

"Let's go down there and make it official. I believe in marriage. It's a commitment for life, dude . . . Wait till I get out. I have people watching you."

Blame, minimize, rationalize, and apology and promise: they were all right there, laid out in his words. The coercion, the manipulation, the emotional and verbal abuse, the threats, the dehumanizing. His attempts to make her believe that he is stronger than the system, that he knows more than the system. The tapes went on for more than an hour in court that day, far more than what I've included here, and in that time I noticed this, too: he failed to use her proper name even once.

BATTERER INTERVENTION GROUPS LIKE Emerge and ManAlive have proliferated over the past two decades; there are now more than fifteen hundred nationwide. While they aim to stop physical abuse and intimidation, the more nuanced programs also work to help an abuser recognize destructive patterns, understand the harm they cause, develop empathy for their partners, and offer them an education in emotional intelligence. But their methods and philosophies vary widely. There is a persistent attitude, particularly among law enforcement, that they are a waste of time and money, which Adams finds perpetually frustrating. Certifications vary from state to state. The court orders vary. The curriculum varies. The quality of the group leader varies. The length of time in the program varies. And in terms of social impact, it's a new field, still finding its way. Judges, too, are often not trained in the differences between, say, batterer intervention and anger management, so you might have a judge order an offender to anger management, even in a jurisdiction where batterer intervention groups proliferate. The fact that only 55% of the men who go through Emerge actually complete the program is a sign of its rigor and efficacy, Adams says.[2] "I'm always distrustful of programs that complete higher numbers. It's like bad schools. They graduate everybody."

If it takes the average victim seven or eight times to leave an abuser, why do we expect offenders to get it right the first time? So many studies on efficacy measure all offenders equally, meaning both those who drop out of programs and those who finish, he told me. And of course those who finish will have different outcomes. The longer participants stay in the program, the more likely lasting change can be. "It's not an all or nothing thing," Adams said. An expansive book by Edward W. Gondolf that looks at the current state of batterer intervention, *The Future of Batterer Programs*, says essentially that we are still in an early phase of such treatment and he cautions against putting too much stock in the idea of a predictive risk assessment: "The tough question facing batterer programs, and the criminal justice field in general, is how to identify the especially dangerous men . . . The shift, therefore, has been from prediction to ongoing risk management that entails repeated assessments, monitoring compliance, and revising interventions along the way."[3]

Anger management is often conflated with batterer intervention as if they are equivalent—indeed courts across the country today still often sentence abusers to anger management courses, as happened with Ray Rice in 2014. After he clocked his girlfriend—now wife—in an elevator so hard he knocked her unconscious, a New Jersey judge tossed the domestic violence charges and sent him to anger management counseling.[4] Such outcomes speak to a deep misunderstanding of the nature of abuse. (The NFL, despite public promises, has made almost no progress when it comes to domestic violence. In the fall of 2017, at least half a dozen new players faced domestic violence charges, but were drafted anyway, and at the time of this writing the NFL had failed to implement a single reform recommended to it by a commission formed in the aftermath of the Ray Rice scandal, according to Deborah Epstein, a law professor at Georgetown University, who resigned from the commission in protest in 2018 as a result of the NFL's failure to take seriously the problem of domestic violence.[5]) A 2008 assessment of 190 batterer programs, in fact, showed that most participants did not have substantial levels of anger, and that only a small percentage were in the unusually high range.[6]

ADAMS'S GROUP AND OTHERS like it typically provide information to the courts about the compliance and authenticity of an abuser's willingness to change. They file a monthly report with probation officers on each abuser and are in regular contact with victims about a batterer's participation in the group. It's one of the most useful elements of any batterer intervention group, frankly. Accountability to probation, court, and the victims. "We can be the eyes and ears of the court," Adams said. "Victims are trying to make decisions about staying or leaving; if she's hearing back from us that he's still blaming her, that's useful to know."

One night, I attend a session at Emerge. The sessions are held in a basement conference room in a generic building in Cambridge, outside of Boston. It's not the leafy, red-bricked Cambridge of Harvard University, but the less rarified, squat gray industrial Cambridge of the working class.

Seven men file in and sit in folding chairs, joking around uncomfortably with one another. The demographics run across age, race, and economic spectrums, though they are not the inner-city, underprivileged culture I would later see in San Bruno. One wears a suit and tie and smells of aftershave. Another has plaster caked on his jeans. It is my first time sitting in on an offenders' group. I don't yet know ManAlive or Hamish Sinclair. By now, I've been talking to victims for years, but haven't spent any time with perpetrators. I still carry a picture in my mind of an abuser who is a rageaholic, a monster, a person visibly and uncontrollably angry. Someone easily identifiable as a "bad guy." I may even have operated under the idea that my own gut instincts would alert me to such a man. And what strikes me immediately—in fact, deeply unsettles me in a way—is how incredibly *normal* they all seem. Like a bunch of guys I'd go have a beer with. They *are* charming. They are funny, gregarious, shy, high-strung. Good-looking or not, well-dressed or not. They are Everyman. One of the hallmarks of domestic violence, Adams told me, is this false idea that abusers are somehow angry generally; rather, their anger is targeted—at a partner or at the partner's immediate family. As a result, friends and acquaintances of abusers are often surprised to hear that they committed an assault. "The most surprising thing is that [abusers] seem like such normal guys," says Adams. "The average batterer is pretty likable." For Adams this is the whole point: that we look for talons and tails, but find instead charm and affability. It's how abusers attract victims in the first place. "We look for the rageaholic," Adams says. But only about a quarter of batterers fit that definition. What he sees, instead, is an inflexible personality. "A rigid black-or-white thinker is what I most imagine," Adams says.

The night I attend, Adams explores how the attendees felt about their parents and, in particular, their fathers. One of the men came from a home in which his father ran a prominent undergraduate university education program. Another has a father whom he characterized as a sexual predator and addict. At least five of the seven men have witnessed their fathers abusing women. Unlike RSVP and many (perhaps even most) other batterer intervention programs, Emerge always has one woman who is a co-facilitator. The reasons for this are twofold: first, a male and female team operating as equals can model for group members what that looks like. But also, Adams found that in the early days of Emerge, men participants would rarely exhibit the kinds of behaviors that reflected their general attitudes toward women, things like interrupting women, challenging their ideas or ignoring them altogether, and in group they call attention to such attitudes immediately. Adams asks the seven participants to rate their fathers as "good," "bad," or "mixed." Of the seven, only one rates his father as "bad." Yet they tell stories of fathers with alcohol addictions, of fathers bloodying their mothers, of belts taken to them throughout their childhoods. I sit there listening, amazed that they fail to see either themselves or their mothers as victims of their fathers. It struck me in such a specific way at that moment, how men and women truly see and decode the world so differently. Of course, I'd experienced this in my own life, in moments with my then-husband—I remember saying to him, on so many occasions when he'd claim I wasn't listening to him, that I was indeed listening. What I was doing was *disagreeing*. But sitting there that night, maybe because I was on the outside of these lives looking in rather than trying to argue a point from inside my own life, the concrete illustration of this abstract idea somehow chilled me. I remember thinking it was a marvel that anyone stayed married for the long haul.

At several points, Adams has to remind them that they can love their fathers and still be critical. Over and over, the men talk about how their mothers had provoked their fathers.

When I speak to Adams later about it, he isn't at all surprised that the men excused and contextualized the bad behavior of their fathers, while demonizing their mothers. "That's part of what happens," Adams tells me afterward. "They've internalized a selfish, narcissistic father . . . [But] you can't lecture people. You give them information, and hopefully over time it begins to make a difference."

The next day, I had lunch with one of the attendees from Adams's group. We rode in his truck to a burger place in Cambridge; he opened doors for me, told me to order first, made sure the restaurant was to my liking. He was, in other words, polite, charming. He wore a baseball cap with the brim low over his freckled face. Though I knew he was in his late twenties, he had the baby-faced appearance of someone who'd started shaving a week earlier. He had been court-ordered to complete Adams's program and he admitted to me that he had lied to his group the night before about using alcohol—a violation of his probation. He minimized the abuse he'd perpetrated on his former partner, telling me that yes, while he had choked her until she nearly lost consciousness, he had *only* done it once, after *she'd* come at him and scratched him. His view was that they were both responsible for the violence done to each other, but only he was having to pay the price for it. He failed to see that scratches didn't carry the lethality of strangulation and so he saw his behavior as simply quid pro quo. It would turn out that this man would never finish the program; he would move out west and, presumably, bring all of his bad behavior with him. But maybe I'm wrong. Maybe something from those weeks he attended stayed with him, even though he didn't complete the program. Just before we'd finished with our lunch, he'd admitted to me that once he had overcome his initial hostility to the group, the program had made an impact on him. "When you find yourself in a class like that, you can't lie to yourself about the decisions you made," he said. "My life has taken me to a point where I can't tell myself I'm not that bad."

WHEN ADAMS FIRST BEGAN studying how to change the behavior of abusive men, before he'd made the connections to narcissism, nearly all the research from the 1960s and '70s described violence in the home as the product of a manipulative woman who incited her husband. That victims provoke their own abuse is an attitude that persists today. In the early 1980s, Ellen Pence, a domestic violence advocate in Minnesota created the Power and Control Wheel.[7] The Wheel highlights the eight ways a batterer maintains power and control: fear, emotional abuse, isolation, denial and blame, using children, bullying, financial control, and brute force and verbal threats. Advocates point out that abusers don't walk around with a conscious notion that they're seeking power and control. Instead, they say things like, "I just want her to be sweet [obedient and subservient] and have dinner on the table at six." Or, "I just want her to have the house cleaned, and the kids in bed." Or, "I just pushed her a little. She's overreacting." Or, "I wouldn't have broken that plate if she hadn't screamed." All of these are variations on the same thing. (Later, I would hear Jimmy Espinoza tell a group of men to be on guard for the words "just," "if," and "but," which seemed to me a fairly decent summation).

Like Sinclair, Adams believes that men make choices to be violent. In a 2002 paper he cowrote with Susan Cayouette, the codirector of Emerge, on abusive intervention and prevention, he wrote, "Many batterers conduct some, if not most, of their nonfamilial relationships in a respectful manner, which indicates that they already know how to practice respectful treatment of others when they *decide* to."

For Adams this extreme narcissism is at the root of understanding batterers, and while we may think of narcissists as conspicuous misfits who can't stop talking about themselves, in fact they are often high-functioning, charismatic, and professionally successful. The narcissists are "hiding among us," Adams says, "and they're clustered at the top." Such people are not easy to identify, in part because they have outsized people skills, and "we live in a world that is increasingly narcissistic. We extol success more than we extol anything," he says. Adams points to the kind of "charismatic narcissist who is worshipped by others." This is the kind of white-collar batterer who—through money and connections—manages to evade judicial and law enforcement systems. A man for whom status and reputation are everything. He and other researchers I spoke with often talk about our collective vision of criminals, especially murderers; how we tend to picture rageaholics when the reality is that they are impossible to divine from the general population.

The average batterer, Adams told me, "is more likable than his victim, because domestic violence affects victims a lot more than it affects batterers. Batterers don't lose sleep like victims do. They don't lose their jobs; they don't lose their kids." In fact batterers often see themselves as saviors of a sort. "They feel they're rescuing a woman in distress. It's another aspect of narcissism . . . And there's a sense of wanting to be eternally appreciated for that." In contrast, he said, "a lot of victims come across as messed up. Because that's exactly the point for him: 'I'm going to make it so no one wants you.'"

Victims' lives are messy. Often they are substance abusers, or they live in extreme poverty. Many have suffered traumatic, abusive childhoods. Such cases are the most difficult to prosecute, not least because the victims can be unreliable witnesses. "This is why batterers are so often able to fool the system," one domestic violence advocate told me. "They're so charming, and the victim comes off as very negative." Even in court, a detective named Robert Wile told me some years ago how he has come to understand that "the majority of [victims] who we're going to bring into court are going to be people who have a lot of mental health issues, and we have to portray them as good people so we can put away the knucklehead who beat them up. And who gets to say not a word? Him. He just sits there."

Wile's remark reminded me of a woman I'd met once just as she was managing to get her life back together after years of abuse. One of the questions that is so difficult to really explain is how abuse slowly erodes a person, how often survivors talk about emotional abuse being so much worse than physical abuse. Indeed, Gondolf's book talks about domestic violence as a process, rather than a single incident, and yet our entire criminal justice system is set up to address incidents, not processes. This particular woman had a social work background, and I spent many hours with her as she tried to explain how her ex-husband's abuse just whittled away at her. The first time, she said, was so sudden and so strange she assumed it was just a onetime event. They'd been walking on a busy Manhattan street, arguing, when he suddenly leaned over and bit her on the cheek so hard that half her face bruised up and she had teeth marks for days. When he saw what he had done, he took her to the drugstore to buy makeup to cover it. Like so many others, he claimed to be deeply remorseful. Horrified by what he'd done. He cried. He apologized. He made promises. "I was still like, this is unacceptable," she told me, "before I had just got so broken down and it was just about survival." And yet he continued to abuse her, escalating the abuse year after year. He'd throw golf balls at her face as she drove down the highway, or toss a blanket over her head and strangle her. By the time things had reached the level where she feared for her life, he could go to the store on his own, buy the makeup she needed to cover up his assault, and present it to her without apology. By then, she says, she was so beaten down as a person she felt as if there was nothing left, a husk of skin and bone with no spirit, no agency of her own, only a kind of slow, painful slog toward unconsciousness. And yet, at the same time, she felt if she could only help him see himself through her eyes, he'd change, become the person she'd always felt him capable of being. It's a common narrative. Women are given the message over and over that we are the holders of the emotional life and health of the family, that the responsibility for a man to change lies, in fact, with us. "The only way that I can really describe what happened to me is like part of me, like, died, and then part of me got ignited in terms of, like, my love will heal us," she said. "But I had to stop loving myself and *only* love him." His narcissism, in other words, didn't even allow the room for her to care for herself.

She was ashamed by the turn her life and marriage had taken, so much so that she didn't admit it to anyone for a long time. After all, she told herself, she had a promising career and a graduate degree; she'd been raised to "know better" by a feminist. She wasn't impoverished. She wasn't uneducated. She was liberal, middle class, white. She had long blond hair, a white-toothed California smile. And still, here she was, with this man who'd somehow carved away the humanity in her. The abuse must have somehow been partly her fault, she thought. He had post-traumatic stress disorder. She needed to be more patient. He'd fought for his country, serving in overseas wars. She owed it to him, she told herself. Hadn't everyone else in the world given up on him? Wasn't she the only person he really had? Wasn't that the promise she'd made him? Love, honor, sickness, health, poverty, wealth. It was her duty to stay, to help him see clear to fixing his own pain. She couldn't imagine what he'd been through. Where was her empathy? Her patience? Someday, somehow, she thought he'd get better and the abuse would end and it would all be okay.

And then one day she woke up and she fled. And her case was so extreme that she qualified for a witness protection program that kept her address confidential, that had her mail delivered by private courier, that installed security cameras at her doors and windows. It took her years to return to herself. Years where he was put on a GPS ankle bracelet and given a lifetime restraining order and barred from even entering the county, never mind the town, where she lived and worked. He did jail time. And eventually, several years after she left him, she did something she'd forgotten she once loved: she went jogging. Outside. In the open air. And that was when she knew she was really free.

The Haunting Presence of
the Inexplicable

One night, Patrick O'Hanlon and his wife, Dawn, stayed up till the early morning hours. Their daughter, April, had gone to bed hours earlier. O'Hanlon had suffered from chronic insomnia for months, such that he had taken to sometimes sleeping in April's bedroom while she slept with her mother. He found this humiliating, but everything woke him: Dawn's snoring, their cramped living conditions, stress from work. He had a long commute and was often so exhausted he'd fall asleep on the train. Once, Dawn had found him sleeping in a closet.

He'd retired from his career about a year earlier and the transition had been difficult. Only a handful of people knew that he was going through a hard time—Dawn, April, his mother, his boss. But no one realized how bad things had gotten. He suffered from severe depression—"major depressive disorder," it would later be called—and he had begun to hear voices telling him there was "no way out" and he should "end it all."[1] He avoided any place where he might have to interact with strangers—elevators, for example. He repeatedly scoped out one of the railings at the apartment complex where his family was temporarily living to gauge whether it would hold his weight if he hanged himself. He imagined jumping off high places, driving into walls, swerving into oncoming traffic. He hoarded his medications. For weeks, Dawn had been calling her mother-in-law saying she was scared for her husband; Alice O'Hanlon began to call her son more and more frequently, worried that he might harm himself.

Suicide was everyone's primary concern. No one knew the extent of his anguish until the night Patrick O'Hanlon went into his daughter's room, where, as he suffocated her, he told her he was "sending her to Jesus." She did not fight back. From there, he went into his own bedroom and bludgeoned Dawn before suffocating her as well. Then he drove around for a number of hours; he stopped at a convenience store. He stopped to buy a rope. He stopped to call a minister and tell him what he'd done.

LEGALLY DEFINED, FAMILICIDE, OR family annihilation, includes the killing of an intimate partner and at least one child. (Some researchers define it as killing the whole family.) As a crime, it is indisputably rare, though rarer still as an area of research for social scientists. I have found only a handful of researchers who even touched on it in their published work. One called it a mere "footnote" in violence studies.

The first known annihilation in the United States can be traced back to the mid-eighteenth century. Over the course of the next two centuries, such cases averaged three per decade. Then, in the 1990s, there were thirty-six cases. And between 2000 and 2007, sixty cases. And from 2008 through 2013, in research done by the Family Violence Institute, there were 163 cases of familicide that claimed a total of 435 victims. This did not include cases where children killed parents (patricide) or where a parent only killed children (filicide). From the time of the 2008 economic crash, we began averaging, says Neil Websdale, director of the Family Violence Institute and author of the book *Familicidal Hearts*, around three a month. In other words, while nearly all other forms of homicide steadily declined over the past several decades in the United States, familicide appears to be on the rise.

IF BATTERER INTERVENTION PROGRAMS are most often populated by working-class white men and minorities, and jails are overwhelmingly poor white and people of color, it is in familicide where white middle- and upper-middle class men dominate. The disparity between minorities and whites of course is most visible in prisons across the country, where minorities are disproportionately incarcerated for things that Caucasian men get away with all the time because they have the money or the connections or the education. Think Rob Porter, Eric Schneiderman, Donald Trump, and you'll see white male privilege and economics at work. But in familicide, the reverse is true: the overwhelming majority of men who kill their entire families *are* white, middle or middle-upper class, often educated, often well-off, or well-off until just before the murders. Some of the better known incidents, like Scott Peterson, who's on death row for killing his wife and unborn child, or Chris Watts, sentenced to life in prison in November 2018 for killing his wife, two daughters, and unborn son, dominate national headlines for months.[2] Familicide is the one area of domestic violence homicide that often doesn't seem to easily follow any of the other patterns. And perhaps because the crime is so unthinkable and so dark, and perpetrators almost always kill themselves as well, it is rarely studied by researchers. Websdale, in fact, who is also the director of the National Domestic Violence Fatality Review Initiative (NDVFRI), is perhaps the only researcher in the United States who targets his academic research at this act specifically.

Perhaps it's obvious, but these are among the most difficult kinds of stories to report on. With both the darkness they inhabit and the emotional fortitude required for such reporting, it's no wonder that stories of familicide are underreported. But the challenge is also simply practical: most perpetrators kill themselves. And those who *do* live tend not to want to talk to reporters.

Patrick O'Hanlon was that rare find for me: someone who lived after the act and was also willing to talk to me. I believe he had initially thought of our interviews as a way toward absolution, a way to try to explain himself to the world. He fit David Adams's definition of narcissism in every way, even saying at several points how he believed the world was waiting for his words. But at some point, it must have become clear to him that absolution through me is impossible. He decided, after months of interviews, that he did not want to participate. We went back and forth on it. As a journalist, the ethics and practices are clear: one cannot go "off the record" once the record, as it were, is complete. I had maybe fourteen hours of interviews with him, several notebooks' worth. I was within my rights to publish his story. At the same time, I am living and reporting in a country in which the media is deemed an "enemy of the people" by its commander in chief. We are insulted, threatened, sued (and, yes, even killed) for the work we do, and so such decisions cannot be made lightly. Admittedly, one also does not want to run afoul of a person who has killed his whole family.

So in the end, I felt my only option to explore the question of why these crimes are increasing was through his story, but heavily redacted. His name and the names of his family members have been changed, and other identifying information has been withheld. Much of the information I've included comes from court transcripts, police records, or other public documents.

* * *

PATRICK O'HANLON IS AN erect, wound-tight man with salted black hair; he wears jeans, a short-sleeved shirt, and work boots—the prison uniform. His glasses are held together by tape. He is clean-shaven and tucked in. O'Hanlon's voice is quiet. Our talks take place in a window-less conference room at the prison where the walls are lined with inspi-rational posters of soaring eagles and fuchsia sunsets and waterfalls with messages to "believe" in the possibility of change, to never give up hope. Costco art. O'Hanlon does not wear shackles, but is accom-panied by a guard, who remains in the room with us the entire time, along with the prison communications liaison and a videographer, who tapes every conversation. I interviewed O'Hanlon in five- and six-hour stints where he is serving two consecutive sentences for the murders of Dawn and April. O'Hanlon describes a small area, a kind of prison patio, where sometimes he can smell the countryside, occasionally see the tops of trees. "Prison's not so bad," he says. *Compared to what?* I wonder.

O'Hanlon's father had had a small business that went bankrupt, so his mother supported the family. "He had to get money from my mom," O'Hanlon says. "It was humiliating." As a result O'Hanlon's father drank too much and yelled too much and sometimes terrified his family with his outbursts. One time he pulled a knife on his family and threat-ened to use it on anyone who took a step toward him. O'Hanlon remembers standing up to his dad, until a neighbor came over and took his father away. (O'Hanlon's mother claims not to remember the knife incident, and will say only that her husband yelled and sometimes threw things.) Still, O'Hanlon says, "I wouldn't categorize my father as abusive, but loving."

Like many children who grow up in homes with domestic violence—verbal or physical—O'Hanlon did not describe his father as violent. O'Hanlon fit the mold of the men I'd seen in David Adams's group the night they discussed their fathers. He downplayed the violence of his father and talked more often about his mother's behavior. "My mother was no angel," he told me. "If she had been less provocative, more respectful of his position as a husband . . ."

I asked O'Hanlon one time what violence looked like to him. He described yelling and screaming, someone throwing furniture, the neighbors all hearing the ruckus. He cites the knife incident as proof that his father wasn't abusive. "Another [more] violent man would have used that knife," he says. O'Hanlon seemed not to realize that his house, to anyone outside, would have sounded just like his own description of violence.

THE FAMILY VIOLENCE INSTITUTE sits in a squat one-story building shared with the ROTC and a secondhand office furniture supply warehouse on the main campus of Flagstaff's Northern Arizona University. The door stays locked with security cameras stationed outside because Neil Websdale has had death threats against him in the past, mostly from domestic violence abusers from cases he has consulted on as a criminologist.

Years ago, he began combing the archives for familicides in America for a course he was teaching when he came across the case of a man named William Beadle. Beadle had been a respected businessman who was facing bankruptcy in 1782, and subsequently killed his wife and four children with his hatchet. It piqued Websdale's interest and so he began to comb through archives, finding more and more similar cases. "There seemed to be this link to these line of cases from the 1780s to straight through today," Websdale said. Incidents where an otherwise upstanding man falls into extreme economic hardship and the only way out he can conceive of is to kill his family and then himself. Indeed, Beadle himself wrote of the humiliation of bankruptcy: "If a man who has once lived well, meant well and done well, falls by unavoidable accident in poverty, and then submits to be laughed at . . . he must become meaner than meanness itself."

Websdale began to gather centuries of data from familicides all over the country, research that culminated in his 2010 book, *Familicidal Hearts*, in which he identifies two primary types of family killer: livid coercive, or those with long histories of domestic violence, and civil reputable, in which perpetrators are respectable members of society—like William Beadle—with no obvious histories of violence and who kill out of a warped sense of altruism. There is overlap between the two, but it is the latter that mystifies researchers. (Jacquelyn Campbell rejects these categories to some extent, arguing that domestic violence is always a shadowy background in cases of familicide, even if there's a lack of evidence. She and Websdale have a friendly rivalry in which they often disagree with each other in the most polite way possible.) Civil reputable is the category most affected by, for example, an economic recession. It is certainly the category to which Patrick O'Hanlon belongs, the kind of well-respected, upstanding citizen who seems to just "snap" one day.

"What we miss in the 'he just snaps' theory is the accumulation of emotional repression," Websdale says. Civil reputable killers tend to be middle or middle-upper class. Very often they are Caucasian. (Men make up 95% of all familicide perpetrators in the United States; Websdale's research showed 154 men versus 7 women perpetrators between 2008 and 2013.) Their families tend to be traditionally gendered, which means the man is the primary support, while the woman takes care of the family and home. (This is not to say women don't work, but rather they carry the emotional needs of the home.) Rocky Mosure is such an example. They're often religious compared to the general population, with a fundamentalist outlook, and they can be rigidly constrained in their emotional range, all of which fit with Patrick O'Hanlon. Often they're extremely socially isolated. Economics—loss of a job or rank or status, a pending bankruptcy—can be a catalyst for the final act of killing.

The altruism materializes with the idea that the family is being saved from a worse fate than the murder itself. A famous case from Florida in 2010, for example, involved an unemployed mortgage broker named Neal Jacobson, who killed his wife and twin sons on their seventh birthday; the family lived in a gated community in Wellington, Florida, and were on the verge of losing their home to bankruptcy. In another famous case, from Wales, Robert Mochrie killed his wife and four children and was facing bankruptcy. It appears that in both cases—and many others—the wives had no idea of the financial ruin facing their families. Such secrets are another hallmark of these killers, Websdale said. "I'm astounded at the level of secrecy in these men's lives."

David Adams rejects, to some extent, these categories of Websdale's in part because he believes they frame the offender as "victim." To Adams, the categories are less germane than his theory of narcissism. "If you have this outsized sense of yourself, and you suffer narcissistic injury, you'll lash out," Adams says. He's speaking here, not simply of someone with a colossal sense of self-confidence, but with a recognized personality disorder. Such narcissists, Adams says, "live and die by their image." When that image is compromised, say they're discovered lying or a secret they've borne is discovered, they lash out and "impose" their solution on their partners and children. The solution, in extreme cases, is homicide.

The financial situations of many in Websdale's civil reputable category suggest a link between what perpetrators perceive as economic catastrophe and the murder of their families. Indeed, in the 161 cases Websdale's team identified between 2008 and 2013, 81 happened in 2009 and 2010. The Northeastern University criminologist Jack Levin looked at familicides in the first four months of 2008—seven cases— and found they had nearly doubled compared to the first four months of 2009—to twelve. (While we're talking about small numbers here, we are also talking about extreme acts.) By then, the unemployment rate had also nearly doubled after the recession. "I think there is a definitely a relationship between unemployment and the DOW and the familicide rate, particularly with civil reputable offenders," Websdale says. "I would describe it as a lag inverse relationship."

James Gilligan, author of *Violence: Reflections on a National Epidemic* and the evaluator on RSVP at its inception, sees evidence of both homicide and suicide rates rising under economic duress in his research. "There's a clear line," he said. "If a man loses his job, he can feel castrated and emasculated and prone to suicide or homicide or both . . . It's an apocalyptic mentality." Richard Gelles, director of the Center for Research on Youth and Social Policy at the University of Pennsylvania, points to economic stressors as well, but warns that under our current social and political conditions things are likely to only get worse. "You can still play by the rules and lose your pension, lose your job, lose your house, and have 50K in college loans still to pay, and when you declare bankruptcy you still have to pay those loans," he said. "It really is the perfect storm of screwing one section of the population." The dissolution of the American middle class, he told me, is "a canary in a coal mine."

There are others who find the economic angle more debatable. Marieke Liem, a postdoctoral fellow at Harvard who studies family violence, found a strong correlation between the unemployment rate and familicide from 1976–2007; but a second analysis covering 2000–2009 found the two only "weakly related." Jacquelyn Campbell believes that economics and joblessness are "stressors" for all forms of domestic violence, but not stand-alone causes themselves.

AFTER HE GRADUATED FROM high school, O'Hanlon applied to a prestigious university. He believed no one thought he could do it. His siblings didn't take his aspirations seriously and sometimes ridiculed him. "I believed in God. I said, 'If you're real, help me.'" And God, he says, answered his prayer. He was accepted and he began his life with all the respect that bestowed on him.

Patrick O'Hanlon met his wife, Dawn, just after he'd graduated. He says she impressed him. She was ambitious, working full time while attending college at night, and she was desperately broke. O'Hanlon said it was love at first sight; he worried that she couldn't pay her rent and felt he had a duty to help her. So he asked himself, "What would Jesus do?" And the answer he heard was to save her. The couple married shortly after they met. O'Hanlon says Dawn was always driven; she eventually earned her degree and got a job. After a few years, they had a daughter named April.

When they were still dating, O'Hanlon remembered how Dawn was often too busy to see him. One week she had a paper to write and O'Hanlon took the assignment and wrote the paper for her. He wanted to see her, he explained, and that paper was "getting in the way." What about cheating? I asked him. He had often tried to insist that he was an honorable man. "As far as I'm concerned," he said, waving away my question, "I'm not the one who handed it in."

And then came September 11, 2001, the crash at the Pentagon. From the moment he learned of it, until later that same morning when he called Dawn, he says he doesn't remember a thing. He walked about a mile and a half, but has no memory of the walk. He cites this as the moment "Patrick O'Hanlon began to lose his mind."

NEIL WEBSDALE POINTS TO many possibilities for the increase in familicides. He says masculinity exacts a heavy burden on men who cannot accept feminism. Domestic violence theory points to an abuser's need for power and control and asks why the victim doesn't just leave. But Websdale argues that abusers are just as vulnerable in a sense by their own inability to live without that victim. "My question isn't 'Why doesn't *she* leave?'" he says, "It's 'Why does *he* stay?' Many of these men are terribly dependent on their female partners. They see them as a conduit to the world of feeling that they don't inhabit, generally. Often these men have an inchoate sense of shame about their masculinity that they don't understand." Websdale calls it the great paradox of domestic violence, how an abuser can be both controlling over his or her partner, while simultaneously unable to control that dependency.

Gilligan agrees with Websdale's assessment of changing gender roles. "Any time any major social change occurs—as happened with the civil rights movement when legal segregation ended—that produced a huge backlash, and I would say the changing sexual mores and gender roles is also producing a huge backlash. [We hear] some of the most bigoted, sexist, homophobic attitudes, even while the public in general is becoming more tolerant." Gilligan believes violence should be approached as a public health problem, which in its most radical form means that he believes it is preventable. "We talk as if once people are grown up they should be able to deal with whatever happens," he said, "but the fact is that human beings are so much more vulnerable and fragile than we recognize. Then we're surprised when we see how vulnerable and fragile they are that they break."

Certainly, we are living in an age in which progress and the attendant backlash that Gilligan cites are extreme. Plenty of men are spewing bigoted, racist, misogynistic rhetoric in manifestos before they kill— Dylann Roof, Elliot Rodger, Alek Minassian. At times our highest leaders in office today seem to normalize these killers' brand of sexist and racist vitriol, their sense of entitlement. It's hardly a secret that presidents from Thomas Jefferson to Ronald Reagan to Bill Clinton have all been accused of rape (in Jefferson's case, of course, the accusations have long been confirmed). The difference to me compared to all of these other moments—from Jefferson's pre-suffrage systemic rape to John Kennedy and Bill Clinton's serial philandering and even to Donald Trump's bleating misogyny—is not only that today's heated rhetoric unleashes, in my view, extreme violence, mostly in the form of mass shootings—but also that such violence is happening at the same time the majority of women are very publicly and very vociferously demanding better. It is no longer assumed that we will endure harassment at work, or assaults on campus, or even endless womanizing from our partners. Women are fighting for more and better laws from our legislators, for more and better treatment from the judiciary and law enforcement. As I write this, thousands of women are marching on the steps of the Supreme Court after a white upper-class man accused of attempted rape has just ascended to the highest court in the country. Thousands of women are running for office, more than ever before, and historic numbers of women now serve in Congress. So are we living in an age in which progress will prevail as it has in other modern cultural and social movements? Ask me in twenty years. But I certainly hope James Gilligan's theory— that progress follows moments of great social upheaval—is right.

Many researchers, including Websdale and Adams, also talk about the incendiary possibilities of extreme shame. In a now-famous TED talk called "Listening to Shame," Brené Brown, who calls herself a "vulnerability researcher," talked about the correlation of shame with violence, depression, and aggression, among others. She said shame is "organized by gender." For women, it's about a competing set of expectations around family, work, relationships; for men it's simply, "do not be perceived as . . . weak." Calling shame "an epidemic in our culture," Brown cites the research of James Mahalik at Boston College, who studied what our ideas were of gender norms across American society. For women those norms involved "nice, thin, modest, and use all available resources for appearance." For men, the norms included "show emotional control, work is first, pursue status, and violence."

I called Mahalik for further context and he said it isn't so much about individual men endorsing violence as it is about a general cultural response in the United States. He cited foreign policy and civil unrest and how our collective first response veers toward violence: police in riot gear in Ferguson, for example, or military action in the Middle East. Even in Hollywood's portrayal of men, violence is "a prominent part of moviegoing," he said. "Somehow we've equated violence with problem-solving."

In O'Hanlon's psychiatric records, shame comes up again and again. He is ashamed that he didn't get promoted, ashamed that he'd been transferred to a job he felt ill-equipped to handle, ashamed that he couldn't shake himself out of his despair. In one of his final therapy sessions before he retired, his treating psychologist wrote, *He has learned that having a bit of humility is actually strengthening rather than weakening . . . Low risk for self-harm or harm to others.*

If you ask O'Hanlon why he did it, he'll say he does not know. If you ask him what advice he'd offer in terms of prevention, his answers vary. And I asked him every time I ever spoke to him. Here is a compilation of what he said over the course of our interviews: "Don't take on too much. Don't be prideful. Don't be greedy for promotion, for financial gain. Don't work so hard. Lower your expectations. Don't be too ambitious. September 11th. We need to address how we treat mental illness in this country. We need to look at the medication they're taking. Survivor's guilt. I should have read the Book of Job. You don't know how far I drive on my commute, what my life is like. Insomnia. When you have cancer, you can ask your friend for help. Not so with depression."

The thing is, he's not really wrong about any of this.

* * *

AFTER SEPTEMBER IITH, O'HANLON WORKED in a supporting role for a federal organization. He also began to have trouble sleeping. O'Hanlon said the images of body bags[3] and flag-draped coffins wouldn't leave him. I asked him one time why he didn't go overseas for his job and his normally placid demeanor erupted. "A lot of people ask me, 'You're a wimp. Why not go to Iraq? Afghanistan?'" he said, his voice suddenly loud in the conference room. "I was nineteen with arms pointed at us. I volunteered. The Berlin Wall was still up. I was out there with howitzers, tanks pointed at us in Germany. Don't tell me I was a wimp. After 9/II I was put on watch, on the highest level of security. All these men putting boots on the ground? They were supported by *my* office."

O'Hanlon's answer made it clear I'd tapped a sensitive area. When pressed, O'Hanlon later says no one called him a wimp to his face, but he sensed it. "A four-star general would say, 'Don't measure a soldier by the proximity of combat,'" O'Hanlon told me, adding, "Don't tell me I'm not brave. I'm not a patriot."

As O'Hanlon's insomnia worsened, so too did his depression. He continued to see a psychiatrist, who prescribed many different types and doses of drugs, which O'Hanlon believes may have contributed to his stress. He also had cognitive behavioral therapy and attended general therapy on and off until he retired. On evaluation sheets from this time when asked if he was having suicidal thoughts, O'Hanlon always checked the "no" box, but he says that wasn't true. He *was* having suicidal thoughts. But he didn't want to mark that box, because he would have lost his security clearance and possibly his job. He couldn't think how to support the family without his work. He knew he was sick, very sick, but he also knew in every practical sense that he couldn't admit to it.

As his retirement approached, he says the stress began to weigh down on him. At the same time, April began rebelling. She felt stifled by her parents, overly controlled, always pushed to maintain her grades; she wasn't allowed to sleep at friends' houses or vice versa. One time, her parents caught her cheating and spanked her. Shortly after, the family moved to a small temporary apartment and put money down on a house that was still under construction.

Then O'Hanlon retired.

SOMETIMES THE CRIME SCENE of a familicide shows a degree of care that is chilling and offers clues to the killer's motivation. William

Beadle collected the blood of his family in a receptacle so as to not make a mess, and then laid the bodies of his three daughters out on the floor, covering them with a blanket. Jacobson's and Mochrie's children were left lying in bed, covered up; Mochrie had mopped up the blood from his daughter's wall and ingested weed killer before hanging himself. Another left gold coins on his family's eyelids, presumably to help them on their journey into the next life. Websdale refers to this kind of symbolism as the emotional architecture of a case. "At the level of metaphor it speaks to the understanding of their plight that is misguided. This defies social science understanding; it requires a literary insight." Instances where the use of a dumbbell as a murder weapon, for example, suggest to Websdale that a perpetrator is "killing with his masculinity. He may not mean to. It may be unintentional . . . an undeveloped understanding of what it means to be ashamed."

In today's interpretation of Christianity, God literally sacrifices his own son, the ultimate filicide, so that the world can be saved. The Romans may have committed the act of putting Jesus on the cross, but it was all part of God's master plan. Other examples abound in the Bible. Abraham brought his son, Isaac, to the altar, prepared to sacrifice him, but God stopped him at the eleventh hour, the knife at Isaac's throat, his arms and legs bound up. God said Abraham had passed the test, had proven his love. O'Hanlon refers to Isaiah 53:8–9: *He was taken from prison and from judgment; and who shall declare his generation? For he was cut off out of the land of the living: for the transgression of my people was he stricken. And he made his grave with the wicked, and with the rich in his death; because he had done no violence, neither was any deceit in his mouth.* In a religion in which family killing is not only rationalized, but also celebrated as the ultimate form of love, devotion, and faith, perhaps the connection is not a stretch today. O'Hanlon himself says it took three lives to save his: Jesus Christ, Dawn O'Hanlon, and April O'Hanlon.

He was, by his own admission, a "lukewarm" Christian until the murders. "I ask God, 'Why? Why? Couldn't there have been *any* other way?'" In his interpretation, the murders seemed to be a way for God to get O'Hanlon's attention, to straighten up, to restore his faith in the Lord, to serve. He said God is working miracles through him, saving other prisoners. At several points he suggests I title this chapter "Triumph Over Tragedy." Where is the triumph? I ask him. Because the tragedy part is clear. He says it hasn't come yet, but it will. He tells me to research the pastor Rick Warren and his son's suicide, or Creigh Deeds, the former congressman whose son stabbed him before killing himself. O'Hanlon sees mental illness and turning a negative into a positive as the link between himself and these others. But he also sees them all, himself included, as victims.

Why? I ask. I ask him this over and over. Why did you? He asks himself, too, fills in the blank for me sometimes. How could you? I ask even though I don't expect O'Hanlon will ever be able to adequately answer. "God didn't answer any of Job's questions. He said, 'Where were you when I created the world?' God was redirecting Job's sight toward the sovereign God that we can't comprehend," O'Hanlon says. "He's telling me the same thing he told Job. Don't focus on what happened; focus on what you can do for me."

O'Hanlon says his insomnia worsened after he retired, and he began to have homicidal and suicidal thoughts. In a journal he kept from this time, his notes become increasingly desperate. Two months before the homicide, he wrote, *Please help!* five times. Two weeks later, *Please spare my life. Please help. Lord help! Spare Dawn and April.* In a psychiatric evaluation after the murder a forensic psychologist wrote, *He described persistent, intrusive thoughts of killing himself, as well as killing his wife and daughter to spare them any further burdens and suffering. Mr. O'Hanlon believed he could overcome these thoughts on his own, and he did not want to speak them out loud lest they become more real.*

FOR MANY MEN AND women, retirement is a painful, difficult transition. And O'Hanlon took a menial job after retiring that he felt was beneath him. O'Hanlon himself once sent me a list of possible research areas—survivor's guilt was one, suicide another—and his suggestions felt less manipulation than a man also in search of answers. Researchers use the term "multi-determined" to explain a situation in which there are potentially many causes for an event or action. Depression, insomnia, shame, loss of status. But Websdale rejects this term. "People think that if they can find enough variables they can do the odds ratio, put them into a formula, and spew out the cases where there's very, very high risk, and I think that flies in the face of the complexity of the human condition," he says. "At some level, we're talking about the haunting presence of the inexplicable."

O'Hanlon considered suicide, but the prospect filled him with shame and he could not envision leaving Dawn and April to live through the humiliation of such an act. Over the years, he had been prescribed medication: Ambien, Zoloft, Klonopin, Wellbutrin, Oleptro, Remeron, Paxil, Ativan, Lunesta. He admitted that sometimes he'd cut the doses and save half in a basket in his bathroom that Dawn didn't know about. He couldn't stand the mental haze that he felt when he took the drugs, and because, he said, "I knew I'd need them someday."

He started to believe people were laughing at him. He didn't go out. He sat in a chair at his house and stared at the ceiling, his head thrown back, his body limp. April would see him and say things like, "Cheer up, Daddy." O'Hanlon's mother told April to make her father feel better, and she tried. But every time she tried, he felt worse, guilty for making his problems—his delusions—her responsibility. He should have been strong enough; he was the man of the house. What was *wrong* with him?

The pressure increased. There was his daughter's rebellion, his terrible commute to a new job he hated, his family crammed into a tiny living space, he no longer had professional status; the condo he and Dawn owned was underwater with the recession. At the same time, the builder on their new house was giving them trouble, not following the code, O'Hanlon said. They fought over the construction, and O'Hanlon says the builder eventually allowed them to pull out of the deal. Though O'Hanlon says they were financially solvent and the builder returned their down payment, court records state that he was tens of thousands of dollars in debt as a result. In the days before the murders, Dawn had taken to returning all the new furniture they'd purchased for their new home. "It was as if," O'Hanlon says, "we were all doomed."

O'HANLON SAYS HE LOVED his family. Loved and loved them. "I did not hate them," he says. "I had not one iota of hatred for my family the night before. No negative feelings, nada, nothing. I have no motive." After the murders, O'Hanlon drove around with that rope looking for a place to hang himself, before realizing that he'd have to wait till nightfall. He swallowed more than a dozen Ambien before calling the pastor, who called the police. O'Hanlon was interrogated while he was so high on Ambien he holds no memory of it. (He was read his Miranda rights while under the influence of Ambien and maintains that his rights were violated.) After his arrest, he attempted suicide by hurling himself headfirst into the metal frame of his cell door. He passed out in a pool of his own blood, a six-inch gash in his head and a spinal injury that should have left him paralyzed. The fact of his survival—he required multiple surgeries—that he can move at all, in fact, is proof to O'Hanlon that God kept him alive for a reason. In a psychiatric consult at the time, O'Hanlon was reported to have rammed so hard into that doorframe that there could be no question about his intent. "If this isn't mental illness, I don't know what is," the doctor wrote.

Each time I visited O'Hanlon, he sat down and stressed again that he was not the man, the murderer, he'd been painted to be. "As far as I am concerned," he would say, "I have been corrected. Here I am at this *correctional* facility. And I have been corrected." He has a radio in his cell. He is allowed thirteen books, and Amazon shipments are approved by the prison. There is a small track where he recently began running again after an ankle sprain finally healed. It takes him three minutes per lap; he does twelve laps. He calls himself a model inmate, by which he means that he does not get in fights and does not harass correctional officers. He leads a Bible study for his fellow inmates and often he helps them write letters and sends them to friends and family. He breaks the rules with his three-way calling, but this rule seems somehow not to count for him.

In O'Hanlon's case, several experts point to mental health likely playing a role in his familicide, though a jury rejected his "not guilty by reason of insanity" defense. (Websdale's team told me the familicides they'd found often used this defense strategy when the perpetrator lived, and it almost never worked; a fatality review team member also told me that she had yet to come across an investigation where there were not "unmet mental health needs.") How much of this refusal to attribute O'Hanlon's actions to mental health may or may not stem from mental health biases in this country? We tend to have easy empathy for people suffering mental health issues when they are universally beloved and when their actions affect only themselves (a Robin Williams, say), but our empathy falters, perhaps rightly so, when those actions affect the lives of others, such as what happened with O'Hanlon.

James Gilligan says we ought to treat people like O'Hanlon as research subjects. "We must be able to look horror in the face if we are ever to understand the causes of the human propensity toward violence well enough to prevent its most destructive manifestations," he wrote in *Violence*. "Suicide is no solution to the problem of homicide; both forms of violence are equally lethal."

One of the first questions I ever asked O'Hanlon was whether or not he thought he was going to heaven. "Absolutely," he said. Dawn and April, of course, were already there.

Then he told me how God keeps a jar for all the crying we do in our lifetimes; our tears collected and held by Him. He paused a moment, then said, "I think when I go to heaven, I'll be welcomed with open arms."

Though he also believes his own grieving will never end. He says he still cannot look at pictures of April. Recently, he noted, she'd have graduated from high school. "As I'm jogging around the yard or eating, I pray I could be sitting down with my family, you know," he tells me, but he begins to cry a little and he shifts in his seat and tries to right himself with his mantra: "I have a choice. I can go forward or back; I can be negative or positive, and I choose . . ." He cannot finish. He throws his head back violently, then sobs, his arms straight out in front of him, hands clenched in a prayer or a fist, I cannot tell. I do not interrupt him, but it is an unbearable sound, a sound I've never heard come from another human. He howls and howls, trying to hold it in, regain control, his body in an absolute visible war with itself. When our interview finishes that day, I sit in the stillness for a minute with the prison liaison and the videographer, and none of us speaks; it is as if we have been dragged to a place so dark and so full of misery that it will take no small effort to claw our way back into the daylight.

And it strikes me that this is why O'Hanlon agreed to talk to me at all, to try to find some way to live with himself in this world. The tutoring, the letter writing, the Bible studying. Clawing his own way out of the darkness just enough to get through each hour of each day. This is the state of purgatory in which he will reside in this life: trying to extricate his pain through a thousand small gestures and kindnesses and prayers from that one colossal, horrifying moment.

There is a narrative that emerges with Patrick O'Hanlon, of not giving up, of determination and persistence. It is a peculiarly American narrative of hard work and defying rejection before, finally at long last, the inevitable success that was promised all along. But what if the key to all this isn't hard work, isn't dogged determination, but rather resilience in one's own failure, the grace to accept defeat and move on? What might have been had Patrick O'Hanlon chosen another path? Gone into real estate? Become a software engineer? It's the kind of question most of us ask about our own lives. How decision X led to action Y. A chance encounter. A flip decision. A left rather than right and it might have all unfolded so, so differently.

A Superhero's Kneecaps

A man's voice comes through the speaker of a black phone sitting in the center of a faux-wood table. Whiteboards span one wall, windows along another. More tables sit haphazardly inside this conference room, which is the generic color of offices across the country: taupes, creams, beiges. A dozen police officers in plain clothes are poised around the phone in silence, listening. "Leave us the fuck alone," the voice says. "Just leave us the fuck alone."

Then the line goes dead.

Two police officers are huddled over the phone. They have just seconds to make a decision about what to say when they call the man back. Do they tell him the house is surrounded by tactical officers—a SWAT team? Do they tell him to come out with his hands up? One of the officers dials. The man picks up: "What the fuck do you want?"

"Listen, Ronnie," the officer says, "the quickest way to make us go away is for you and Melissa to come out." Melissa is Ronnie's girlfriend. He has barricaded himself in the house with her.

"I didn't do any fucking thing wrong," Ronnie says. "Melissa and I just need to work this shit out. I'm having my eyes fucking opened as to what's been going on."

"I don't want anyone to get hurt," the officer says. His name is Matt. "But we heard a gunshot—"

"There wasn't no damn gunshot," Ronnie says, then adds, "It was just a shot to the ceiling."

"I need to know Melissa's okay."

"She's fine as fuck. What I'm doing is none of your fucking business. Stay out my business and I'll stay out yours." Ronnie hangs up. We are on the outskirts of San Diego, on a quintessentially sunny July afternoon.

Besides the officer next to Matt—his name is Chris—there are several others around. One keeps track on a second-by-second basis every time

175

Ronnie hangs up the phone or his anger ramps up. 1:00 p.m. 1:01 p.m. 1:03 p.m. 1:08 p.m. 1:09 p.m. 1:15 p.m. The hours will start to stack up and they can see if there are certain triggering moments or topics. Another, the supervisor, feeds information to Matt and the others based on real-time interviews that are going on elsewhere by other police officers or detectives—with friends, family members, acquaintances of Ronnie and Melissa. They learn about previous relationships, family incidents of violence, maybe street fights or run-ins with the law or employment histories. Several large sheets of paper are tacked up along the whiteboards with information about Ronnie and Melissa, their history, their family members, what can be gleaned about their relationship dynamic. Several officers are writing madly as the information comes in, dates of the relationship, and employment. Other incidents of violence. Past hurts in Ronnie's childhood. It is disjointed, appearing in pieces in real time in the hope that they can square Ronnie's personality and past with what's happening here today. They learn that this morning a coworker went to pick Melissa up for work, and when she came to the door, she had a bloody lip, appeared nervous and scared, and said she wasn't going to be able to come in. That coworker, Denise, called the police; they refer to her as the reporting party. Officers have spoken with Ronnie's sister and brother. Learned his father was sometimes abusive, that Ronnie had a strained relationship with him. They have also learned that Ronnie cheated on Melissa with one of her friends, and that Melissa hasn't been going out with their mutual friends much anymore. She goes to work and goes home, and they rarely see her. One of Ronnie's ex-girlfriends tells officers she's never seen him violent in any way; she also says she thinks maybe he still loves her, and they suspect she harbors feelings for him and so the information is suspect.

They've been at this for several hours already. Officers around Matt are quietly trying to piece together all the information that's coming in and gauge the dangerousness of the situation. Of them all, the most pressure is on Matt to keep Ronnie talking, to calm him down, to let Melissa come out unscathed. Though there is a kinetic energy in the room, it is also strangely quiet, like a group of kids whisper-yelling in the corner of a library. The ringing phone and the voices of Ronnie and Matt are the primary sounds despite the flurry of activity. One wrong word or sound could set Ronnie off. One right phrase and Matt will connect with him. In law enforcement parlance, they refer to these as hooks and barbs. Hooks pull Ronnie in, calm him down; barbs set him off. Matt has already walked into a barb with Ronnie several minutes earlier when he brought up Melissa's coworker, Mack. Ronnie, it turns out, believes Mack and Melissa have been having an affair.

"I'm letting him spout for a while, burn off that energy," Matt says. "At least he's mad at me and not her."

"He's going to get tired," another officer says.

But it's speculation, because Ronnie keeps hanging up on them pissed off, and he's made no sign to release Melissa. For all they know she could be dead already. Or the house could be booby-trapped. He could have multiple weapons, high-powered weapons in there with him. He's already blockaded the doors so she can't leave.

Matt calls back. "Hey, Ronnie, you hung up on me. I'm just making sure we're all right."

"Everybody's cool," Ronnie says, sounding not at all cool.

"Okay, okay," Matt says. His voice is a little shaky. He's young, only in his late twenties. "Hey, tell me what you do for work?"

Instantly, it's clear this was a mistake.

"I'm not here to give you my life story, motherfucker! You know everything about me. You slicker than a can of oil. What the fuck is wrong with you? Who you think I am?"

Slam.

Matt is shaking his head. He knows he fucked up. His colleague, Chris, is sitting beside him telling him it's all right. Rookie mistake. But it's clear that Matt's lost the ability to connect with Ronnie like he needs to, and they decide to turn it over to Chris. The handoff in a hostage situation is critical. It can't look like a handoff. And Chris and his team can't lie. They can't tell these guys that they won't be charged, that it'll all be okay if they just come out with their hands up. And yet they have to compel them, basically, to walk straight out of that house and into a jail cell.

They have only seconds between each call to discuss strategy. Unlike other crisis situations, where an offender takes strangers as hostages and time can often help deescalate a situation, such time is not on their side in a domestic violence situation. The longer it goes on, the more likely it could escalate and end in violence. They have to be approachable yet firm, confident yet empathetic. They have only their words. It's a complete departure from how officers normally operate, where there is a clear delineation of powerful and powerless. Using the tools of what Hamish Sinclair would call "to intimate," they have to compel an offender to relinquish control. They cannot bark orders. They cannot make demands. They cannot throw a noncompliant offender to the ground and handcuff him. All they have, in this moment, are words. And some officers, it's fair to say, are better with words than others.

They decide to do the handoff this way: Matt will tell Ronnie he's going to look into the Mack situation, interview Mack a little about his relationship with Melissa, and in the meantime, Matt's going to turn the phone over to his partner, Chris.

They call again. "Ronnie, it's true. We do have a lot of information about you," Matt says.

"Fuck you, you lyin' motherfucker," Ronnie says. "Lyin' Matt."

Matt lets him spew, then tries out the plan, tells him he's going to look into this Mack guy, turn Ronnie over to Chris. Ronnie is spewing on the other end, calling Matt a liar, telling him he's not interested in being friends. It goes on. Ronnie hangs up. Matt calls back over and over again. "Listen," Matt says in a rare moment when Ronnie is quiet, "this Mack. He's an old guy. Like sixty-five, seventy years old. Did you know that?" The implication is clear. Melissa is young, in her twenties still. No way she'd be sleeping with someone so much older. (I wonder if these officers have ever seen Hollywood movies.)

Ronnie picks up on it. "Are you familiar with modern chemistry, motherfucker?" he says. "They make a blue pill that keeps your dick harder than a superhero's kneecaps." *Click*.

When Matt calls back, he tells Ronnie he's going to talk to Mack, that Chris is going to be on the phone with him.

"Is Chris a liar, too?" Ronnie asks. "You put someone on the phone, you make sure it's a fucking honest cocksucker, all right?"

Chris takes over and says this: "Hey, Ronnie, it's Chris. What's going on?"

Instant mistake. Because of course, Matt, Ronnie, Chris . . . they all know "what's going on." But you can't blame Chris. It's a generic phone greeting. It's how any of us would get on the line, probably. But every word is crucial in a hostage situation, every second matters, and it's not just the words themselves but how they're delivered, and the emotional context with which they're offered. The authenticity. And Ronnie's sharp, attuned to all of this. His response is this: "Are you a lying motherfucker, too?"

Back and forth they go, with Chris calling, trying to find an in, a hook, some way to connect, and Ronnie hanging up on him. Three, four, five, seven, fifteen times he calls.

"I can hear you're upset," Chris says.

"No shit, Sherlock. You must be a great investigator," Ronnie says. "Why can't you just leave me alone? You guys ain't getting nowhere."

"We want to get somewhere, Ronnie, but we need to make sure everyone's okay, first," Chris tells him. "Can I talk to Melissa? Is she okay?"

"You want the bitch on the phone, I'll put the bitch on the phone. I'll throw the bitch out the goddamn window if you want her." Ronnie turns his head away from the phone and yells into the void. "Bitch, these cops want to talk to your fucking ass!" But he doesn't put her on the phone. Instead, he offers to throw her out the window again, says it'll be so quick she won't even feel it.

"Ronnie, Ronnie," Chris says, "it concerns me when you talk like that. I don't want anyone to get hurt."

"Oh my golly, oh my Jesus Christ," Ronnie says. "Oh my soul. What the fuck you want me to do? Why don't you all get the fuck out of here?"

He hangs up.

Chris takes a moment to confer with his supervisor, who advises him to go over what Chris knows so far with Ronnie. "Say, 'Hey, this is what we know. Denise came to pick up Melissa. Someone heard some shots, but maybe not.'"

"So you want me to downplay the whole thing?" Chris asks.

"Just tell him what you know, why we can't leave. That her friend came to get her and saw a little blood. That the gunshot's a little concerning. I'm not saying minimize it completely, but don't make it sound like he's Al Capone, either."

Chris nods. He hits the redial button on the phone.

I decide to go down the hall and see Ronnie for myself.

RONNIE IS ACTUALLY RETIRED officer Lou Johns. We are in San Diego at a crisis negotiations training for law enforcement officers, specifically targeted toward domestic violence situations. When I told friends I was going to a hostage negotiation and training session, they immediately imagined banks and a small gaggle of men in ski masks. Though the numbers are not tracked consistently, around 80% of all hostage situations in this country are a result of domestic violence, said William Kidd, who is leading this week's training. The FBI has only recently begun to track hostage situations, but only when jurisdictions voluntarily submit their numbers. Currently, there are more than seven thousand in their database. And while there are crisis negotiation trainings all over the country for the FBI, for law enforcement, for any number of similar agencies, this one in San Diego is the only one that puts intimate partner terrorism at the center of the training.

The end goal of a hostage situation with domestic violence at the center versus strangers changes the entire scenario, infuses a tense situation with an extremely dangerous emotional charge. Gary Gregson, another facilitator this week and a division manager at DPREP, a law enforcement training and consulting firm, says that in a traditional hostage situation involving strangers, hostages are a bargaining chip. "A bank robber will use his hostages to gain escape." But with domestic violence, it's the exact opposite. The hostage taker wants to stay exactly where he is. His end goal is not to escape; it isn't even necessarily to stay alive. It is to maintain control. "The abuser wants her to recant, to apologize," Gregson says. "Or pay a penalty for not going along with him." That crucial difference factors into every aspect of a negotiation. The relationship between abuser and victim, because it is emotionally charged, intensifies the dangerousness. Violence may be ongoing throughout the negotiation. And coercion. Gregson reminds the participants that they're dealing with manipulative people, that they must guard against displays of friendship or trust. He reminds them that battered spouses or children will frequently display Stockholm syndrome, identifying or aligning with one's attacker, even in the aftermath of a hostage situation. (It is sometimes called trauma bonding.)

Gregson says the most difficult aspect of any negotiation for a police officer is to "take off your cop hat and put on your negotiator hat." In an earlier training, one of the officers was tasked with interviewing the sister of "Ronnie." It became clear that he didn't appreciate the difference between an interview and an interrogation. "We don't want her to feel pushed," Gregson said later. "We want her to feel invited, comfortable in this environment. Think of it as social rather than investigatory."

Law enforcement, it's fair to say, has a troubled relationship to domestic violence. Police are often, though not always, the first responders to a violent situation in the home. And research has shown that even if there is no arrest, a police response can be a significant deterrent for re-abuse, as well as increase the likelihood that a victim will access local domestic violence services, like protective orders.[1] But police can also be the perpetrators themselves—rates of domestic violence among police officers are two to four times higher than the general population. In one recent video, I watched police officers on a call to the ex-wife of a colleague of theirs. She described how he broke in to her home, threatened to kill her and her new boyfriend, how she'd endured years of abuse when she was married to him. Seconds later, in bodycam footage, those same officers stand at the foot of her driveway joking around with the perpetrator—their coworker. They don't dismiss entirely the incident, but they tell him to just lie low. He swears he didn't break down her door. He minimizes. Just days later, both she and her new boyfriend are killed by her ex-husband before he turns the gun on himself. In an earlier scenario in San Diego, I listened in as William Kidd played the part of a former SWAT commander named David Powell. In real life, Powell had broken a restraining order and been called in to police headquarters by his superior. When he refused to show, calling to say he had hostages, the SWAT team that he once commanded surrounded his house. A seven-hour standoff followed, after which Powell stepped onto the porch and opened fire on his former colleagues. They shot back and killed him.

In a local New Jersey article covering the incident, the police chief said the incident followed a "domestic situation."[2] This, too, is part of the problem. The language we use to describe what is, by any measure, a crime. Domestic disputes, domestic violence, private conflicts, volatile relationships, mistreatment, domestic abuse. All of these are passive constructions, eradicating responsibility not only on behalf of the abuser, but on behalf of law enforcement as well. That domestic violence is a crime shouldn't be obscured, not least of all by those charged with protecting the public from violence. In my view, although I use the term "domestic violence" in this book because it is the most commonly used reference for what I am investigating, a far more accurate term, and one that captures the particular psychological, emotional and physical dynamics, is "intimate partner terrorism."

The training in San Diego addressed directly the potential bias of cops arresting or negotiating with other cops in a crisis situation in the David Powell scenario. Gregson asked what impact it might have on them knowing they were negotiating with another officer. Those attending the training admitted such a scenario would be difficult, but insisted they'd follow the procedures as they would with any other crisis negotiation.

Yet still police departments around the country routinely fail to discipline officers for domestic violence complaints. In a study done in Los Angeles of ninety-one cases of officer-involved domestic violence, three-quarters of the time the complaints weren't even included in performance reviews.[3] And a situation such as what happened with David Powell, in which an officer's actions are not addressed immediately, or possibly at all, isn't, frankly, the exception.[4] Police departments across the country fail to discipline officers for the same crimes that civilians are arrested for every day. A study from Florida between 2008 and 2012 noted that while only about 1% of officers remained on the job following a failed drug test, and 7% remained after a theft, nearly 30% of officers with domestic violence complaints were still employed in their same positions a year later.[5] Victims are reluctant to report domestic violence, fearing retaliation, and police officers not only have access to guns, but they also know the law, and they have relationships with prosecutors, judges, administrators. A police officer's partner knows, surely, that any call that comes through 911 will show up on the zone car computers of law enforcement across a jurisdiction, showing the address where the call originated, the name of the perpetrator, the incident being reported, and other information that can instantly alert an officer's friends or colleagues. And even when it comes to specialized training of law enforcement, at least a quarter of departments around the country have no written procedures on how to deal with domestic violence calls.[6]

But the code of silence that often keeps fellow officers from outing colleagues they know or suspect to be violent isn't simply tribalism: an "us against them," cop-versus-civilian philosophy (though most police officers I've met feel this to some degree). Domestic violence charges brought against law officers can carry an outsized weight for the perpetrator; they often equate to an officer losing his or her job, since convicted abusers are not allowed to possess firearms. At the same time, the stresses of the job result in higher rates of familial violence, as well as alcoholism, divorce, and suicide. The lessons of the male role belief system that I'd learned sitting in classes by Jimmy Espinoza operate every bit as strongly in any given police department as they do in the San Bruno jail.

LOU JOHNS, PLAYING RONNIE in San Diego today, was the longest serving crisis negotiator in San Diego's history. He jokes that he spends an inordinate amount of time on the golf course these days. That is, when he's not here, helping to train new recruits, such as the twenty-one participants who are here from jurisdictions all over the state of California this week. Johns's reputation preceded him, his "way with words" as his fellow facilitators say. ("Did you hear that one, about the superhero's kneecaps?" he asked, when I walked into the office where he was playing Ronnie. He laughed a little. He had the phone on mute. I could hear Chris on the other line, trying to connect, trying to find a "hook." Johns tossed back a pistachio.)

The first time Johns was ever called out to a negotiation it was a suicide. A man on a bridge. Johns was filled with an electric anxiety. It was freezing, a cold rain falling on them, wind at maybe twenty miles an hour, three a.m. The guy's girlfriend had slept with his brother. Johns told him that was fucked up. It wasn't a reason to kill yourself, but it was fucked up. The guy asked for one reason he should live, one excuse, something he hadn't heard before. "You mean like a joke?" Johns asked him. "Yeah," he said. "Tell me a joke I've never heard before." Johns said, "You'll come off this bridge if I tell you something you ain't never heard before?" The guy said he would. So Johns goes, "Okay, how about this one: I'm standing up here freezing my Black ass off. Stick a pole up my ass and you got yourself a fucking Fudgsicle."

The guy crawled down off the bridge.

Johns is full of these kinds of stories, the unexpected, the ridiculous. Once he came to a scene, SWAT team in full gear, surrounding the building. They'd been out there a few hours. No one had made contact yet with the offender. Johns got on the phone, said, "Hey, man. Why don't you come on out." And the guy did. Just like that. The stories without happy endings, the ones where that person didn't climb down from the bridge, that spouse didn't let his wife go, Johns talks less about. Those are the narratives that run through an entire precinct, that compel nearly every one of the participants here this week.

Johns spent twenty years as a negotiator for San Diego. In the early days, which were the late '90s, no one was really thinking about domestic violence, he told me. "It used to be, okay, motherfucker, you're going to jail. Then if the woman is talking shit, you say, 'I don't give a fuck if I have to come back and put both of you in jail.'"

He hangs up on Chris. The phone rings one second later. "Ronnie," says Chris, "it really frustrates me when you keep hanging up."

"Hey, motherfucker, you know what? I don't give a fuck if you frustrated," Lou/Ronnie says. "One, two, three. Hang up!" Click.

Johns turns back to me. "When the domestic violence stuff came into effect, I could actually see how it made everything more clear," he says. "It channeled things as to what was going on." Domestic violence trainings and awareness in the early 2000s began to give police officers a context for why and how abusers were violent, the particular ways that abusers manipulate, how police sometimes re-traumatized the victims, why victims sometimes appeared to want to stay in these abusive relationships. Earlier in the training, Kit Gruelle, one of the facilitators, had shown a situation not unlike Michelle Monson Mosure's, which illustrated to them how a victim could be out picking up the kids from school, going to the grocery store, running errands, appearing "free," and still be a passive hostage, under the control of a partner who had convinced her she'd never get away from him alive.

The scenario goes on for another hour. Despite what it may sound like, Johns has a script in front of him. He doesn't know how the officers on the phone will respond, but he has certain indicators as to the emotional tenor of the situation that he wants the officers to pick up on and those indicators dictate what he says. He knows, for example, that he needs to get them to a point of frustration by hanging up and swearing. He knows his responses should point out when they make a mistake—such as when they do too many handoffs. He also knows he can't be entirely noncompliant. He has to allow them moments of both hooks and barbs. He also will appear to get suicidal later in the scenario, and he'll say things like, "I dunno, man. Just fuck all of it. It's all bullshit. None of this shit really matters. Melissa don't love me anymore anyway." Officers on the other end should pick up that change in tone, situate it as a sign of increased danger. If a perpetrator doesn't think he has anything to live for, a lethal situation can turn fatal. It's no accident that suicide is one of Jacquelyn Campbell's risk factors.

In another set of rooms down the hall, another retired officer plays "Ronnie" with another set of trainees. It's difficult to watch the police try out this first negotiation. You can often hear the nervousness in their voices and the scenario is chillingly authentic, for them and for me. It doesn't matter that we're in a generic set of brick office buildings beside a San Diego highway. Most negotiations happen over the phone, between people who don't lay eyes on each other until it's over (and in many cases never). While we're in the second day of training, Kit Gruelle e-mails around a news article. A former lieutenant in Georgia killed his estranged wife and her boyfriend. Bodycam footage from an earlier incident shows him at three a.m. lunging for her even as the police are standing there. He threatens her in front of the police, saying, "You know what's going to happen." And yet he was not arrested that night. He was ordered to turn in all his guns. He still managed to get his hands on one. Another one, just weeks before this class began, happened in Orlando, an estranged boyfriend with a history of battering ended a twenty-one-hour standoff by killing his four hostages—all of whom were children—before killing himself.

The real-life stories thread through the entire session. Stories from the facilitators and their years on the force (most of them are retired now). Stories happening in real time, as the trainees sit in class learning. Stories close by and across the country. Daily stories of angry men, scared women, vulnerable children. The constant stream of stories give these scenarios the feel of real life, the weight of real life. And the officers doing the talking, you can hear in their disembodied voices over the speaker phones the insecurity and anxiety of getting it wrong, the desperate attempts to find that one gem of a phrase that will be their bridge.

And all of the scenarios they conduct in this training come from real-life cases. Ronnie and Melissa were an actual couple once, in the exact situation the officers this week enacted. The next day, Gruelle e-mails another domestic violence hostage situation. And from the airport that night, when we're all at our various gates waiting to fly home, another one. And when I get home from my red eye flight, two more are waiting for me in my inbox.

IN NEARLY EVERY GEOGRAPHY I visited throughout the course of writing this book, I also did a ride along with the local police. I tried to make these on weekend nights as often as possible. (It perhaps goes without saying that I was almost always assigned to their department's most liberal, gregarious officer, though once—in Washington, D.C.—I was assigned to a female officer who was only on her fourth night out and seemed wild with nervousness, as if I were secretly spying on her for some higher-up. I got slightly nervous when she inquired as to whether I'd brought my bulletproof vest.) I asked them all about officer-involved domestic violence and about guns and domestic violence calls more generally. From California to Massachusetts and places in between, they answered that they would do nothing differently with a colleague than with a civilian abuser.

To a one, I did not believe them.

About guns, they all said they wished there were fewer among civilians.

And this I believed.

Guns made their jobs exponentially more dangerous, far less predictable, and unlike many pro-gun civilians, they were all too aware of how chaotic and unreadable a scenario with guns can get. My ex-husband used to say, "You can't negotiate with a gun." Diplomacy, he believed, offered more chances for everyone to come out alive, not just the perpetrator.

The idea that a gun can "save" anyone in any situation has always seemed suspect to me. A gun is a passive instrument; it does what it's told to do by a human. And humans make mistakes. I picture a home invasion, someone in bed, asleep, who wakes suddenly to find a stranger in the dark perched over the bed. How does the gun get into the home-owner's hands? How does the safety get turned off? How does the bullet find its way into the target in those sheer seconds? Maybe it's a quiet house; the homeowner is awakened, reaches under the mattress, silently gets out the gun, silently clicks off the safety, silently tiptoes downstairs. He can hear the thief, but the thief cannot hear him. Silently, he finds the thief holding a flat-screen TV and he shoots. Maybe it's a movie theater. Guy walks in in the dark, starts shooting. Somewhere in the audience is another gun, a good guy. He shoots, too. Maybe it's a hotel room. Guy starts shooting. A dozen people in the crowd have guns, but they're good guys. Good guns. They start shooting back. How do you identify the good from the bad? The intentional from the accidental? Maybe it's a sniper at a gas station. Someone with a Toyota has a gun. He's a good guy. He shoots, too. Maybe it's a kid, and another kid has a gun. A good kid with a gun. A good teacher with a gun. How do you know, how do I know, how does anyone know who is who, and which gun is which, in those panicky milliseconds? Where to run, how to hide? How does a plastic seat with a fabric top stop a bullet anyway? A car door? A locker door? A speaker? A particle board desktop? Doesn't matter who's good and who's not. Bullets have no moral preference. Every domestic violence scenario I've ever known has had this one thing in common when guns are present: there is never, ever time to think. A knife gives you a second to run. A bullet does not. Guns supercharge the dangerousness for all parties involved. I think of that woman in Montana all the time at the fatality review, the retired nurse with her knitting needles saying, "Get rid of the fucking guns." She says it in a room where more than half the people around her, she knows, are carrying guns. *Get rid of the fucking guns.*

FOR SEVERAL DECADES BOTH researchers and law enforcement themselves said domestic violence calls were among the most dangerous the police encountered. And certainly they are among the least predictable. It's also true that plenty of police across the country have been killed or wounded on domestic violence calls. In a fourteen-year study of 771 police officers killed (just over fifty a year, on average), about 14% are killed on domestic violence calls—97% from firearms.[7] In my first years of asking ride-along questions, police would almost unequivocally answer that domestic violence calls were their most dangerous (occasionally, someone might also include traffic stops). But in the past two or three years, officers have begun to say to me, anecdotally, that it's active shooters. That's the scenario they fear most. In a law enforcement report that studied FBI data on active shooter incidents between 2008 and 2012, the authors found that the perpetrator stopped shooting about 40% of the time when police arrived; of those incidents that were ongoing even after police arrived, the law enforcement officers were shot about 15% of the time. Active shooter events, called ASEs in law enforcement parlance, were both on the rise and now among the deadliest for police, the study concluded.[8] The idea that many of the active shooter situations officers were likely to encounter *began* as domestic violence wasn't mentioned anywhere in the report.

Officers aren't the only ones who would like to see fewer guns among civilians. A third of women in the United States today live with guns in their homes, yet fewer than 20% say those guns make them feel safer, and more than half want stricter gun laws in the country.[9] The risk of homicide to a person in an abusive situation increases eightfold when guns are present.[10] A decades-old gun ban referred to as the Lautenberg Amendment, which passed in 1996, was intended to ban convicted abusers with misdemeanor domestic violence charges from possessing or purchasing firearms, but research has shown that this is rarely enforced.[11] Misdemeanors, it's important to point out, have a wide range of definitions from a simple slap all the way to a near-fatal strangulation, depending on the state. States must enact their own statutes requiring abusers to turn in their guns and at the time of this writing, only sixteen states had such a statute in their governance laws.[12] The federal law does not generally apply to those who are not recognized legally as married[13] (often called the "boyfriend loophole"). Stalking is also not included in Lautenberg, which means that tens of thousands of stalkers are legally in possession of firearms in America today.[14]

In a study done by April Zeoli, one of the country's leading experts on guns and domestic violence and an associate professor at Michigan State University, she and her colleague Daniel Webster looked at the forty-six largest cities in America to see what effect, if any, these gun restrictions had on intimate partner homicides. Surprisingly, they found that the federal domestic violence misdemeanor firearm prohibition offered no reduction in such killings.[15] Zeoli says there are likely multiple reasons for this, including a lack of enforcement, a lack of knowledge about the restrictions by local jurisdictions, and judges in some states with wide discretion when it comes to putting the prohibition in place. The laws can also be confusing. "If you have a law that says this person can't have a firearm, but doesn't follow up with who's supposed to take it, how it's removed, where it's stored and who shoulders the cost . . . you're leaving it to local jurisdictions to figure out what may work for them . . . this gives people who may not want to put the law in place a lot of discretion."

Where the laws do seem to have significant impact, however, is in the twenty-four states that have firearm restrictions for those with restraining orders, temporary or otherwise. Currently, eighteen states also have laws that allow police to confiscate firearms at the scene of a domestic violence incident.[16] Zeoli's study found that intimate partner homicide decreased by 25% in cities where the restraining order laws were clear and enforced.

"It's not always an issue of being shot," says Teresa Garvey, a former prosecutor and attorney advisor for AEquitas, a prosecutor's resource for domestic violence law. "[Guns are] used to make threats, to back up threats, or to add to the environment of intimidation."[17] They are used as blunt force instruments, and as reminders of who holds the power. Like Donte Lewis, who hit his girlfriend so hard with his gun, she foamed at the mouth. Thirty-three thousand domestic violence firearm incidents occur annually in the United States—far exceeding the number of intimate partner homicides.[18] Guns take away any bargaining power a victim may have once had.

The single most common argument in favor of gun ownership is that it makes women safer. That it doesn't matter if you prohibit abusers from purchasing or possessing firearms; if they want to inflict harm on another person, they will find a way to do it. But Zeoli says, "This simply isn't true . . . Would-be [perpetrators] aren't replacing guns with other things."[19] In chilling testimony before the Joint Committee on Public Safety and Homeland Security, David Adams said that he, too, had decided to test this theory among fourteen killers that he interviewed. "Eleven of the fourteen men who used a gun said that they would not have killed if the gun were not available," Adams told the committee.

"Many serious abusers already have the motive to kill their intimate partner or ex-partner; let's stop making it so easy for them to have the means to do so."[20]

Kit Gruelle told me this was the most significant misunderstanding about guns and domestic violence. "[Guns] increase women's danger exponentially," she told me. "Until a gun comes into the relationship, she still feels like she has some capacity to deal with what's going on, whether it's to run, to lock the bedroom door, or whatever."[21] The pro-gun argument that asks women to arm themselves is asking them to behave as their abusers behave, Gruelle notes. Such views have conscripted the narrative, putting the blame on victims for not doing all they could to protect themselves. "It's not a character flaw if [women] don't have a natural tendency to turn and fire on the father of [their] children," she said. Gruelle told me that if she had ever pulled a gun on her abusive husband "he'd have taken it away and laughed at it."

MY RIDE ALONGS TAUGHT me that no matter how often police superiors talk about domestic violence, it is really the culture of any given department and the belief system of any given officer that will dictate what happens out on the streets. One Saturday night in Montana, I was out with a cop who'd been on the force for more than a decade.[22] A little after midnight, he got a call for a "domestic." We showed up at a trailer, the third squad car to arrive. A woman with a loose bun stood crying at the end of a pickup truck, while her husband was at the bottom of the driveway talking to several officers. The man I was riding with—I'll call him Dan—made his way around the woman and to the entrance of their trailer. Two bug-eyed kids under the age of five were wandering in and out of the house. Another officer was in a field next to the house looking for a knife. The man had called the police on the woman after she threatened him with the knife. After he called, she ran out of the trailer and threw the knife into the field. Both of them had been drinking.

There were eight police officers on the scene by now, all white men. The woman was in a stretched out black T-shirt and leggings. She watched the officers as they wandered into her trailer and back out, around the field and the yard. Three were talking to her husband; none were talking to her. "He hit me first," she said, wiping at her cheeks. I'd been standing beside the trailer taking notes.

I looked at her to acknowledge I'd heard, but didn't want to say anything. She clearly thought I was on their team somehow.

She said she got the knife to protect herself, because he'd come at her after they'd returned home from a party. Just then an older girl, a teenager, emerged from the doorway and collected the two smaller children and brought them in the house. The woman was wearing forest green Crocs.

"Did you tell the police?" I asked her.

She nodded.

"Has he hit you before?"

She nodded again, and her face crumpled into tears. I waited to see if any of the officers were going to come and ask her any questions, maybe do a lethality assessment, but none did. I asked her some of the questions I knew from the Danger Assessment myself. Had she been strangled? (Yes.) Were the kids all his? (No.) Did he have a gun? (Yes.) Did he have a job? (Yes.) But then an officer came up and told her she was going to have to come with him. I went over to Dan, my ride, and told him she claimed to have a history of abuse from the guy. Dan nodded. "Unfortunately, he's the one who called. So we have to arrest her."

The teenager came back out just then and began screaming at the police. "You're arresting her? *Her*?" The officer in the field found the knife and held it up. "You should be arresting him!"

"He's the one who called us," said Dan.

The two kids came back outside. It was clear that emotions were ramping up. The woman was now in the back of a cruiser, watching through the window, her eyes wide.

"Can you at least not arrest her in front of the kids?" the teenager said. "I'll take them somewhere."

"Where can you take them?" Dan asked.

"I'll take them to the park." It was nearing one o'clock in the morning.

"You're going to take them to a park in the middle of the night?" Dan said.

She nodded like it was a completely reasonable idea.

"Let's go inside," Dan said, shuttling her back toward the entrance of the house. I followed and when we went inside the small trailer, the disarray was shocking. The combined kitchen/living room was filthy. The counters piled with dishes, pots, paper plates that had food encrusted on them. Flies abounded. The window screens were broken. The place smelled of cigarettes, body odor, mold, old food. A bunk bed had only one mattress. A balloon made from an old condom sat on the floor. Half a dozen police filed into the cramped room, shoulder to shoulder.

"I don't want him to stay here," the girl said. "If you're going to arrest her, you have to arrest him, too."

Dan asked if the girl was scared to stay alone in the house with him. In typical teenager style, she rolled her eyes at him.

"Has he hit you in the past?"

She nodded. "With a hanger."

A large TV dominated the room, playing cartoons. The two younger kids were glassy-eyed with exhaustion. They displayed no emotion at all. No fear, no joy, no curiosity, no surprise. The teenager was combative with the officers, and I wondered what it all looked like from her point of view, six large men standing in her living room, looming over her as she sat on the couch. One or two walked down the hall, shined a flashlight into chaotic rooms. She wasn't forthcoming with any information, and I thought of the negotiation class. *It's not an interrogation; it's an interview.* None of these officers seemed able to step back and read the room for a minute, to crouch down to her level, to offer her just a simple comforting phrase, to ask, for example, how they could help. Was there someone she could call? Did she need food? Instead, they towered over her collectively with their bulletproof vests and their guns and their gear and their hissing radios. They were leaving her in this disastrous house where a grown man who abused them would return, probably in a matter of hours, and a grown woman who may have been equally abusive but was at least a sometime protective presence may or may not return. It was shocking to me in a sense. None of these officers was anything but polite. They knew the law. But they were also absolutely ill-equipped to act or think in any way that suggested they recognized the psychological complications at play, the implications of what they looked like from a child's view. This was trauma happening in real time. They weren't interested in either the messiness of human emotion or any future fallout from this moment. At the same time, their jobs had prepared them only for right and wrong, criminal and civilian.

In Massachusetts, I'd been on a call once where a brother had assaulted his sister. She'd come in, crying, to the station to make the report. The officer took her statement, and then offered her a drink of water or a cup of coffee, asked if she'd like to stay at the station for a while just to get ahold of herself (she agreed). Then he talked to her just for a minute or two about familial violence, how hard it could be on people, how it was good she'd come in. Just general stuff. He hadn't done much—offered her a drink, a minute to gather herself, a statement of empathy. But that is sort of the point. He had done *so little* and yet still it amounted to an acknowledgment of their shared humanity and in the end would mean so much to her.

When we got back to the squad car, Dan said they'd be calling the department of children and families, and the two little kids would have to be placed somewhere, at least temporarily, and quite possibly permanently unless the woman could prove she was a fit mother. And with the house as disgusting as it was, I couldn't imagine how that would be possible. "We could have handled that better," he said to me. That at least was something, his acknowledgment. I did not disagree. And yet, many months later, I'd see for myself just how difficult it can be to act even in one's own best interest when I'd have my own mini confrontation with an officer of the law.

In the Season of
Unmitigated Discovery

I'm driving through coal country, on the border between Pennsylvania and New York. Summer of 2018. Rainy. Several months earlier, a text message came to my phone from a number I didn't recognize. (*Hey Ray, I'm not getting in trouble! I'm chilling like the wind.*) It was Donte Lewis, resurfacing in Pennsylvania at the Canaan federal penitentiary.

After several months of back and forth, I'd been cleared to visit him. I could do a media visit, but I tried that at Atwater in California and it never went through. Then he was transferred, and so we just decided to do a visit the way everyone else does it, which turned out to be both informative and stupid on my part and could have turned out very badly for both of us.

What I want to know, but suspect there is no real way to, is whether Donte can possibly remain nonviolent in a place like Canaan and manage to stay alive. Can violence be something he can turn on when he needs to survive, say, in a federal penitentiary, and something he can turn off when he's back on the outside? I would see firsthand how the tiny injustices here are crushing. The vending machines, for example. There's a sign that says use them at your own risk. And, indeed, I lose at least five bucks, see a soda like a drunk soldier, half out of its plastic ring and leaning against the glass without falling. It's such a small, small thing, to have a vending machine that works, that doesn't peel off precious dollar bills from people who hardly have many to spare.

But everything here is authoritarian, whether it makes sense or not, whether it seems logical or is merely establishing who has the power and who does not. This is true for visitors and inmates alike. There are lines on the floor you can't step over, retractable belts such as those you might see at airport security to keep people corralled in one place or another. The visitors' waiting area before we go through security is quiet as a church during a prayer. But tense, too. As if a single too-loud sneeze could upset the careful balance. This is a no-emotion zone. No laughing.

No small talk. No direct eye contact. The guard in front is serious, youthful, maybe new to the job. He doesn't have the hard edge of other guards I've met, the wearied experience and tense demeanor of someone who's been in charge of other people, and particularly other men, for a very long time. I call it the "I know better" stance. I know better than you how this system works. I know better than you how bad these men are. I know better than you the full range of human depravity.

I get to the prison at two minutes after nine a.m. Like all prisons I've ever been to, this one is in the middle of nowhere, atop a rolling, green set of hills, with a working-class family neighborhood circling it. One of the houses has a beat-up wooden porch and is overflowing with faded plastic toys and chipped flower pots, and a sign on the porch says *Shangri La*.

"You missed the processing by two minutes," the guard at the desk tells me. On the website, the visiting hours are eight a.m. to three p.m. "They're doing a count at ten. Come back then."

I go and sit in my car. Listen to NPR. Read the *Times*. Play a stupid game on my phone called *Township*. Walk back in at ten.

"They just started the count. It takes about an hour."

I go back to my car. NPR. The *Times. Township*. Walk back in at eleven. There's a line of about a dozen people now who seem to have just materialized. I am one of three whites, so far as I can tell. The lopsided racial injustice of incarceration spelled out right there in the anecdotal demographics of the waiting room. It's also nearly all women.

The guard gives me a locker key, tells me to lock up my car key in the locker. "So I take this key"—I hold up the tiny locker key—"to lock up this other key." I hold up my car's fob. He nods.

I don't know why I say these kinds of things out loud. My best friend has told me for twenty-five years that I have trouble with authority. I lock my fob by itself in the locker.

I am allowed a single clear baggie, in which I have my locker key, some money, some lip gloss, a Post-it notepad, and a pen. Three of the five of these, it turns out, are contraband.

Finally, at a little after noon, we are taken to the main meeting room, a windowless cement-block square with blue tape on the floor to signify the lines inmates and visitors cannot cross. A small group of guards with what appear to be steroid-soaked muscles sit at a station in the center of one wall. Everything about this moment is a cliché. Especially the no-bullshit guards, who yell at us for having too many people in the

vending machine area and point to a tiny sign that says no more than
two at a time are allowed. I try to decode the logic of this. We have
been emptied of all possible paraphernalia, so what does it matter if four
or five of us are at vending machines at once? (There are six vending
machines . . . all of them, by the time my visit is over, will be broken.)
I consider myself a decent reader, and still this sign was not in any
obvious place. We are insulted, shamed. "You can read, can't you?" says
the guard. My ego wants to scream at him that I am a fucking tenured
professor. I can probably read him right back under the rock he crawled
out from. Instead, I look at him, as I hold a wad of dollar bills, and say,
"I was told there'd be a buffet." He looks taken aback for a moment.
I know it's a double, or maybe a triple, privilege. I am a visitor, not an
inmate. I am white. I am educated. I am not proud that I sometimes
act this way, inserting humor where it clearly doesn't belong. I wish I
didn't ignore my inner editor as often as I do. (Actually, I wish I *had* an
inner editor.) Instead, he looks at me for a minute, then walks away.
Later, I will learn that a guard was killed at this prison by an inmate in
2013. These guards may have their lives threatened every day. They are
probably underpaid, overworked, exhausted. It's a luxury of my life that
I don't know.

I wonder if I'll recognize Donte; it's been nearly three years. At
around twelve thirty, I see him emerge from the locked hallway in
mustard yellow scrubs, beige rubber sandals. He's so, so much older.
His face is dull and matte. He's put on a lot of weight. He looks like
himself, but also like someone totally different. Like an older-brother
version of himself. His hair still has the blond tips, but now the dreadlocks are bunched up behind his head like a long tail. A tiny tattoo peeks
from the corner of his forehead, like a curl. He has a black eye.

Basketball. That's how he got the eye. It's nothing, he says, giving
me a hug.

I wish he didn't feel the need to lie to me.

Canaan is divided into geographies, he says. Your loyalty is to your
geography. Gangs on the outside who'd be arch rivals join together in
here, like the Crips and the Bloods, who have an alliance. "There's like
a hundred dudes from New York," he tells me, "and only four of us from
Cali." They have to stick together. While I was waiting, some of the
women told me this prison is a tough one. Call before you come or
you'll get here and they'll have gone on lockdown. There's a Somali
pirate incarcerated here, an Al-Qaeda sympathizer, and members of a
notorious Tijuana drug cartel. An associate of the Gambino crime family

murdered his cellmate here in 2010, just five years after the prison opened. Next door to Canaan is a minimum security satellite prison that a guard tells me houses mostly nonviolent or white-collar criminals. They have a lot more freedom. They can see the sun.

Donte is in a drug program here, though drugs were not a problem for him as they were for Jimmy. If he goes through this program, he says he'll be eligible to get out a little early. By the time this book is published, he'll have just under a year left.

Donte tells me he still uses the ManAlive curriculum, but sometimes what he's learning here seems to contradict it and it confuses him. "I internalized the lessons, you know? But no one here has." When they call their morning meeting, one or another of the guys has to lead the group and when it's his turn, they tell him he talks like a white guy. "I can't help what I know, you feel me?" he says. "The things I learned from Jimmy and Leo. I say shit like 'I feel this' and 'I feel that' and these dudes don't want to intimate with me. They ain't interested."

So he's alone. In a psychic way, he's alone. Also, his grandmother died a little over a year ago and it broke his heart. He doesn't talk to his mom much. He's still a little mad at his sister, who keeps her ex in her life, the guy driving the car the night of Donte's arrest. He says he turns the lessons he got in California on and off as he needs them, says he's a lot more mature now. Sometimes he wants to help a friend in here, and he'll talk about emotional intelligence or expectations of masculinity. Other times he's making deals with other guys for protection, working the system however he can, knowing full well he's in fatal peril but he's got to be for his own survival. He says he tries to stay "chill."

So I ask him: how'd you really get the black eye?

He throws his head back and laughs. He's missing one tooth in front. He holds one bicep with the palm of his hand. "Yeahhhhhhh . . ." he says, drawing it out. "I had a altercation, you might say."

I nod, say, "No kidding."

"It really wasn't nothing," he says. His cellmate got pissed at him, wanted to fight. Donte told him, "Man, I don't want to fight you. We both from Cali. We got to stick together." Plus, Donte thinks he could probably pummel the guy. He's not very big. Donte is like six foot two, somewhere just shy of two hundred pounds. Knows how to fight. But also, isn't this what all men think? I say to him. That they're the ones who could, if they only wanted to, win this fight, but suddenly they're all altruists, saving the other guy from the fury they *could* unleash, but won't. Such largesse.

Donte laughs, nodding, tells me I'm not wrong. "Seriously, though, man. He ain't a big dude, you feel me?"

But the cellmate hauled off and punched him anyway. Donte said it was nothing, but he was pissed because he was meeting me and it would *look* really bad. And, yeah, it kinda does.

Behind me on the wall is a picture of a park scene with a bench that appears to have been painted by a middle schooler or a high schooler. Every once in a while, an inmate goes up with a woman and a kid and takes a picture with the fake park in the background. One little girl, maybe six years old, has a purple glitter shirt that says *Best Day Ever.*

Donte is hoping Community Works will have a job for him when he gets out. He wants to complete his internship again. He doesn't know. Jimmy, Leo, no one's been in touch with him, but still he hopes. And then maybe, he says, maybe he can come east. Patterson, New Jersey. Or Jersey City. He has some relatives. It'd be away from the familiarity of Oakland. He thinks they need ManAlive there. Maybe he could start something.

His cellmate got a letter back when Donte was still in Atwater, from a girl who knew Kayla Walker, the old love of his life. The letter allegedly claimed Kayla clocked some other girl with a bottle of Rémy Martin. And Donte's first thought was that maybe he was responsible for ruining her life. "I wonder if I taught her that," he says, remorse blanketing his face.

Later, when I leave the jail, one of the guards takes my Post-it notebook from me, where I've spent three hours taking notes. I knew it wasn't allowed, but I figured they'd take it away when I went through security if I couldn't have it. Same with my lip gloss. And my underwire bra. Like TSA. Hold it up to the light, and toss it in the garbage. The supervisor tells me he could call the FBI based on the first page of my notes, in which I describe the room where we meet the inmates, the blue tape on the floor. I laugh out loud (which, it's worth underscoring, is exactly the wrong response). We both know the FBI wouldn't want to be bothered with this on a Sunday afternoon, but we also both know that I should not laugh out loud at a guard who is in the middle of disciplining me. Then I tell him it doesn't matter because the picture of the room is in my brain now.

He says the notebook is contraband. I hold up my lip gloss and offer it to him. It's also contraband, no? I put my hands behind my back and start to take off my bra. "You want this, too?" I ask him. I am smiling.

Six guards stand behind him. I can see my notebook sticking out of his cargo pant pocket.

"It doesn't say anything on the website about a Post-it pad," I tell him.

He has the rules right there in his other pocket. He pulls them out and starts to read them to me. It actually doesn't say anything about a notebook. "See?" I say. "See?"

"If it doesn't say, it's not allowed."

I use the parallel of a tampon. Also not mentioned. Also then not allowed? Women'll just bleed all over the damn floor?

The thing is, I know by this point that I'm not getting my notebook back. That while I'm in my pissing match, he's also in his—and he has an audience behind him for which he will not back down. To use program words: I'm in fatal peril, and so is he, and he has colluders standing behind him and only one of us has any actual power here. Plus, I recognize my own sense of entitlement in this moment. I am a journalist. I am white. I am educated. But what is the point of my challenging him? What am I doing? Have I learned nothing from Jimmy Espinoza and Donte Lewis and Hamish Sinclair and David Adams and Neil Websdale and all the other men I've been interviewing these last few years? What *am* I doing?

And I know, then, because I'm suddenly filled with shame. I turn and walk out of the prison to my waiting car, where I grab my computer and type all that I can recall from my three hours with Donte. His black eye, the prison alliances, the little girl with the purple shirt, the vending machines, his remorse over Kayla. It's there, sitting in my car in the parking lot, that I will come to understand that it's not that I broke the rules that really bothers me. It's not even that I fail to recognize the privilege afforded me by even trying to break them. (Imagine one of the regular visitors, the Black woman who comes every Sunday, trying to get away with what I'd tried to get away with.) What matters is that I know better. I wish I'd done exactly the opposite in the moment. I wish, when that supervisor came out with my notebook in his pocket and told me it was contraband, I wish I'd said this to him: "You're right. I'm really sorry."

Just before I left Donte, after a promise to return and see him, and also to send him some books, I asked him how he thought of his time at Community Works, back for those few months when he was working with Jimmy out of the sheriff's office, working with violent men but not one of them. That brief respite. His life, for a decade, has been prison, has been surrounded by violence, apart from those few months. It was the first time he remembered being surrounded by people who believed in him, he said. And it made him believe in himself. He summed it up in one word. "Discovery." That's how he saw it. A time of unmitigated "discovery."

Maybe he can get back there again someday.

Those Who Break

When I see Jimmy Espinoza again, several years have gone by. All those months he'd been unable to keep the weight on? All those lunches of giant burritos and refried beans, but he'd stayed skinny as a swizzle stick? Turns out he'd relapsed. Gone back to drugs. Dove right back into the shit he'd worked so hard to pull himself out of. Took himself to a live-in facility just blocks away from the sheriff's outpost where he taught ManAlive. He called me on my cell on a Saturday night. It'd been a tough road, he said, but this time he was determined to keep at it. To stay nonviolent. To kick his drinking. To keep his job. To be better, stronger, tougher at all of it, to admit to his weaknesses and through admitting them, by copping to the struggle, he'd grow stronger. Community Works held his job for him. When I asked him how he felt about the book, whether or not he still wanted me to write about him, he paused on the phone for a moment. Then said, "Fuck yeah. This is the real shit. My life is a struggle every day. Every damn day."

He finished a yearlong live-in rehab and was back at the sheriff's office, teaching the curriculum. He's healthier than he's ever been. He's got weight on him now, starts his days with push-ups, ends them with visits to the weight room at his local gym. We compare biceps. He lived in a rehab house for addicts for a few months and then got his own place. He raises his hand first if anyone asks who here is a fuckup, needs to remind each and every class that he's one of them. He leads not just the ManAlive curriculum at San Bruno now, but a narcotics anonymous group for the guys, and then he speaks at churches and community centers around the area, and he doesn't pretend that any of it is easy.

This is the battle, for him and for all the guys he works with, this pull toward their previous life. Toward drugs, toward the streets, toward the life he used to live. He feels it in his stomach, in his mind. He refers to heroin and coke as princesses, fairy-tale women, Snow White and Cinderella, he calls them. The parallel makes me squirm, but I don't call him on the potential misogyny, because it feels unfair to point this out at the moment when he has the fortitude to take himself to rehab and he is really truly trying. The drugs are beautiful, sexy, gorgeous, beckoning women, women lying on white sheets in soft lighting, calling to him, seducing him. Not three-dimensional, in-your-life women, but temporary lovers. Terrible temptresses, tormentors. He knows that they would offer a moment of ecstasy in exchange for that dread-filled, belly-deep knowledge that comes with failure, with committing violence against his own body, as he might put it.

He's been granted a second chance. And a third. And a fourth. He's lived one life, two, three, seven. He's on his last life, he thinks. He makes vows to the guys in his groups, to his family, to the men and women who live at the treatment center with him, to the batterers and the alcoholics and the users and the addicts, to the man who takes his monthly rent check, to his children and the women he once both loved and abused, and to his coworkers like Reggie and Leo. He vows and vows and vows and most days he gets to the end of the day and feels a kind of bone-deep relief to have made it once more. Of all the vows he offers the vast constellations of people, his deepest vow, he says, is to himself.

He writes on a private Facebook page about the struggle. The seduction of those two. Snow White and Cinderella. How beautiful they are to him. How tantalizing. But he won't succumb. Not this night. And hopefully not the next either. Beyond that, he can't see, or won't look. He's not hibernating, he says. Not hiding out. Just staying away from the places that suck him in, the visceral, associative memories with certain corners in the Haight, certain windows where he can look up and remember entire universes: "This girl, she lived up there in that apartment," he had told me one afternoon, pointing up above a storefront that sold expensive urban menswear, "and I used to sit up there and watch my girls." *His* girls, it's in the image. Man. Window. Muscles clenched. Response system on high alert. I can picture him as the bear.

He'd go somewhere else to get high. Kept that shit to himself. A wasted pimp is a vulnerable pimp. A strung-out pimp loses girls, loses territory. No one knew for a long time that he was using. He'd shoot up in some motel room, lay diagonal across the bed and feel like shit. Beat himself up in his mind for being a waste of a human. But it didn't stop him. None of it stopped him.

A scar above his right eye, nearly hidden by an eyebrow, six teeth missing. He laughs at what he looks like. Like a gangster. Like a hoodlum. Like the kind of guy you'd never bring to meet your daddy.

But he talks about love. His grandmother died at ninety-seven, and it tore him up, and he wrote about how much she loved him. How she'd watch ten, twelve cop cars career up the street at night and pray they weren't coming for her grandson, Jimmy. How she knew he pimped. He'd sometimes bring his girls over to her house, and she'd fix them all something to eat, and she'd look at those girls and say, "You know you working in monkey business and this one here's the monkey," and she'd point to Jimmy.

I GO WITH HIM to the sheriff's satellite office, see one of his new classes. It's the place I visited years ago, when Donte was still his intern, except tonight he's in an upstairs room. About a third of the class are newcomers, which means they'll be tuned out. They sit in their circle of seniority. They wear oversized sports jerseys, too-big jeans, paint-splattered T-shirts. There is an exhaustion to these men, many of whom have put in full days at work and are now court-mandated to be here. Some of them began this program in San Bruno and are finishing it out here as part of their probation. I sense open hostility from more than one. A calendar from the prior year is stuck in June. Several tables are pushed to one side of the room.

The airy rush of traffic whooshes outside. County jail is nearby and the headquarters of Airbnb is just beyond the jail. That's what San Francisco is like to people like Jimmy who don't live off the Silicon Valley gravy train: it's a place of dichotomy. Chain-link fences with busted-up liquor bottles on one curb and a block down a local brewpub sells fifteen-dollar pints to hipsters.

Jimmy starts with the first point of the curriculum. Accountability, he says. What does it mean?

"Stage one: it's to stop my violence," one man says.

IN SAN BRUNO ALL the guys in his program are pre-sentencing, which translates to their best behavior. Sitting up straight like the best kids in the class. They've been plucked away by all those triggers in the external world—relationships, drugs, alcohol, gangs, guns, whatever. In jail it's just them and their stories and time. And let's be clear: Jimmy's included in that. His job helps immensely. He's not fooled himself enough to believe that his determination to live a clean, violent-free life isn't bolstered by the mere fact that he's surrounded by support, including a paycheck. But out here in civil society, all those old triggers and ways of living are pulling at these guys. Their friends, their hustle, their women. Half the room looks like they're one good breath away from dreamland. One guy has his elbows on his knees, staring into the carpet. Another's eyelids flutter. Three of the men here tonight are wearing ankle monitors under their pant legs. One has a monitor on each leg.

But Jimmy's not some PhD from a fancy university. He's one of them. He understands their struggle from the inside out. Not from a book and not from research—not, frankly, how someone like me understands it, intellectually—but from the gut. And I've watched enough sessions with him to know that he sees those guys who think they're invisible. The ones who come in drunk. The ones who fall asleep. Who slump over. Who stare him down while he talks. He sees them. He knows. Once in a while, he'll have to "bounce" someone out of class, someone who comes wasted, or who won't participate, and then the courts will find out, and Jimmy says sometimes the dude winds up right back in the classroom he was bounced from.

"Accountability," Jimmy says. Four ways they get into a moment of fatal peril. The first is denial. "I didn't do it. It wasn't me." The next is minimize. "To lessen the impact of my violence," he tells them. Words like "but" and "only" are clues. "I *only* hit her once. I *only* pushed her a little. *But* she came at me first." Blame and collusion are the other two ways. "*She* hit me first," he says. "*She* was in my face." That's blame. Collusion is, say another guy is sitting there beside you. "Oh, dog, you going to let her talk to you like that? Yo, man, if I was you, I'd let her know what's what."

Jimmy tells them if they stay away from those four behaviors, they'll never see him again ". . . unless you're at the park watching the Giants."

They laugh. Jimmy reminds them of the story of Kelly, how he kidnapped her. The second of his three defining stories; most of them have heard it before. "Everything that was on that police report was 125% true. Everything she said was absolutely true," he says. He lowers his voice and takes a step toward them, his body bent in an arc, leaning toward them, pulling them into the moment. And it works. They're starting to sit up and pay attention to him. "And you know what? Every police report that's involved me, ever? I did it. I don't have the experience of being falsely arrested. I don't have the experience of having someone lie on me. And that's what I'm trying to get you guys to see. I know that and it don't make me special, but I know no one's ever lied on me. It's all true. And that's what keeps me here. I don't want to have to live looking over my shoulder. I don't want to live with my partner and every time I walk in the house, she's frightened, because of my impact."

He steps back toward the whiteboard, straightens up, rubs his hands together. He's wearing beige Dickies and trainers. "You guys following me a little?" he asks.

One guy says, "No."

Jimmy smiles, says, "Well, you're going to hear it every week, dog. Don't even worry. The work starts at fatal peril. Break that word in two. Fatal means dead, right? Peril. Deadly danger. You know, you're driving down the highway and someone cuts you off and you're like, 'Fuck!' Your hands come up"—he demonstrates with his hands, a defensive posture.

One of the guys says, "Your manhood's been challenged."

Jimmy nods. He tells them their heart rate increases, their muscles go hard, their face goes into a grimace. It's all subconscious. They won't know it, but it's the limbic system's response to threat. He demonstrates, outsized, clownish, and they laugh.

He says how they all learned as little kids that boys don't cry. "Our dad or mom said, 'Don't cry now. Shake it off,' right? Why not? It hurt. Why not cry? What's wrong with crying? Boys didn't get to cry because they were in pain, falling on gravel, but my daughter? Man. She was scooped up and held and kissed, and my son was told to stop crying." He shakes his head. "Now, with the education I got, I'm like, 'Come here, little man. I feel like crying with you. I know that hurt. It's okay. Cry.'"

He talks about how he grew up believing women served men because he watched his grandmother and his female cousins all make the food and bring the food and clean up the food, and the boys sat watching the ball game. What were they all being taught? And now he's a grown man and he knows, because he had to learn, how to feed himself, how to make his own damn omelet. "I had no concept of appreciation," he says of his past girlfriends, of Kelly. "I never had a bad partner. I had a bad attitude."

"You sure did," one of the guys says. Jimmy laughs.

"I got a lot of people that love me," he says, but in his younger days, he says he wasn't worried about them. How ridiculous it seems to him now. He used to worry about impressing other men, other pimps, other street punk gangsters like he used to be. "I'm worried about the motherfuckers I don't know. I want to be this male-figure motherfucker. And when I'm busy impressing the person I don't know, I'm hurting the people that love me." He says this was his inner hit man. The inner compulsion that tells men to be violent, that hides men from their authentic feelings, that reinforces this male belief system. "We call our image the hit man. Why? 'Cause the hit man moves in silence. The hit man doesn't come outside in the street. He's not driving around in a big ole Cadillac, blasting tunes and smoking a blunt. Motherfucker's out in the suburbs, owns a construction company, you know? Three kids in Catholic schools." He's moving around the room now, bouncing back and forth like he's boxing. Every hit man is different. Depends on the inner lies he makes you believe. Jimmy says his is the "manipulating, womanizing, aggressive bastard." He stops moving. "Every one of those words is deep when you're talking about a crime against your daughters."

It's that thing, right, where men can relate to wanting their own daughters kept safe, kept from men like themselves, but somehow it doesn't extend to their partners. This view has always sat uncomfortably with me; must we always see ourselves, our own stories, to make someone else's mean something? Can't we just believe that all people should be safe and not just those who resemble our own mothers and daughters? Is *relatability* necessary for *empathy*? And there was something else, too, about Jimmy. When I told him I had to talk to Kelly, get her side of the story, talk to his kids, maybe, or his parents, he would go quiet. I talked to his dad once, but his dad didn't seem too happy to see him talking to a reporter. He said so right in front of me. "You gonna talk to her all about you?" he said, gesturing toward me. Jimmy said it was all right, but his father shook his head a little. But then Jimmy just sort of disappeared when it came to me talking to these people, his family. He said he didn't want them re-traumatized, which I understood. We all keep our families safe. But here's the other question I asked: "Why do you get to decide for grown women— daughter, mother, ex-girlfriend—who they can talk to and who they can't?"

That's when Jimmy stopped talking to me.

Eventually, I did talk to Kelly, his ex. She agreed to go on the record. All of their mutual friends, their family members, everyone already knew the story of Jimmy and Kelly, she told me. Kelly called herself Jimmy's "lead story." She understood that her history was part of his mission toward nonviolence, and toward his own recovery. She didn't particularly like that she had to sacrifice her own privacy for his recovery, and for the recovery of men she'd never meet. But she'd made her peace with Jimmy, rebuilt her life, and said she'd learned enough that she would never take shit from any man ever again.

She told me Jimmy had been the first person she felt ever treated her well, at least in the early days. He had a lot of money, and he was nice, though she also says he was a "predator." Years later, when she did finally work up the courage to leave him, she said people told her she was "giving up" on him. She felt a lot of guilt, but she never went back. Her daughter, she says, has a great relationship with her dad now, but it's got nothing to do with Kelly. She and Jimmy are co-parents, nothing more to her. When I questioned whether she believed he really had changed, she said yes, but she also said she believed she could probably trigger him again in a minute. It kept her at arm's length from him.

Just before we hung up, I asked if she thought a violent man could ever truly become nonviolent. She thought about it a moment. "I think they can become ninety percent nonviolent. But there's a small part of them that you can never fix."

For his part, Jimmy never spoke to me again.

JIMMY TOLD ME ONCE about how he knows women want to "fix him." That he recognizes a certain fetish women have with a survivor story, a formerly violent man who's been reborn as a man who doesn't fear his own vulnerabilities and feelings. Nothing sexier than a man in touch with his emotions, right? When I look at his Facebook page, I can see that he's not lying. With every post, women are dripping with platitudes, inspired by his story of survival. He said one woman once flew across the country to meet him.

And it makes me a little uncomfortable. It might even piss me off a little. Men like Jimmy are not remarkable. They're not noteworthy. They're doing what they're supposed to be doing—which is not beating up women. If there's any triumph at all, it is in their very averageness. David Adams is skeptical, too, of this potential fetishization our culture has with a good survival story. It's the potential narcissism, again, the charisma they all naturally seem to have in the first place. "They can become charismatic loose cannons," he told me once, "who never really took responsibility for their own abuse."

Jimmy leans against the whiteboard, his voice with that gravelly whisper again. "I was born and bred in a street gang," he says. "I could go right back fully into the life right now. Right now. I had a four-month relapse in 2014. I came back in April 2015. You know what, guys? I live a beautiful life. I keep myself around positive people. I'm going to hit the gym after this, and then I'm going to have something good to eat. Grab a shower and get in bed."

"That's a good life!" one of the guys says.

"It is," he nods. "I might even hit a ten-o'clock AA meeting. I'm a fucking mess. I got room to work. I don't need to fix you. I need to fix me, because I'm the problem. And I want you all to make it, but you know what? The reality is, the guy on the right won't make it, but the guy on the left will. Ten percent of you will make it. I sat in those seats for two years. I didn't get it. I didn't want to put down drugs, stop my unhealthy relationships, the streets. I stayed fucked up. And you're not going to make me lose no sleep. That's the bottom hard truth. I'm not an enabler and I'm not a babysitter. So if you want to come to sleep every week, I feel bad, bro. Because whatever got you here, that same situation is going to happen again, hella times, and if you don't know this material, man, you're going to do exactly what you did last time . . . and I'll just sit like a motherfucking bird watcher. Jail's like Lake Tahoe, man. It's always open. Be here, and be present."

And this brings Jimmy to his third story, the one I only heard once and could never verify with anyone from his family. The one that guts him the most. It's not a long story, or an unusual story. But he calls it the most painful day of his life. "Twelve years old," he says. His daughter was sexually molested, by someone they all knew.

"I had to make some serious decisions," he tells them. "Either I go and knock this motherfucker's head off, because I had all the right reasons, you know? Do some time for the next thirty years, but it's not a big deal. I'm a gangbanger anyway. I live comfortably in every facility, any facility. Do I kill this motherfucker or do I not do a thing?"

THAT'S WHAT HE *thinks* his decision was in the moment when he received the news. Kill the guy, or not. But really, he says, he realized that wasn't his decision at all. The decision was actually "Do I make it about me and go kill this motherfucker? Or do I make it about my daughter, and be there for her?" If he kills the guy, he takes himself out of his daughter's life at the moment she needs him the most.

"Shit," one new guy whispers.

"I'm going to make sure, each and every one of you, that your partners are not afraid when you go home," Jimmy says quietly. "I work front line for the victim, and I want to see you better your life, because that's one more safe woman in the world."

PART III

The Middle

In the Cracks

A round the same time that Rocky killed Michelle and his children, a woman on the other side of the country named Dorothy Giunta-Cotter was on the run from her abusive husband, William. She'd fled to a shelter in Maine with her youngest daughter, Kristen, and had just had a temporary restraining order refused by a local judge. The judge claimed to have no jurisdiction to issue an order of protection, since Dorothy was a Massachusetts resident.

So Dorothy called the hotline of a domestic violence center in her hometown of Amesbury, Massachusetts. She'd never called the Jeanne Geiger Crisis Center before, and no one there knew her history. But she spoke to an advocate named Kelly Dunne. Dunne normally didn't work on Sundays, but this particular day she had, and something about Dorothy's voice over the phone made her instinctively know she was dealing with an unusually volatile situation. Dunne found a place for Dorothy and Kristen in a shelter in Salem. She met them there later that day, and listened to Dorothy recount an almost unthinkably dire situation.

They spoke for four long hours. Dunne remembers the preternatural patience of Kristen, who sat outside the door of the room for all those hours while her mother detailed decades of such extreme abuse that Dunne still will not share some of the particulars (a promise she says she made that day to Dorothy and that she has kept). William had pushed Dorothy down the stairs, given her black eyes, kidnapped her and held her overnight in a warehouse, beaten her when she was pregnant, and threatened to kill her and drive her body so far out into the middle of nowhere that no one would ever find her. On the rare occasions when Dorothy had visited an emergency room, William would sometimes throw away her pain medication. He didn't allow her to work and she had almost no life outside of the couple's two daughters. Because he was a cable installer William had convinced her that he knew the locations of all the shelters in New England.

Dorothy also understood that under the law fathers had a right to see their children. Any custody agreement or visitation schedule would require a constant negotiation with William. So even if she could prove abuse—which she couldn't, since she'd never called the police on him—William had rights in the eyes of the law. At least if she was in the same house, she reasoned, there was a chance she could protect her daughters. So she'd returned, again and again.

But this time, she swore to Dunne, she was finished. This time, he had crossed a line: William had abused Kristen, who was eleven, for the first time ever. He'd sat on her chest until she couldn't breathe—and that was what spurred Dorothy to action. For many abuse victims, this is what eventually pushes them, when their child gets hurt. It's one thing for an adult to abuse another adult, but a child? This is often the moment victims decide enough is enough.

Like many abusers, William was savvy enough to work the system. After this last escape to Maine, William had sent a letter to Kristen's school saying his wife was mentally unstable and had taken their child without his consent; he told the school that if Dorothy tried to get Kristen's records—which she would need to enroll Kristen anywhere else—that he should be contacted immediately. He noted in his letter that none of this was a result of any abuse in the Cotter home, a remark that struck the school as odd enough that they contacted the local police to come in and talk about the situation. At the same time, William Cotter went to the Amesbury Police Department and filed a missing person's report with an officer named Rick Poulin. Poulin told me that Cotter was concerned his wife would use their credit cards. "He was very defensive for a missing person's [report]," Poulin said. "Alarm bells went off in me." Poulin was also the officer who spoke to school officials, and he even walked down the block to the Jeanne Geiger Crisis Center and spoke to an advocate there. The case was strange, but so far as they could tell, no one had broken any laws. There was no record of abuse, no criminal history for anyone in the family, and no reason to have William on the law enforcement radar at all. Dorothy hadn't yet called the hotline from Maine, and William appeared to be an upstanding citizen.

Dunne says William's behavior is typical of abusers. They want to show victims they know how to play the system to their advantage. Dorothy was in Maine, and with that letter to the school, William, she said, "was trying to smoke her out."

Dunne told Dorothy to stay in shelter, that she'd talk with their crisis center attorney and come up with a strategy after they filed for a restraining order—which they planned to do first thing the next morning. And then Dorothy told Dunne something that stunned her: *I am done with shelter.*

Dorothy had been in and out of shelters all over New England; she'd even gone as far as Pennsylvania. And every time she eventually returned, because she couldn't hide forever. William would never just let her go. He'd never willingly agree to a divorce. Her kids needed to be enrolled in a school no matter where she was or what she was running from. Her own family lived in Massachusetts. How could she leave her mother and her sister? Her closest network of support? She'd someday have to have a job that could cover expenses for her daughters and herself.

DOROTHY TOLD DUNNE SHE hadn't done anything wrong, so why was she the one who always had to leave? She believed that William knew most shelter locations anyway, so there was no point hiding from him. She would not go. Not this time, and never again. Later, Dunne called this their "oh shit" moment. "We had no plan for a woman who refused shelter," she told me. "Shelter *was* our plan."

Dorothy and Kristen spent that Sunday night in the Salem shelter, and went to court the next day with Dunne and the center's lawyer. The court granted her a restraining order—with one caveat: William told the judge he needed access to the garage or he wouldn't be able to get his work tools. So the judge allowed William to pick up his tools from the house in the morning and return them in the evening. It was an unusual ruling, but William had no record as an abuser and, presumably, needed to be able to maintain employment while he and Dorothy sorted out their marital issues.

After court, William vacated the house. And Dorothy and Kristen moved back in.

Dorothy's house was two stories built atop a ground-level garage. It sat beside a small parking lot for their neighbors, whose houses were so cloistered one could barely fit a hand between them. Dorothy's rental house had white clapboard siding with green trim; a flight of rickety wooden stairs led to a narrow porch with two entry doors. The crisis center changed the locks, installed a security system, and gave cell phones to Dorothy and her daughters. They also gave her an emergency response necklace to wear. But one night while she was cooking, she accidentally hit the button and half a dozen police cars showed up. She was so embarrassed, she took the necklace and hung it in her bedroom.

Ten days after she had moved back in, Dorothy walked into the garage to get into her car. She was due for a job interview at Shaw's supermarket. Suddenly, William—who had an active restraining order against him—grabbed her from behind and covered her mouth with his hand. "Stop screaming or I'll shoot you," he warned her. Kaitlyn, their elder daughter, heard the struggle and ran downstairs to find her mother being held hostage by her father. "Her mouth was bleeding . . . and she appeared terrified," Kaitlyn later wrote in an affidavit. "I . . . stood with my mom and dad to make sure nothing was going to happen." After two and a half hours, William left; the next day, Dorothy went to the police station and filed a report about William breaking the restraining order with a detective named Robert Wile. She and Wile spoke for a long time; it was the first he'd ever met her. She told Wile of her husband, "Every time I talk to him, he scares me."

Dorothy was calm, rational, he said. She told him that in a shelter, she'd have to share a room with her two daughters, increasing the likelihood that if William did actually find them, he'd kill all three of them. In her own home, he remembers her telling him, there was a better chance "it would be just me." Wile was struck silent. "She was basically telling me, 'I'm preparing for my own death, and what are you doing?'" Wile told me. "And I was speechless."

By the time Wile, who goes by Bobby, met Dorothy, he'd been in law enforcement for nearly two decades, working his way up to detective. He was often the first one called to the scene of some of the area's most gruesome crimes—kids killed by their parents, wives killed by husbands. Amesbury, Massachusetts, didn't tend to have random crimes, a drive-by shooting, say, or mugging-turned-accidental-homicide. Boston, just an hour away, had random crime, but Amesbury was one of those working-class Massachusetts towns with small central squares and red-bricked sidewalk charm, a New England colonial aesthetic. Still, it had the dubious distinction of having the highest rate of domestic violence in Essex County. And what murders they experienced tended to be where the perpetrator and the victim knew each other, which is to say that they were nearly always private violence. For Wile, the "domestics" were frustrating. Like practically everyone in law enforcement, he hadn't gotten into police work to break up some dispute over butter between husbands and wives. His attitude was basically, "You gotta be kidding me. I'm getting called back to this house *again*?" And even though Dorothy's case, her fatalist vision of her future, stood out to him in its severity, this interpretation of "domestics" was still the way he thought of them at the time.

WILE ISSUED A WARRANT for Cotter's arrest. On March 21, 2002, William, accompanied by his lawyer, turned himself in at the Newburyport District Court. Dunne said Cotter knew what he was doing. He knew the system, showing up at the end of the day on a Friday, all lawyered up. His previous record showed only a few traffic violations and bad checks. He had a steady job as a cable installer and coached a local youth sports team. The judge that day didn't know of his decades of abuse against Dorothy, didn't know the particulars of how he'd broken the restraining order, didn't know he'd once stalked his wife, then kidnapped her. He didn't know William had pushed her down the stairs when she was pregnant once, or how he'd strangled her with a phone cord. The prosecutor in court that day also didn't have Dorothy's affidavit, which chronicled her two decades of abuse. Maybe if Wile had known Cotter would be in court that afternoon, he could have made an appearance, given the judge more information. Maybe he could have called over to someone in the courthouse, warned them about Cotter, but Wile only had Dorothy's affidavit from the day she'd gone in to see him. He knew she was scared of her husband, but he didn't know the extent of the abuse. Dunne knew, but she and Wile had never communicated. Dunne had learned about her abuse only in the final weeks of Dorothy's life, but never spoke to the police about her. At the time, Detective Wile didn't even know any of the advocates at the local domestic violence agency, including Kelly Dunne or Suzanne Dubus, both of whom would become pivotal in Wile's orbit in years to come. No one in the courthouse knew enough to have Cotter on their radar.

All of these critical gaps in the system often make the biggest difference between who lives and who dies—including the lack of communication between criminal and civil courts—and it still persists not only in this particular county in Massachusetts, but also in states and counties across the nation. The very fact that intimate partner violence is so often addressed in civil court, rather than criminal court, gives insight into how we as a society still view it. The country's first "family court," as it was called, began in Buffalo, New York. At the time, it seemed a great judicial innovation to have a place where families could work out issues related to divorce and child custody that didn't require a visit to criminal court. In the ensuing decades, however, what this has meant is that domestic violence has been lumped in with other family matters, like custody and divorce, rather than being the criminal matter that it is. Imagine a man, a stranger, strangling another man with a phone cord, pushing another man down the stairs, punching another man so hard he breaks an orbital eye socket. Such assaults happen daily with domestic violence, but I have yet to speak with a prosecutor who sees these crimes treated as seriously as when they happen in the context of domestic violence. "It shocked me, the things someone would do to a family member that they wouldn't do on the street, or in a bar fight," a former prosecutor from Ohio named Anne Tamashasky told me. The day William Cotter showed up in court, he paid $500 and bailed out minutes after he'd turned himself in.

Five days later, William arrived at Dorothy's house wearing a tactical vest and armed with pepper spray, handcuffs, ammunition belts, and a sawed-off shotgun. Kaitlyn was at a friend's house; Kristen unwittingly opened the front door. As soon as she heard his voice, Dorothy barricaded herself in her bedroom. William pushed past Kristen and broke down the door to Dorothy's bedroom, dragging her out in seconds. Kristen ran upstairs and called a neighbor, who called 911—an arrangement Dunne had worked out so Kristen didn't have the psychological burden of calling the police on her father. The police arrived within minutes.

I freeze the scene in this crucial moment sometimes: Dorothy, still alive, held hostage by her abusive husband, and the police there—half the force, it seemed—guns drawn and ready. The family was known in the department now both because of Officer Poulin and because of Detective Wile and the day Dorothy went to see him. Wile understood by now that Cotter was dangerous, maybe more dangerous than most, and he shared it around the station to be on the lookout. And this is the moment: William is alive. Dorothy is alive. Dispatch is on the phone. The police are there.

Was this a scene she had ever imagined, sitting there with Detective Wile, telling him how she would die in her own house? She was thirty-two years old, not even halfway through her life. She had the glamorous look of an actress from the 1940s, a more ordinary Hedy Lamarr or Loretta Young.

Did Dorothy have time to remember that fateful day when she was fifteen years old and she met a boy who claimed to fall in love with her at first sight? Did she blame that young version of herself? Did she consider how her culture pushes little girls toward love, tells them love conquers all? Did she ever wonder why we don't tell more stories of love's defeat? I don't believe love conquers all. So many things in this world seem more powerful than love. Duty. Rage. Fear. Violence.

I picture Kristen, eleven years old, hiding under her bed, blind to what was happening. The unbearable weight of knowing she'd let her father in. She'd thought it was going to be her friend at the door. I lost my own mother when I was around Kristen's age. It was cancer, a civilized death, if there is such a thing. But I understand just a fraction of the raging desperation Kristen must have felt, the promise she was maybe making to any available invisible god in the blazing heat of the moment to protect her mother. And I understand this, too: that however terrible the singular moment of death is, however haunting those brittle final seconds, the loss will come to be defined by the buildup of years still to come. The scale of it, the cruel forever of it, a steel gate the size of the world itself shutting before you have time to blink.

The scene unfreezes. When the dispatcher called Kristen back to confirm the police arrival, William picked up the downstairs phone. He told the dispatcher to call off the police or "someone's gonna get hurt real bad." His voice was stern, but oddly flat, as if he still believed all of this was well within his purview, as if he thought this was just a colossal misunderstanding, his own private matter to manage. Officer David Noyes was the first to their door. He could hear Dorothy screaming, "He's gonna kill me! He's gonna kill me!" Noyes had his gun cocked, too, his Kevlar on. It was raining. They were all in their police-issued rain gear. The Kevlar and the equipment belt and the rain poncho made it difficult to maneuver. The dispatcher did not, of course, call the police off. Noyes kicked down the door at the same moment William shot Dorothy; Noyes said the muzzle flash was so sharp it blinded him for a moment, long enough for William to turn the gun on himself. The entire episode was captured by dispatch. Dorothy screaming in the background, a boom and instant cessation of her voice, then men's voices barking orders. Above all the chaotic racket you can hear a single wail: *"Noooooooooo!"* screamed into the receiver by an eleven-year-old girl.

AS NEWS OF DOROTHY's murder spread across the police station and then to neighbors, family, friends, media, domestic violence communities, and the courthouse and judge who'd seen William and allowed him out on bail, it was as if the entire town went into mourning. Those who hadn't known her were just as shattered as those who had. Dorothy's became the highest-profile murder Amesbury could recall. Kaitlyn and Kristen had lost both parents at once. Dorothy's mother and her sister, her entire family, were all shattered. And for Dunne and Dubus it was a reckoning. "We fell into an institutional funk after Dorothy's murder," Dubus told me. The fact that they'd known Dorothy was in as dangerous a situation as anyone could be, short of camping on the front line of a war zone, did not in any way alleviate their feelings of anguish and guilt. In fact, it seemed to make them worse.

When I asked Dunne to explain why, she had no hesitation in her answer: because Dorothy's death had seemed "instantly preventable." If they couldn't save the most obvious cases, the ones like Dorothy who predicted their own murders, the ones who absolutely knew they were in unmitigated danger, then what was the point of any of the work they did? Shelter was a part of this, too: Why was their only answer to take an innocent victim and essentially lock her away? Afterward, newspaper editorials skewered the local police and the judge who had released William Cotter on bail; some news commentators called for the judge's resignation. Dubus, then the chief executive officer of the Jeanne Geiger Crisis Center, called a meeting between the district attorney and members of the police department, including Detective Wile, in order to analyze why the standard response procedures had failed. Everyone appeared to have done his or her job correctly. The only real digression from protocol had come from Dorothy herself, when she refused to return to shelter. To Dunne, this meant their protocol was wrong.

IN THE MIDST OF this reckoning, in 2003, Dunne flew to San Diego and attended a conference on domestic violence. The keynote speaker was Jacquelyn Campbell. Campbell spoke about the Danger Assessment. As Dunne listened, she was struck partly by the information Campbell was sharing, but also by how Campbell was offering a whole new way of quantifying the information to illustrate increased dangerousness. The single biggest indicator for domestic violence homicide is a prior incidence of physical domestic violence, Campbell said. It seems obvious. But often it's the escalation that is missed. And her assessment showed where to rank dangerous behavior, like threats of suicide, or access to a gun. Dunne listened as Campbell talked about how half of women killed by their partners had sought help from the police or the criminal justice system at least once. These were opportunities to catalog risk markers. The risk of homicide unfolds on a timeline, Campbell said, spiking, for example, when a victim attempts to leave an abuser, or when the situation at home changes—a pregnancy, a new job, a move. The danger remains high for three months after a couple splits, dips slightly for the next nine, and drops significantly after a year.

There were other risk markers new to Dunne, too. Like how strangulation is a different category of violence than, say, a punch to the face. Or that abusers tended to fall into two categories when it comes to their pregnant partners: those whose abuse escalates, and those who lay off entirely for those nine months. Forced sex is a risk marker, as is controlling most of a partner's daily activities. Dunne sat in the audience growing more and more agitated as Campbell went on. In her mind, an entirely different narrative was running that went something like this: "Dorothy had that. Dorothy had that one. Dorothy, again. Yup. Dorothy. Dorothy, Dorothy, Dorothy."

For the first time, she learned about the Danger Assessment tool—what Campbell had thought would only ever be used in an emergency room. Dunne did a postmortem Danger Assessment on Dorothy and saw that she would have scored an eighteen, around the same as Michelle Monson Mosure. Dorothy had been in the highest possible category for domestic violence homicide, and none of them had even known it. This was why her death seemed so instantly preventable, Dunne realized. Because it *was*. It was protocol in the making. For the first time since Dorothy had been killed, Dunne began to feel a tiny bit of hope.

When Dunne returned from California, she and Dubus immediately began to think of how they might use Campbell's work to predict which domestic-abuse cases were more likely to end in homicide. Dunne's goal was twofold: one, identify and create action plans for high risk cases; and two, keep victims out of shelters as much as possible. They knew they needed to devise a program that would identify the potentially lethal cases, the Dorothys-in-waiting. And if these victims could be scored and categorized, then maybe the protections they'd build around them could operate on that same timeline of dangerousness that Campbell identified. Because if they could predict them, it stood to reason they could prevent them. They brought Campbell up to Massachusetts from her home in Baltimore to work with them on the design and implementation of what they had in mind. During the following year, Dunne and her staff met with police officers in Amesbury and Newburyport, district attorneys, probation and parole officers, batterer intervention counselors, and hospital representatives. They knew it was about information flow, breaking down communications barriers. If everyone in each of the various offices around town—the judge in the courthouse, the detective in the police department, the advocate in the crisis center, the social worker at school, the nurse in the emergency room, et cetera—had had all the information about William and Dorothy, instead of different offices having various different bits of information, there was a very good chance Dorothy may have lived. William might not have been allowed to bail out. He might have had to relinquish his guns. He might have been on a GPS bracelet. It was all these gaps that Dunne and Dubus needed to figure out how to fill. They went over what services they could try to incorporate into the safety plan for any given scenario. Could the office of probation help with getting judges more informed? Could police identify some of the risk factors on a call? Could the emergency room help identify potential domestic violence victims? Could police share reports with the crisis center advocates? Could batterer intervention groups share their information with the crisis center? At each stage, they talked through the practices, the legal issues, the privacy standards, and most of all how they could share information across bureaucratic lines. They scoured state statutes and privacy laws, learned what kind of information they could legally share with other offices and what they could not.

Sharing information meant departments that had been siloed were communicating. Perhaps the most significant cultural barrier existed between the police department and the crisis center. Every possible gendered stereotype that exists about these two entities had to be addressed on a personal level. Dunne's office was primarily made up of women, the police department primarily men. Wile told me once that, prior to the formation of the High Risk Team, the local police officers viewed Dunne and the other crisis center advocates as the "Men Hate Us Club." "We didn't deal with them," he said, because the common feeling among police officers was that the women who worked in places like crisis centers, well, "they don't like us." Dunne laughed at this characterization. "We were the feminazis, and they were the assholes who cared only about overtime," she told me. But as they talked to one another, advocates to officers, they learned about the unique set of problems and barriers each faced. In talking to Wile, Dunne began to see how officers could get frustrated going to the same house again and again. And officers like Wile began to understand the intractable circumstances that keep victims in place. Dunne was able to explain how victims who appear hostile and show solidarity with their abusers when the police show up are often taking a safety measure, sending a message not to police but to their abusers. *See my loyalty? Please don't kill me when the cops leave.*

In this new system, the crisis center would serve as the central point of communication. They formed a team, one representative from every possible organization that could be involved—from the emergency rooms to the judiciary to the prison to the police to the advocates and half a dozen others in between. They decided to meet monthly, discuss those cases deemed high risk, and within the tangled bounds of confidentiality agreements and HIPAA laws, share as much as they knew about each potential homicide. Offices working in isolation would no longer be the modus operandi. "It's in the cracks that murders happen," Dunne would later say.

In early 2005, the country's first official Domestic Violence High Risk Team began accepting cases. Their mandate? Fill in the cracks.

Shelter in Place

Back when the women's movement brought domestic violence into the national consciousness, shelter seemed the most viable answer to the problem. Get the victim out of harm's way. Many states still did not have laws against battering one's wife. Intimate partner violence was seen as a private family matter and what research existed around domestic violence still carried a residue of such incidents being the fault of victims inciting their abusers. It would be decades before the idea of men being held accountable for their violent behavior even became part of the national conversation. Creating shelters was the first nationally coordinated attempt to address intimate partner violence, and throughout the 1960s, '70s, '80s, even well into the '90s, it was more or less the only solution offered to women in dangerous situations. In 1964, California opened a shelter for female victims of alcoholic partners who were also abused, though Maine and Minnesota are generally credited with the first shelters devoted solely to battered women. Shelter saved, undoubtedly, many thousands of women's lives, and continues to do so today. Over the course of four decades, the shelter movement expanded, and today there are more than three thousand.[1]

The definition of shelter varies widely; it can mean a bed in a hotel room for a night, or a group house with two dozen families. Cities with dense populations sometimes have small apartment buildings or single occupancy motel-type residences. Outside of major cities, shelters tend to be single-family homes in residential areas, where victims and their children are allotted one room and share kitchens, bathrooms, and dining and living rooms with five to eight other families. There are rules governing curfews and chores. Historically, boys over the age of twelve and pets have not been allowed in shelters, and most contact with friends or family, including a victim's employer, had been discouraged, for safety's sake. (New York is currently creating what it's calling the country's first 100% pet-friendly shelter; Arkansas, meanwhile, opened the country's first shelter for men in 2015.) Shelter doesn't simply mean a safe place to sleep; it means walking entirely out of your life, having your children walk entirely out of their lives. It means disappearing from view.

This is what came into focus for Kelly Dunne when Dorothy refused shelter. Kelly Dunne once told me the "dirty little secret" of shelter was that it was a "ticket to welfare." If a woman needed shelter and the closest bed was across the state, she had to take it immediately, even if that meant leaving a job or a kid's school and friends behind. Dunne said some of the most haunting images she carries with her in her twenty-five-year career include watching women standing on the curb with their suitcases and their children, waiting for a bus to take them across the state to the only place that had a shelter bed available that night. It is profoundly disruptive. Necessary sometimes, still, but wrenching.

More and more victims resist staying in shelters, Dunne said. They wonder whether they can continue in their job or care for their elderly parents; whether they will be able to make a doctor's appointment or a dinner date with friends; whether their child can still be in the school play; whether they can bring family heirlooms; whether they can post on Facebook or Instagram. "The answer to all those questions is no," Dunne said. "Shelter was this way to get the criminal justice system off the hook. They'd say, 'If she's really that afraid, she'll go into shelter,' and when women didn't, we'd surmise that they really weren't that afraid." Dorothy taught her how dangerous such an assumption could be.

In recent years, shelters and clinical-treatment providers have worked to better accommodate the needs of abuse victims. Jobs are often encouraged; sophisticated security systems have been installed in shelters that can afford it. Some shelters now allow teenage boys to stay with their mothers and families to bring their pets; others permit contact with friends and family. One afternoon Candace Waldron, the former executive director of Healing Abuse Working for Change, a crisis agency in Salem, Massachusetts, arranged for me to visit their new state-of-the-art shelter. It had replaced the one where Dorothy and Kristen stayed, which had been a tiny house on a side street close enough to the ocean that sand skittered across its narrow sidewalks. Situated in an elegantly renovated Queen Anne Victorian on a wide boulevard with security cameras discreetly tucked away throughout, the new shelter had room for eight families with three separate cooking areas. There was an elevator and a children's playroom piled with toys; the hallways and staircases were brightly painted and hung with flower paintings. A small sandbox was set up in the backyard. It was, so far as shelters go, large and airy, while also being devoid of the kinds of personal touches that most of us have in our homes: photos of family, say, or posters, kids' art, tchotchkes, toys, books, CDs.

This is top of the line: play areas are provided, security is tight, conditions are decent. And yet even at their best, shelters represent a total disruption. Still, speaking out against shelters has cast advocates like Dunne outside the mainstream. "It's not a popular opinion to be putting forth in the domestic violence world," she said. This despite the fact that most shelters remain chronically underfunded, opening and closing at the whim of state or county budgets, and that the evidence suggests that shelters provide victims and their families neither an easy respite nor a long-term solution.

In response to a *New Yorker* article in which I covered many of these same points, a reader wrote in:

As the founder of one of the country's first shelters, I reject the statement . . . that shelters are, in effect, a 'ticket to welfare.' High Risk Teams are an important innovation, but they reach only a fraction of victims who are already known to law enforcement or service providers. The model is most effective as part of a comprehensive approach to preventing domestic violence that includes shelter. Shelters provide safe housing and trauma support for individuals and families, the vast majority of whom have endured chronic abuse, poverty, and homelessness. It's the place where survivors report feeling safe for the first time in their lives. Support services emphasize education, employment, and a pathway to stable, affordable housing. Indeed, our High Risk Team, a partnership of more than twenty-five local agencies, has sent families to shelters on numerous occasions, when shelter was truly their only option.[2]

I cannot argue with this letter writer's statement. So I must concede that these two realities uneasily coexist: that shelter is necessary and saves lives, but it is also an abysmal fix.

Dunne, too, concedes that shelter is necessary sometimes. She described an ongoing case in which the assailant had been ordered by the court to wear a GPS bracelet so that his movements could be monitored. He failed to appear at probation for the fitting and was effectively on the run and at large; for his victim, shelter was the safest option. Often shelter can be helpful even just for a night or two to let tempers calm down. But Dunne also characterizes shelters as prisons for women, with strict rules and curfews, and says that children, removed from the famil-iarity of home and friends, can emerge from them traumatized. Even in the best shelters, like the one I saw in Massachusetts, you're housing traumatized people with other traumatized people. Families are most often allotted a single large bedroom.

Imagine any other crime where the impetus for change, and the loss of civil liberties, lies with the victim, Dunne said. "Shelters have saved the lives of battered women," she said. "But it seemed inherently unfair to me, that this was our answer."

THESE DAYS, THERE IS a push to try to keep victims in their commu-nities and out of shelter, to build a kind of safety wall around the victim. One of the methods of this is called transitional housing. Transitional housing differs from shelter in that it offers more long-term accommo-dation, and in most cases, more autonomy. Many cities have some version of transitional housing today, so to find out what transitional housing actually looked like, and how it differed from shelter, I went one afternoon to meet with a woman named Peg Hacksylo. Hacksylo is the former executive director of the District Alliance for Safe Housing in Washington, D.C., and founder of a transitional housing program lauded nationally as a model to emulate.

I visited one summer afternoon. The building bore no signs out front or any indication at all of what it was. A small children's playground was built in a side yard behind a fence that spanned the building's perim-eter. I had been told in advance I'd have to be buzzed in—a camera was stationed at the entrance, along with other cameras at key locations around the city block taken up by the building. Tall iron fencing—nearly impossible to climb—terraced both sides of the walkway.

The building itself is in one of D.C.'s gritty neighborhoods, with gentrification curling in from the edges, and so affordable housing—D.C. is the fifth most expensive city in the nation—has gotten even more difficult to find. As of this writing, the average rent for a one-bedroom apartment is more than $2,200 a month.[3] It's an issue that every city in America grapples with, but particularly those with fast-eroding afford-able housing: San Francisco, New York, Boston, Washington D.C., Chicago, Los Angeles, and many others.

"Historically, if a victim of domestic violence went to the services in the city to get help or shelter and she would explain that she was homeless because of [domestic violence], they would say, 'You should go to a domestic violence shelter; we don't deal with that,'" Hacksylo told me. "And the domestic violence shelter system was so small and lacked so much capacity that . . . what would happen is that victims would go into domestic violence shelters and when they would time out of those shelters, they would go back to the family intake system to say, 'Okay, I need housing.' And the [intake system] would say, 'Are you at a shelter?' And the victim would say, 'Yes.' So the intake people would say, 'Okay, then you're not homeless.'"

Hacksylo says to get around this, programs had a practice whereby they'd have to make survivors homeless by basically evicting them from whatever program they were being housed by in order for them to be able to say, legitimately, that they were now homeless and needed housing.

For many, this resulted in an endless loop of recurrent homelessness and violence and shelter and homelessness and violence and shelter. Even today, a task force headed by the D.C. Coalition Against Domestic Violence reported that a third of homeless women in the District were homeless directly because of violence in their home.

HACKSYLO'S OFFICE HAD PURPLE walls and a red ceiling. She was dressed in an olive linen sheath that gave her the appearance of floating. Her braided hair had a colorful scarf in it. Back in 2006, Hacksylo told me, the city had just two shelters, which between them offered forty-eight beds for women and kids only (no men). The police department, meanwhile, got more than thirty-one thousand domestic violence calls a year. (Domestic violence didn't become a crime in Washington, D.C., until 1991.[4]) Between D.C.'s two primary agencies—House of Ruth and My Sister's Place—seventeen hundred victims annually were getting some kind of assistance. The gap between needs and services was gigantic and overwhelming.

At the time Hacksylo had left her role as deputy director of My Sister's Place and taken a job with the Office of Violence Against Women (OVW). After a coalition of domestic violence groups convinced the D.C. city council of the District's overwhelming need for shelter, the council allocated a million dollars to anyone willing to create additional safe housing. If funding is the most significant challenge any nonprofit organization has, this seemed like a no-brainer; here was basically a bank account just waiting to be used by someone to address an obvious and huge social need. The recipe was all right there: need plus funding.

But no one came forward to apply for the funds.

It was an unusual situation, to have a vast pool of funding, and no applicants.

Hacksylo, who knew her way around the D.C. domestic violence community, was tasked with finding out why. She set up a series of focus groups and for four months tried to figure out what the problem was. It turned out to be maddeningly simple: existing domestic violence agencies were so overwhelmed on a day-to-day and hour-to-hour basis, need for them was so great, that none was in a position to be able to implement such a vast, new program. It wasn't a lack of vision, necessarily; rather, these agencies all suffered, individually and collectively, from a lack of people power. So Hacksylo went to her boss at the Office of Victim Services and said, "Look, this is my passion, my love. If you don't mind, I'll start a nonprofit and do it myself."

Hacksylo laughs about it today. "It really was a backwards way for a nonprofit to get started."

But within six months she'd pulled together a board of directors, filed the paperwork for her nonprofit status, got a funding sponsor, wrote her grant proposal, and found a building to purchase. She's not a religious person, she told me, but the fact that so many things fell into place so quickly suggested to her that "something bigger than me was happening."

In July of 2007, Hacksylo's new domestic violence agency— DASH—put a contract on the building where I met her in the summer of 2017. They called it the Cornerstone Housing Program. It took three more years before building renovations, staff hires, and program planning allowed them to begin admitting survivors and their children. In the meantime, Hacksylo did more focus groups that confirmed what she already knew: that many survivors either ended up in the homeless shelter system, or they went back to abusers for lack of housing alternatives. Anywhere from 25 to 80% of homeless women, depending upon which study is cited, have domestic violence histories. And it gets worse. In cities where police can give nuisance citations, domestic violence winds up being a major cause of eviction. Matthew Desmond writes in his book *Evicted* how domestic violence nuisance cases surpassed all other forms of nuisance citations combined (things like disorderly conduct or drug charges) in Milwaukee, and that 83% of landlords who were issued such citations either evicted those tenants or threatened to evict them, meaning that victims who were abused became not only less likely to call the police next time, but they were also often victimized a second time through eviction. Later, Desmond recounts how the chief of police in Milwaukee was baffled when rates of domestic violence homicide increased and, as Desmond writes, "his department's own rules presented battered women with a devil's bargain: keep quiet and face abuse, or call the police and face eviction."[5]

Once Cornerstone opened, Hacksylo was surprised to learn that DASH was getting just as many calls from advocates at other domestic violence or social service agencies as they were from women in abusive situations in need of housing. They were saying, "I have a victim of [domestic violence] right here and I don't know what to do." Hacksylo began to realize how siloed the services are for homeless versus domestic violence, how little any of these groups tend to communicate with one another to work together. "What's happening is that victims are falling through the cracks as a result," she said, citing a kind of circular inferno that so many victims found themselves in.

While Hacksylo was busy putting together Cornerstone, she also began looking for scattered site transitional housing; scattered sites are basically units that DASH has negotiated for with landlords to lease to their clients. In the hyper-expensive housing market that is Washington, D.C., these scattered sites are a constant source of need, and DASH has had to go farther and farther beyond the city limits to find affordable housing and willing partners. At the same time, with transitional housing all across the country now offering survivors a pathway to stability, Hacksylo says the Housing and Urban Development Agency (HUD) is moving away from transitional housing, claiming that it's overly expensive for what it provides. Instead, HUD is moving toward what it calls "rapid re-housing," getting domestic violence survivors in and out of a subsidized housing situation in just four or six months.

Hacksylo says for most people, this is simply not enough time. Often, they have significant debt or their credit has been ruined by their abuser, or they haven't had a job in a long time. Sometimes they want to finish a degree or vocational training. At DASH, their rent is covered for two years. They can sometimes apply to extend that for another six months, and after that, DASH has a project to help with another two years of partially subsidized housing. And even then, Hacksylo says, it's sometimes not enough time. I think of Michelle Monson Mosure and the long view she had for her own survival. She was going to school, putting things in place to buy the house from her father and slowly establishing credit in her own name, and then she was going to get a nursing job. Would four to six months have done much of anything for her?

The frustration for Hacksylo is clear, but she knows she has to work within the world that exists, not the world that she wishes. Wherever she can, she'll create it. Today, she is working on a national model (NASH—the National Alliance for Safe Housing) based on what she created at DASH. She told me that in 2013, she began a new pilot program that has changed entirely the way she thinks about surviving domestic violence. It's called the Survivor Resilience Fund and it's just that: a pool of money to help survivors. "The conventional wisdom is that if a victim wants to get out of a situation, then she must leave her home and uproot her family and start all over again, and that typically means going into a shelter, and then going into some other subsidized long-term housing, finding a new job, new schools, putting their lives back together entirely," she told me. Exactly what someone like Dorothy Giunta-Cotter had been facing. But what Hacksylo has found in this pilot project is that there are many survivors who have the ability to sustain their own housing, but they're facing a short-term financial crisis. Maybe they don't have enough money saved for a security deposit and first month's rent; maybe they don't have a way to furnish a place they've moved into. Maybe they have an abuser who racked up credit card debt in their name. Whatever the situation, the Survivor Resilience Fund is simply a means to get them past that first big financial hurdle and keep them in their own communities.

"For me," Hacksylo said, "it's been this total paradigm shift, because I've worked in shelter and transitional housing my whole career." She says basically, the money they can offer helps a survivor avoid homelessness as a result of private violence. But the resilience fund has proven to Hacksylo that conventional wisdom isn't always necessarily true, that survivors don't want to leave their communities, and many don't even want to be cut off from their abusers. They want to be safe, but they also want their children to have both parents in their lives, so the fund provides them with a way to establish their own home in their own community and in many cases keeps the criminal justice system out of the picture. "When survivors have access to income," Hacksylo said, "they necessarily are in a better position to demand safety and justice for themselves."

Before we finish, Hacksylo takes me on a short tour of Cornerstone. It finally opened to clients in 2010, and today has forty-three studio and one-bedroom units; DASH covers rent for two years—long enough, Hacksylo says, for survivors to get their finances together, pay off debts and hopefully save some money, to address whatever other needs they may have, like substance abuse, and to get their children situated in school. There is a small fitness room with a television in one of the units and two communal play areas for kids—one for younger kids and one for older, plus the playground outside. Twice a week they have volunteers trained on children's trauma come in to play, and two former students of the Corcoran School of the Arts and Design have a nonprofit to work on art therapy with the kids. The basement has walls lined with children's art that's been professionally mounted, and she says they do community art shows regularly where the kids are the docents. The units have hardwood floors with newly renovated efficiency kitchens and large windows overlooking the neighborhood, where sunlight streams in on this muggy summer day.

What Cornerstone offers is immediate: it's not a beautiful place to live, but it's an autonomous place to live. Hacksylo says it's like a first apartment out of college. But it's not a place that seems, at all, like a shelter, where everything is shared, everything is a negotiation with someone else. Families have privacy; most of the sixty or so kids who live here at any given time don't even know they're in a domestic violence program. The units are a kind of visual symbol of hope. That a future without violence can exist for them and for their children. Another way to think about it might be this: empowerment comes with sovereignty.

In the Fire

I'm sitting in a conference room with pale green furniture around a long oval conference table in downtown Newburyport. Kelly Dunne sits to my left at the head of the table, wearing a black skirt and flats, her hair blond-tipped. A stack of files sits in manila folders in front of her. Detective Wile, in khaki shorts and running shoes, sits across from Howie Adams, a police sergeant from Newburyport, just back from vacation. Wile has a deep end-of-summer tan. Just outside, the Merrimack River joins the Atlantic Ocean, and white sailboats bob in aquamarine water in a ubiquitous New England summer scene. Signs advertise whale-watching tours and trips to Plum Island. Newburyport itself, which was once a run-down, blue-collar mill town, has gentrified, and now boutiques, organic restaurants, and local galleries proliferate. Probation, parole, the Merrimack police department, batterer intervention programs, and the local hospital all have representatives sitting around the table with us. Dunne and her colleague, Kate Johnson, head the meeting.

I've come to Newburyport because it is one thing to understand, in the abstract, that communication can improve a system, but I wanted to see precisely how a High Risk Team could strategize on the ground to get victims out of danger. I agreed to not identify anyone from Dunne's caseload, and not to quote any healthcare team members who are barred by HIPAA confidentiality. If a detail was part of a public record, say a police report, then I'd use that, but otherwise, the primary way I was able to include specific details from any one case was if the detail is present in multiple cases; for example, there is a case where an abuser threatened to break CDs and slit his wife's throat with them. Seems incredibly specific, identifiable to a certain couple, but as it turns out, Dunne sees this particular threat frequently (though presumably less often with the advent of streaming . . . which I realize sounds a little ridiculous, but is also probably true. Spotify saves lives.). This is how we agreed to maintain the safety of victims while also allowing me to see firsthand how it all worked.

Cases are referred largely by Dunne's team or through one of the police departments, and the team votes on which referrals wind up in their roster. (Cases can remain active for years.) About 10% of all domestic violence cases are high risk for them. They scrutinize each case for changes—a new pregnancy, an attempt to leave, an abuser going off probation or parole, the violation of a restraining order, the loss of a job, an incendiary Facebook posting. They look at case histories and patterns of offender behavior through the lens of Campbell's risk indicators. The day before, sitting in Dunne's office, she handed me a stack of several dozen police reports with the names redacted to give me a sense of what she deals with on a daily basis. I sat on a soft couch in an unused room at the crisis center, white noise machines whirring simultaneously all down the hallway (so clients have privacy when they meet advocates). It reminded me of a yoga studio, all muted colors and soft lighting, and felt like a shocking inverse to the horror of what I sat reading:

> *"It's not clear how I got on the kitchen floor but the next thing I remember is* [X] *on top of me strangling me with both hands."* *"*[X] *made threats to me in the past about killing me, putting me in the chest freezer, & then taking my body out onto his boat & chumming me into the ocean. He also stated that he could kill me and put my body in his septic tank."* *"*[X] *held her repeatedly against the heating pipes."* *"*[He] *would . . . gut her and hang her up like a deer to bleed."* *"If I decide to bring home another woman with me, you'll do what I tell you to do with her. I am your master, you are my slave. If you don't do as I say and keep me happy, I will kill you."* *"*[X] *frequently makes threats to* [her] *life, including breaking her CDs in the car . . . and threatening to slice her neck open with them while she is driving."* *"*[X] *held her hostage with a rifle . . .* [and] *stated he would 'set up' over 1,000 yards away and 'take her out.'"*

Earlier, I'd spoken with one client whose abuser, her ex-husband, had been put on GPS monitoring by the team. (She spent more than a year in protection as part of the Commonwealth of Massachusetts Address Confidentiality Program.) She told me, "He doesn't have the judgment of someone who has something to lose." It reminded me of James

Baldwin, *The Fire Next Time*. "The most dangerous creation of any society is that man who has nothing to lose."

The day I attend, Dunne and Johnson have fourteen cases to discuss. One of the first problems they encounter involves the privacy of medical information. It was a case of severe strangulation by her ex-husband. The woman had called the crisis center, gotten an active restraining order against him, and was put in the high risk roster. He, in turn, was put on probation. But in the past week, he'd called her and threatened suicide. She phoned the paramedics and he was taken to the hospital. Afterward, he was jailed for violation of his probation, where he now was being held. The team has to strategize about what might happen upon his release. Can he be referred involuntarily to a psychiatric ward? Was there any indication of his demeanor at the hospital? The hospital representative, Moe Lord, is mostly silent even though she may well have been there when he came in and recognized his name from an earlier high risk meeting; HIPAA laws restrict her from saying almost anything. She tells Dunne she can't speak to his demeanor. She says generally she often sees guys come into the hospital wearing GPS ankle bracelets and knows it likely means they're abusers on probation. She also sees women with suspicious injuries, but unless a patient discusses the situation with her, she can't even call the police on a restraining order violation. Still, she's here because getting a sense of these cases enables her to try to intervene with known victims should one wind up in her emergency room. She'll at least be able to share information about Dunne's agency, and give a sense of how that victim can get specific help.

"Is there a mechanism at all for when [abusers will] be discharged, to call the police?" Dunne asks Lord.

"If we know about it and he gives us permission to speak," Lord says.

"So he could walk right out of there?" Dunne asks, referring to the hospital. This is a dangerous scenario. He's broken his restraining order, and the victim has called the police on him, which is likely to escalate the situation, and enrage him even more.

Lord nods.

Dunne's face flusters with frustration. She glances down at the file in front of her, forehead creased in concentration. She has always struck me as uniquely unflappable, steady under stress.

A probation officer in attendance says the victim came to see him after she called police, and Detective Wile, it turns out, knows the abuser. He offers a history of accusations from other victims (which I am not allowed to include here). Wile has lived in this part of the country for his whole life. He seems to know every family from every small town around here and in meetings he will often wax on about this family or the other and their years of being in and out of trouble, or years of drug abuse, or what brother married some sister from a family two streets away and now he's watching the kids of those kids start to get in trouble. He's fond of the word "knucklehead."

"I would think the exception would be the Tarasoff warning," Dunne says, finally. She is referring to a warning required of mental health professionals when there is a credible danger to a victim. It's sometimes called, simply, the "duty to warn."

Lord considers this, nodding, and says, "If I know about it." If she knows, in other words, that an abuser she recognizes from their case-load could be a credible danger to a victim upon his release. "I think we just figured a work-around," Dunne says to Lord. "If in the future we had a more dangerous case, if you heard from probation there's just a warrant, you can't do anything. [But] if you heard the information a little differently   like he's made a threat against her life, that's a Tarasoff."

Lord nods at the possibility.

The team strategizes a coordinated plan for each case. Sometimes, the police do extra drive-bys or home visits. They'll note the cars at the house, lights on or off that are unusual. I remember one story of an officer who saw a light on in the upstairs window of a home he was tasked with watching. He stopped in at the house, asked the victim if everything was okay. It turned out her kid had turned on the attic light. When the officer drove away, he circled back—it's a common stalking tactic for abusers to be watching for a police drive-by and then show up just as the officer rounds the corner. But the police in this part of the country are well aware of this tactic from the High Risk Team. So the officer drove around the block, circled back to the house two minutes after he left, and found the abuser there, just getting out of his car.

Other times, an abuser might be put on GPS, or have exclusion zones—usually entire towns—he is barred from entering. They might place a victim in transitional housing or help with legal fees and representation or give safety training. They might change locks or provide new cell phones to the children and the victim. "If you care about the long-term health of a victim, not having them killed is not enough," Dunne says. "When that offender goes to jail, her physical safety may be okay, but her life might unravel [with] the loss of support. You have to restore that victim back to the state they were in before that violence occurred."

To Dunne, this is critical. Victims often come with their own set of issues. Addiction, poverty, unemployment. Dunne is not trying to fix every aspect of someone's life. She's trying to get them out of danger to a space where they may be able to think through solutions to more systemic problems—like employment or addiction. To maybe give them the emotional and physical and mental space to address some of these other issues.

"The key with domestic violence," says Dunne, "is addressing it in misdemeanor phase." One of the more challenging elements of domestic violence is that ideally you want to stop abuse from escalating. But for that to happen, misdemeanors need to be taken far more seriously than they generally are in intimate partner violence cases. Like the case in San Francisco with Tari Ramirez and Claire Joyce Tempongko. Some of the most extreme violence in cases like this are misdemeanors, for which abusers are given shockingly light sentences. Ramirez, recall, was given only six months. Even Donte Lewis was given only four years for kidnapping his girlfriend and hitting her so hard on the head she foamed at the mouth and passed out. And many perpetrators like Ramirez go straight from a misdemeanor to a murder. But for the judiciary, the challenge is what to charge an offender with and how much the court can and will respond in an attempt to stop the behavior.

One of the most effective tools for the High Risk Team is a Massachusetts bail statute called a 58A, or dangerousness hearing. A standard bail hearing is meant to determine an offender's flight risk, whereas a 58A can be requested by the district attorney and allows defendants, even those with clean records, to be held in the misdemeanor phase without bail until trial if they are deemed a sufficient threat to an individual or community. The statute might have prevented the release of William Cotter and saved Dorothy's life, but it was seldom used for domestic violence cases at the time and so not on Dunne's radar, and the details of the Cotters' situation were scattered among agencies. In Massachusetts, offenders can be held for 180 days. "A lot of violence happens between arraignment and disposition," Dunne says. "We contain the offender so the victim doesn't have to be contained." Few states have such a clear dangerousness statute, and in her trainings now Dunne encourages advocates to search their states' bail statutes for something similar. Many advocates simply don't know to look, though even when they do go back and research their own states' bail statutes, they're almost sure to be disappointed. In April 2018, Pennsylvania became only the second state to pass such a statute allowing a judge to take into consideration, specifically, the dangerousness of a domestic violence abuser.[1]

The 58A belongs to a category of bail statutes known as preventive detention, and Dunne says in her trainings across the country, she almost never meets other advocates who have something like the 58A. Most, in fact, ask her how they can get such a statute passed in their jurisdictions. "Many states have preventive detention statutes," said Cherise Fanno Burdeen, the chief executive officer of the Pretrial Justice Institute, an advocacy group that works with communities on effective bail practices. "But they are sorely underused. The systems use work-arounds which unfortunately don't always work, meaning dangerous people leave jails every day, unsupervised."

Preventive detention statutes emerged from federal legislation called the Bail Reform Act of 1984, which allows a defendant to be held pretrial if he or she is deemed dangerous enough to another person or to a community. A determination of dangerousness includes factors like the nature of the crime, the evidence against the defendant, and the history of criminal activity, among others; most often, these statutes have been used in gang or drug cases, though Massachusetts has seen a marked increase in their use for domestic violence.

While no one tracks how often such hearings are held—either in Massachusetts or nationally—each state differs slightly in how preventive detention statutes are implemented and on what grounds. One common thread, however, is the controversy of whether to use preventive detention at all. "The Constitution tends to frown upon punishing prospective behavior," Ronald S. Sullivan Jr., the director of the Harvard Criminal Justice Institute, told me. "We punish past behavior that's been proven. Here we're keeping people in jail because we think they'll be dangerous." But Viktoria Kristiansson, an attorney adviser for AEquitas, cited the importance of the dangerousness hearing, claiming it "automatically provides a different context for a judge to analyze the evidence."

Holding an abuser before trial has helped to keep victims out of shelter; it provides them with the time to find alternative housing, save some money, find counseling, and perhaps find a job. "We know that arrest, in and of itself, is protective," Dunne told me. "You're trying to disrupt that escalating cycle of violence." Holding an abuser in jail prior to a judgment in court allows victims time to regroup, to put their lives in order prior to the trial when the danger levels increase again. Dunne says it's been critical to their success. And of the offenders monitored by GPS bracelets in Dunne's caseload, not a single one has re-assaulted and nearly 60% of them have been held pretrial using a dangerousness hearing in her jurisdiction. Though no one has tracked how much the 58A was used before the High Risk Team was created, anecdotally Dunne said she saw "maybe five in three years" before Dorothy's homicide. "Now we see two a month."

THE LAST CASE OF the day is an immigrant woman and her abusive partner. He is currently in jail for assault and battery—which jeopardizes his immigration status—but the couple has a small child currently staying outside the country with the abuser's family. The family has threatened that if the charges against the abuser are not dropped, the young mother may never see her child again, and if her partner is deported before she gets her child back, she also may never see the child again. What this means is that she cannot testify without potentially losing her child; she cannot, in fact, appear to be siding with the prosecution at all. It's the kind of insurmountable situation that both victims and prosecutors alike find themselves in. Though it hasn't happened yet, the team fully expects her to recant. Sergeant Adams describes the couple's history in the affidavit from the night of the arrest, most of which I cannot recount here, except to say that he had so isolated her that he wouldn't allow her to make calls on her cell phone to anyone but him, and he had set up cameras inside their home to keep tabs on her.

Wile suggests an amendment to the complaint that will add several additional charges that, he says, "will give the DA's office something to work with. If you can get eight or nine charges out of one incident, it's a better shot that she won't have to take the stand, and he'll plead on some of those." Wile is referring to several different elements here. The first is to try to charge an abuser with as many allegations as possible in order to negotiate some kind of plea deal, even beyond the violent incident. Are there possible drug charges? Is there an illegal weapon or firearm in the house? This also offers a better chance that at least *some* of the charges might stick. The other element Wile is referencing is called evidence-based prosecution. Meaning "evidence" rather than "witness" based. A prosecutor can offer up enough evidence in court that a witness wouldn't have to come and testify in front of her abuser. Such evidence may include photos, affidavits, witness testimonies, prior records, or 911 tapes.

This is how, for example, Stacy Tenney and Michelle's family could have prosecuted Rocky Mosure with or without Michelle's testimony had they ever found that snake. They could have coupled that with an affidavit about the time Rocky threatened them all with Michelle's grandfather's gun, or, had they known, about the many times he'd stalked Michelle on her way to and from school or kidnapped the children as leverage. Had they been able to hold him for dangerousness prior to trial, they'd have learned he was in and out of work, on and off drugs. They could have known all of this, acted on this and perhaps more if they'd had, back in 2001, a High Risk Team sharing information, creating a more complete picture of the situation across bureaucratic borders.

Evidence-based prosecution for domestic violence cases existed back when Michelle recanted, too. Ellen Pence, the advocate in Duluth, Minnesota, who'd created the Power and Control Wheel, was advocating for it way back in the 1980s. But it wasn't until Casey Gwinn, then a prosecutor in San Diego, took notice of her efforts and began to bring one such case after another to trial in his jurisdiction that the evidence-based movement in domestic violence really took off. Gwinn traveled to Duluth and met with Pence, learned about her advocacy, and returned to San Diego just in time to try his first evidence-based domestic violence case—against a sitting judge named Joe Davis. Davis's girlfriend had recanted, and then disappeared. But Gwinn pressed charges anyway.

And in front of local media and television cameras, he lost the case.

It was a humiliating defeat. The whole trial had been intensely followed in the region, given that it was against a judge, and Gwinn told me he just "made a fool of himself . . . I didn't know what I was doing."

But after the Davis trial, the San Diego city attorney at the time, John Witt, called Gwinn in to his office and told him it was going to be difficult for both of them, for their entire office, for a while, but that he believed in what Gwinn had attempted to do. "He told me to go out and figure out how to win these cases," Gwinn said.

Gwinn began ordering 911 tapes in all domestic violence cases—something he'd never done prior to Davis. And he asked the police to take pictures of everything: the crime scene, the victims, even the perpetrators if they were raging in the backs of police vehicles. Any possible shred of evidence that existed, Gwinn wanted. He began to go out to roll calls at local police departments, asking them to gather more and more evidence. When one sergeant told him his entire mission was bullshit, that Gwinn was never going to prosecute these cases, Gwinn created a messaging system to let police know how their cases were resolved.

Gwinn tried twenty-one cases in a row, all domestic violence misdemeanors. All without the victim testifying.

He won seventeen of them.

By the time VAWA passed in 1994, Gwinn had trained attorneys around the country on evidence-based prosecutions in domestic violence cases. (It's a bit of a misnomer to call them evidence-based since all trials are, technically, based on evidence.) He came to fervently believe that if we could prosecute murderers without a victim's cooperation, we could prosecute batterers. In 1996, Gwinn was elected city attorney of San Diego and he made good on a campaign promise to devote 10% of his entire office to a domestic violence unit. By now, jurisdictions around the country came to him for training. Gwinn said they went from prosecuting fewer than 5% of domestic violence cases in the 1980s to some jurisdictions prosecuting 80% of such cases by the late 1990s.[2]

Then, in 2004, Crawford came.

In *Crawford v. Washington* the Supreme Court ruled that cross-examination is required of witnesses at trial unless a witness was unavailable (e.g., sick or dead). The court said that a defendant had the Constitutional right to face his accusers, that testimonial statements by witnesses who did not appear at trial were hearsay. And hearsay was not admissible.[3] This meant victims who were too terrified to appear in court but were otherwise healthy could no longer allow prosecutors to use their statements.

Post-*Crawford*, there is still some room for state courts to determine admissible evidence using their own discretion, but generally speaking *Crawford* had a profound effect on the movement of evidence-based domestic violence cases across the country. These days, victim statements are often inadmissible in court proceedings if a witness is uncooperative (as happens in as many as 70% of cases).[4] "The barrier to evidence-based prosecution is not about evidence," Gwinn said. "It's not about the viability of winning these cases. It's about cultural norms and values. And at the heart of it is a stunning amount of misogyny."

ONE OF THE CRITIQUES levied at the Newburyport model is that scaling up to a busy urban setting where resources are scarce and domestic violence calls nonstop would prove difficult. Mark Gagnon, the former chief of police in Amesbury, dismisses this criticism. "A bigger community's going to have more resources," he says. "It can be done, just at a different level." Dunne recognizes the challenge of scaling up, but says it's a matter of dividing territory into manageable jurisdictions. Urban areas in Massachusetts like Framingham, Lynn, and Cambridge have undergone trainings by Dunne and Wile and developed High Risk Teams. "I think one of the benefits of the model is that it not only changes things for the victims, but it changes things for *everyone*," said Mary Gianakis, former director of Framingham's Voices Against Violence and head of their High Risk Team. "It changes the way every spoke on the wheel approaches domestic violence . . . I also think it sends a clear message to perpetrators. That as a community, we're not going to tolerate this kind of violence . . . It's an important message, because it changes the culture."

Today, Kelly Dunne and Robert Wile have trained tens of thousands of people across the entire country. And groups from California to Louisiana, Florida to Illinois, have asked for the training. Campbell did the research, but Dubus and Dunne put theory into practice, she said. "They were informed by my work, and now I'm informed by theirs," Campbell told me. Former vice president Joseph Biden championed the Amesbury program in October of 2010, when he honored Suzanne Dubus at a White House event to mark Domestic Violence Awareness Month. "We need to replace what we have been doing and replicate this kind of success," he said to those gathered.

To Dunne, their success demonstrates how a seemingly intractable problem can be addressed at relatively low cost, through coordination, the sharing of information and pure vigilance. "With Dorothy's case we were looking for a fire alarm while we were in the fire," Dunne said. "And you can't do that. You need a system already in place." Prior to the team's formation in 2005, the town of Amesbury alone had on average one domestic violence homicide per year. Since they began, Dubus and Dunne have not had a single homicide in their caseload. What is of equal importance to Dunne, though, is that they have had to put fewer than 10% of the survivors in shelter; before 2005 that number would have been above 90%. To Dubus, it seems obvious to create a model in which the victims are protected rather than banished. "Here's the outrage," she told me. "It's really cheap to do what we're doing. It's a lot cheaper than murder investigations and prosecutions and jail time."

In late 2012, the Department of Justice's Office on Violence Against Women in Washington, D.C., earmarked half a million dollars to replicate the High Risk Program, along with another out of Maryland called the Lethality Assessment Program. Twelve sites around the country were originally considered, including Rutland, Vermont; Brooklyn, New York; and Miami, Florida. In the end, only one test site got the green light from OVW to replicate Dunne's program: Cleveland, Ohio.[5]

In the state of Ohio, between July 1, 2016 and June 30, 2017, there were 115 domestic violence homicides.[6] The year 2016 alone had more than seventy thousand domestic violence incidents (just over half had charges filed).[7] "Seventy thousand calls," said Tim Boehnlein, of the Cuyahoga County Victim Witness Service Center, who is also one of the two leaders of the High Risk Team in Cleveland. (The other is the Domestic Violence and Child Advocacy Center.) "That's a lot of people whose lives are being affected by domestic violence, a lot of families."

The city of Cleveland is divided into five districts within the police department; the three inner districts had domestic violence officers, but neither the first nor the fifth districts—the city's far east and far west sides—had the capacity to deal with the overwhelming number of domestic violence calls daily. So that's where the city targeted its new high risk experiment, beginning in October 2016.

Dunne called me at home one afternoon just after she'd returned from one of her training sessions in Cleveland. "There's someone you have to go meet," she told me. "Don't ask me anything. Just go."

Grace Under Pressure

In a dim, smoky apartment dominated by chocolate brown springy couches, a barefoot toddler wails. The toddler, whom I'll call Joey, has a head of loopy curls and knocks over a metal kitchen chair. Another boy picks it up. He knocks it over again and vaults over the chairback several times. There is a TV on in the kitchen. A bowl of soggy Cheerios on the table that no one is eating. Across from me is an adolescent boy with pale skin who is hauntingly quiet. I'll call him Mark. He is used to the racket by his little brother, who has autism. He also has other siblings with other special needs. The toddler marches into the living room and runs to his mother's knees, then takes a business card she's set on the end table beside her. "Joey," says the detective sitting next to the mother, "Joey, don't you take that card now."

Detective Martina Latessa speaks with a kind of generic urban accent. The Bronx, maybe. East Coast, gritty neighborhood speak. Except she's never lived outside of Cleveland, where we are now. Joey ignores her; it's unclear if he understands. She's smiling at the boy. "Yo," she says, "you hear me, Joey? Don't you take that card." Joey skip-hops barefoot back to the kitchen, card in hand. He trampolines on the kitchen floor, falls to his bum, scoots away to where I can't see him. Detective Latessa's face is serious again the minute Joey's out the door, and she turns to the mother, "The reason your case is assigned to me is, I'm out of the domestic violence unit. I'm not out of the fifth district [where this house is located]. I'm what's called the Homicide Reduction Unit, a task force." She lets the words vibrate in the atmosphere.

Homicide.

Reduction.

Unit.

She has the woman's full attention now. I'll call her Grace. She pulls her oversized sweater down over her hands, shrinks into the couch. Her focus entirely on Martina. Mark sits on the other side of Martina, rubbing his hands between his knobby knees, watching his mother's face. He is pale as a stone.

"If I handle your case," Martina says, "you're at the highest risk of being killed, okay? You understand?"

Tears begin to slide down Grace's face.

"Is that hard to hear?"

She nods.

In the kitchen, Joey is screeching. Ear-shattering, nerve-racking screeches. We sit on the soft couches, springs worn down from use, and a guinea pig twitches in a cage on a nearby shelf.

"I'm going to need you to let me do my job," Martina tells her, "so I can protect you and your [kids], okay?"

Grace wipes at her nose with her sleeve, nodding. Her hair is pulled back in a ponytail. Someone leads Joey to a back bedroom, where his screeching is muffled, and it's a relief for a moment. But then, within seconds, he's back, and he's jumping again on the back of the chair.

"It's going to be hard," Martina says. She seems not only unfazed by Joey, but also as if she can't hear him at all. "And this is not going to go away. You're going to take back your life and start taking it back today, okay?"

Grace is nodding, nodding, nodding.

Martina turns, suddenly to Mark. "You pet that thing?"

I'm a beat behind her. Then I see what she means: the jittery guinea pig.

"Yeah," Mark whispers in a half statement, half question.

"You better not be mean to that animal," she says. She grins at the boy, pointing with her pen to the guinea pig. It takes a moment to understand how natural this shift was, her emotional read of the room. She's just told a young boy that his mother is standing on the precipice of being killed, and that mother is sobbing. There is almost nothing more terrifying to a child than seeing an adult—who is meant to be in control, who is meant to have all the answers—break down sobbing. Martina has an organic talent for reading an environment, maneuvering around the delicate emotional edges. She's lightening the mood. And if you're someone who has just been told in front of your adolescent son that you are first in line to be the city's next murder victim—you can now take a beat to gather yourself. "He better have food and water at all times," Martina says, in her Very Official "police who can kid with kids" voice. Mark's grinning. He pulls his knees up to his chin and rests his head there, watching her with a blend of awe and shyness.

And then she's back to Grace, holding out a mug shot: "Is this him?"

TO UNDERSTAND HOW EFFECTIVE Martina Latessa is at her job, it might help to think about a small plastic animal she has on her desk. From the front, it has the body of a frog, from the back, a chameleon, and it is so colorful that it's futile to search for clues as to its identification. It's not like anything found in nature. It looks like one thing from one angle, another thing from another angle, and—when viewed as a whole—is something in a category unto itself. It's disarming, also funny, and a little bit ridiculous.

You don't have to go far to find metaphors in Martina's world.

She is one of Cleveland's two domestic violence detectives dedicated to high risk cases. A high risk domestic violence detective, if you will, though the title is clunky. This position—in a demanding, high volume urban area—is brand new. She and her counterpart, Greg Williams, may well be the only ones in the country. (There are many places that have dedicated domestic violence detectives or police officers, but I have yet to meet one who handles a major city's high risk cases, only. Kelly Dunne couldn't confirm that Martina and Greg are the only ones, but she had never come across others.) So the title is also unique.

Martina is preternaturally suited to her job, perhaps the most effective police officer I've ever seen on a domestic violence case. When I mention this to her, she says, "You lie!" But her blush gives her away. (When she introduces me around the department, she says, "This is Rachel I-hate-the-Cleveland-police Snyder." Later, I will learn that my best defense is calling her a Steelers fan.) It's this chameleon-like quality she has about her—in the space of a few moments, she can communicate the unbelievable danger that Grace is in, joke around with Mark like it's just another day in the life of an adolescent boy and his pet, and kid around with Joey that he better watch himself. Most people, myself included, when presented with an autistic toddler, would likely just ignore the child. Maybe ask if someone can watch him for a moment. Martina brings him right into the action. It's a subtle way of telling Grace, "I see how complicated your life is, and it won't put me off." Later, she'll tell me she knew he had autism the second she walked in the door.

That Martina is a woman, frankly, seems entirely meaningful to me, though her supervisor, Shamode Wimberly, disagrees. Gender doesn't matter, Wimberly believes, if someone is good at her job. And Martina seems to do the work of three people. But in my view, the fact that she is a woman speaking mostly to women is significant. That she meets victims in their own homes, or the homes of friends and family, rather than forcing them through a bureaucratic maze of departments and courthouses and crisis centers, is meaningful. That she jokes around, asks about the rest of their lives, spends as many hours as it takes, is meaningful. That she is only one person, a severely limited resource, is also meaningful.

Martina grew up on Cleveland's west side in a family of thirteen kids, one set of parents. She has so many nieces and nephews she rounds up (to forty). The first time I meet her, she tells me she grew up in a house that stared into Ariel Castro's backyard, where he held Michelle Knight, Amanda Berry, and Gina DeJesus for a decade. No one could believe it when the news broke. A house close enough to shoot a damn arrow into. That neighborhood was like a small town; everyone knew someone who knew those girls. The talk of them, how they'd just vanished, came up often throughout the years.

We drive past the house where Martina grew up, a two-story, postwar house, wooden siding, gabled roof. She's driving a dark blue undercover car, one of those V-8s with plush seats, bouncy springs, a radio in front that occasionally crackles a police code. Her curly hair is pulled back in a ponytail as tight as an Olympic gymnast's. She slows the car and points across the street to what was Castro's backyard. The house has since been demolished. Martina, who's been on the Cleveland police for eighteen years, was already a detective by the time the three were found in 2013.

When Martina was a kid, there was a neighbor murdered right next door to her. A man named Nick who used to eat pigeons and toss the bones into her family's backyard. She can't remember his last name. The murderers ended up being Martina's older sister's boyfriend and his friends. ("They served their twenty-five years. They're out now," she told me.) The murder scared the hell out of her. The street was jammed with police, with emergency medical technicians, and the coroner was there. And then suddenly, they were all leaving and she started to cry. She counted the houses: Nick's was first on the block, and then her house was second. She thought her family was next. That tomorrow whoever murdered Nick would come and murder her and the rest of her family. A homicide detective saw her crying, and he came over and sat down on her front porch with her. He promised her he'd come and check up on her. She points to that day, that very moment when she made up her mind not just that she wanted to be a police officer, but that she wanted to be a homicide detective.

This is her three-decade-long dream. It sounds apocryphal. A bit put on for an audience of one reporter. Except I return again and again to Cleveland, spend days with Martina Latessa, and the murder of her neighbor, it becomes clear, exists somewhere in the very front of her mind. She's tried over the years to look up his case, to find out the name of that homicide detective. But homicide paperwork in the 1980s was an entirely different and noncomputerized system, and she's never found anything. Sometimes she'll pass someone in the hall that she knows—a special unit officer, a street cop, a newbie in training—and the murder of her next-door neighbor will work its way into the conversation. She took me down to homicide one day, walked in the door and said to the entire room. "You got a space for me yet? This is Rachel I-hate-the-Cleveland-police Snyder." It's a running joke, how much she wants to move to the homicide unit. A detective calls out and asks if she ever found that old case file, the one she's always talking about. She says, "Nah," but she will one day soon, go marching down to the basement where the old hand-written files are kept. One morning before she is due in court, she runs into one of her old mentors. He's retired now and works as security for the courthouse now and again. She asks him about her chances to get to homicide, if he thinks she'll get the next opening. "Why you want to work down there?" he asks her. "There's nothing to solve. Everyone's dead." He tells me he has a T-shirt that reads, *My day starts when yours ends.* (Months later I recount this slogan to a retired officer in San Diego and he says, "Yeah. I think every PD [police department] has that shirt.")

Lynn Nesbitt, who is a domestic violence advocate with a desk just over from Martina's, says they can't quite bear to think about Martina leaving. And even Martina herself seems torn about it. She won't say it, but I suspect she knows she's unique. She blushes at compliments, bats them away with sarcasm. ("You a damn liar" is one of her favorites. Another, "That's crazy as cat shit.") She's always been one of those women operating in a world of men, and now for maybe the first time in her law enforcement history, the fact that she's a woman is a benefit. She gets victims to talk in ways I've never seen from a man. Even some of the detectives in her own unit, as good as they are, are unlikely to get the kind of victim's cooperation that she manages to get. There are stats that suggest victim cooperation in domestic violence cases is as low as 20% in some jurisdictions. And there are plenty of police around the country who still believe if a victim won't cooperate, then there's no point in even writing a report, let alone a prosecutor filing charges.

Martina grew up going to Catholic school, wore the uniform and everything. A good girl. But her neighborhood was gritty, dangerous. She'd walk home from school skipping around used needles. She knew in only a vague way what they were. Other kids would ask her if she wanted to smoke weed, if she wanted to drink beer, if she wanted to try this or that drug, and her answer was always the same: no. No, no, no. Because she had that idea of being a homicide detective planted in her brain at age nine, and she never wavered from it for a day. She kept herself clean. Lived in the ghetto, but was not of the ghetto. Her parents fought, but there was never any violence. She said her father wore the pants in the family, but her mother picked out the ones he was going wear.

One afternoon, when she was ten or eleven, she was at an older relative's house when the woman's husband came home and started beating on her. It scared the shit out of Martina. She ran out of the house, down the street to the pay phone. She called her older brother, told him what was happening. "It didn't even occur to me to call the police," she said. Her brother came, and they went back to the house, but by then, the husband had left, and Martina's relative said it was all okay and no big deal, and just forget about it.

The single most defining element of Martina's life, beyond police work, is sports. Her senior year of high school, she took the rap for something she says a friend of hers did (she won't tell me what it was), and she was kicked off the basketball team. At the time, she was devastated. Basketball had been her focus ever since junior high. In her family of thirteen kids, she was arguably the most gifted athlete, a natural talent in everything from softball to golf, but basketball was her main love back then. She wound up learning from a friend about a local league run through Cleveland's public recreation centers. Being the talent that she was, she spent her senior year playing on that league all over the city and for her—a sheltered girl from Catholic school—it was like a crash course in street smarts. Suddenly, neighbors who'd lived around her all her life but who'd always been strangers became her friends. She befriended a local family of sisters named the Koziols—all of whom were as serious about sports as she was—and one of them, Maryanne Koziol, offered her a job at Cudell Recreation to coach kids—the same place a young boy named Tamir Rice would someday be killed.

"Those Koziol sisters toughed me up," she says. She coached six- and seven-year-olds, the peewee leagues, and ran the summer T-ball program. Then later, she coached young girls and teenagers. Softball, volleyball, wherever she was needed. She met kids who were abused, kids whose parents were drug addicts, kids in foster care. Kids caught in a relentless system of poverty and violence. She heard street lingo for the first time, saw neighborhood drug dealers just hanging around, drumming up business. "Working with [the Koziols] prepared me for what I would face in the police," she says. "Holy shit. Without that toughness they gave me I would have never, ever, ever made it."

One of the sisters, Sue Koziol, played women's flag football and encouraged Martina to try out. She made the team, effortlessly, and they went on to win eleven national championships, playing all over the country for the next decade of her life. From there, she was recruited to play for the Cleveland Fusion, a team in the National Women's Football Alliance. Tackle football. The first time I Googled her, I found an article on her career with the Fusion and I had not, until that moment, known there was a women's tackle football league. (She is retired from tackle now, but still coaches.) The lessons she learned playing organized sports—not pickup games, or backyard sports, but on formal teams—became essential in her police work.

"In order to play sports, you have to be coached," she says. We're talking in her office, which has the kind of industrial gray desks and brown wheeled office chairs that date back to the Nixon administration. She leans in while we're talking. I'm camped in a half-broken chair on wheels, sitting awkwardly between her desk and Williams's, who sits behind her and who once popped his eyeball out and then back in to show me he could do it. "You have to learn to take someone's advice, criticism. Just shut the fuck up and let them teach you," she says.

This is one of her tools with survivors, too. Martina doesn't treat victims as weak or powerless. She doesn't ask them why they stayed, why they married, why they got pregnant. She'll let them know the situation they're in, and the situation their kids are in, but ultimately the most important thing she can do is listen to them. "These victims of domestic, they never have a voice. They can't have an opinion at home. [Abusers] tell them shut up; don't talk to me," she says. "So if I sit down with them you'll see them struggle to get the story out, same thing with Grace, how she cried and struggled, but sometimes it's good to get stuff off your shoulders. I try to give them that opportunity."

On the desk in front of her sits the chameleon-frog-lizard, along with a stack of case files in varying stages of investigation. The beige phones are so old in their office that they date from the *Barney Miller* era. ("We put people on hold, but we can't transfer anybody," she told me earlier. "People think we're just lazy.") One of her coworkers has brought in some hummus, which Martina thinks is too damn fussy for food. She's partial to Mountain Dew and cereal, but every time I was with her, we only ever stopped for a meal once—and then only because I was so hungry I suspect my eyes had drained of life. "If I had to say what makes someone a good investigator, it's your patience," she says. Then she adds, presumably for my benefit, "I'm going to cuss right now; you're going to hear me cuss for the first time [by "first" she means fiftieth] . . . but sometimes policemen and detectives need to shut the fuck up and just listen."

On the wall beside her desk is a saying by Calvin Coolidge: *Don't expect to build up the weak by pulling down the strong.* Beside that is taped a poster of a player from the Cleveland Cavaliers, his body with Martina's head Photoshopped atop it. If you insult the Cavs, Martina will trounce you. The poster was created by a fellow detective named TJ, who Photoshopped similar posters for everyone in their office. TJ once offered to show me his case files for a single year—2016. We went into a separate office, pulled out a file drawer, then a second, then walked back to his office and he pointed to box after box under a conference table. In their first year of operation, they screened sixteen hundred cases for dangerousness, about half of which were deemed high risk. Prior to the team's formation, they estimated they'd get roughly thirty high risk cases a month. In fact, in their first month of operations, October 2016, they had more than eighty, which shocked all of them.[1] Now they have an average of around fifty every month. Cleveland's violence is a lot of things—gangs, drugs, thuggery. But above all else, Cleveland's violence is domestic violence.

Chambering a Round

At Grace's house, Martina shows her the mug shot. Lynn Nesbitt, the domestic violence advocate, is sitting on the other side of Grace. Grace affirms that it is him, her partner, whom I'll call Byron. She signs her name to the paper in front of her—the sheet that Martina will use in her report on Byron and Grace.

"I get nauseated just looking," Grace says.

"Okay," Martina says, and puts the paper away in a clipboard box she's holding on her lap. "You don't have to look at him ever again." She takes out a blank report, ignoring Joey's constant screeching, the television, and even Grace's tears, and she asks Grace to tell her story.

"All of it, or just . . ." Grace asks.

"All of it," Martina says.

MARTINA HAS A REPUTATION for detail in her reports. In the world of domestic violence, a police report is a first step in what can feel like an endless and incomprehensible system. But it's crucial. An incomplete report means possible charges won't get prosecuted, so an abuser who shows many of the most urgent signs of lethality—for example, Rocky Mosure—can easily be dropped by the system. Martina says she is constantly impressing on patrol officers, in the many trainings she conducts, that it's better to be overly detailed than under. I've spoken to prosecutors across the country who look at the thoroughness of police reports as the single most important element they need to make their case.

This is probably the most common complaint I hear, too: that police reports are unspecific, ambiguous, terribly written, lacking in detail. And, as a result, prosecutors will be left with a weak case or often no case. Take that report from the Training Institute on Strangulation Prevention, for example, which found that officers downplayed the incidents because they weren't properly trained on how to identify strangulation injuries that weren't instantly recognizable, like memory loss, a raspy voice, urination or redness in the sclera of the eye.[1] Such reports leave prosecutors with scant evidence.

I think of what might have happened had someone like Martina gone to the Mosure house—not asked Michelle to come in to the office, but gone there herself—and seen the children, seen the control Rocky had over her, been able to make Michelle believe that the system would protect her. It's important to see the environment they're in, Martina told me once, to go to their homes. "I could have had Grace down here all day long, but I wanted to go where it's comfortable for her," she said. "This gives me an idea of who they are, where this all occurred . . . I always say, 'Shame on me as a detective, if I don't get my ass out of this chair, go to her house, take my own pictures.' I want something you can see."

GRACE BEGINS HER STORY for Martina. She and Byron have lived together for several years.[2] They have children together, and she also has children from her previous relationship. Five days earlier, Byron had come home from work drunk, storming in the front door asking where his gun was. "Under the bed," she told him. He went outside to empty some work gear from his car, so she pulled out the gun from under the bed and went outside to give it to him. When he saw her, she says he began playing around like he was going to run her over with the car. She couldn't gauge his mood, if he was serious or kidding. His intoxication made him hard to read. She was half asleep. So she "held the gun up" and she said it "made him flip." Martina asks her to clarify how she was holding the gun. At him? Toward him? "No, over my head," she says.

"And then what happened?"

Grace says, "He starts playing around like he's gonna murder me. So I went back in the house and put it back under the bed." He followed after her, asking where it was.

Then the doorbell rang. This added to the confusion, to the increasing hostility. It was the middle of the night, somewhere around two a.m. Someone had been doing this recently, ringing their doorbell and then running away. They'd never answered it. But Grace says Byron had been accusing her lately of cheating on him, and he'd used the ringing doorbell as evidence of his theory. She didn't know who was at the door and neither of them answered it, but it was an occurrence they'd experienced several times over the past few weeks.

Martina asks if Grace knows who it was.

"No idea."

Byron got the gun back out from under the bed. Grace was awake now, alert. Joey was asleep on the couch. "He pulls it back." Grace mimes with her hands cocking a gun. She doesn't know the lingo.

"That's called 'chambering a round,'" Martina says. "He's putting one in the chamber."

Grace nods. Her son Mark is clasping his fingers together, hands between his knees, eyes trained on the floor. Joey continues to scream and jump on various pieces of furniture that he's been able to knock over.

"Then he lays me down on the bed," Grace says, "and he put it to my temple." She's sniffling as she tells this story, trying not to cry, wiping at her face with the stretched-out sleeve of her sweater. "I could feel the tip moving. I don't know. I don't know how to say it."

"As if you would click the top of a pen, right?" Martina says, demonstrating with her pen.

Grace nods. "He said, 'I know you're fucking around on me. I'm the only one that's been there for you, and you're fucking around on me' . . . He kept saying we were going to be on the news tonight."

Martina interrupts her every few seconds to clarify one point or another: which temple did he hold the gun to? How long did this go on? Where were the children? How long did the doorbell ring for? What was he saying? What was she saying?

Grace continues with her story. Byron tells her over and over how they'll be on the news, how he's the only one who gives a shit about her, and she's hearing him, but she's not hearing him, because he's got that gun trained on her temple and she can hear the clicking of it, and so all she's doing, she says, is laying there with her eyes squeezed shut, and she's praying.

"What're you praying for?" Martina asks.

"I was saying goodbye to my kids in my head and telling them I loved them, because I was sure he would kill me." She's crying again now and Lynn hands her a tissue. Mark is crying a little, too, but also trying to hold it in, and I can see his chest heaving a little bit. He's a little man, standing right there on the brink of adulthood, stranded between feeling like he wants to save his mom and needing her to protect him.

I want to stop here in this moment and acknowledge how easy it would be to blow past, how important it is to really understand. The

Danger Assessment is one thing that gives an idea of risk, a kind of mathematical calculation of a life in which there are infinite variables. Martina's question is the kind of drilling down detail that many don't think to do—police, advocates, even attorneys. They ask for the facts, the play-by-play of a violent moment, but they may not ask what the person was thinking or feeling in that same moment. But Martina learns, from Grace's answer, not only about Byron's dangerousness, and his carelessness with another life, but also about Grace's vulnerability. *She* thought she was going to die. This is sometimes where the discrepancy comes from when people say victims aren't aware of the dangerousness of their own situations: it's not so much that they're unaware as that they don't know they know. A kind of cognitive dissonance. Martina will underscore then what Grace knows, but may not be fully aware of: that she can trust her own gauge of danger. She is Michelle. She is Dorothy.

Even if Byron didn't mean to kill her, Grace says, he was drunk, and he had the gun cocked back, and he could have slipped, accidentally pulled the trigger.

"Can he hear you praying?" Martina asks.

"No," Grace says. She shakes her head. Martina lets her collect herself. She asks another boy who'd been in a back bedroom to watch Joey, take him out of the living room. After that, Grace says, he pulled her up by her hair off the bed and slapped her. Or maybe he punched her. She doesn't remember exactly. It happened three times. Punches or slaps. Her eye has marks around it, but they're faded now. She couldn't call the police for nearly a week, because he didn't work that whole week and so kept her in the house. The kind of passive hostage Kit Gruelle talks about. Byron didn't have to lay a hand on her after that. He already had her cowering.

She lived with him all during that week, obeying him, listening to him, pretending it was all okay, she was okay, what he had done was okay. Her love was bigger than his violence for a long time, but this time—when he bought her flowers the next day for the first time ever—scared her just enough. She spent five days making him believe that love was still enough to forgive him (and maybe she wanted to keep on believing it, too, for another minute). She pretended to love him to stay alive and to keep her children alive. And the moment she had a window of freedom—the very next time Byron left for work—she ran. Took her kids and ran across town. And that was yesterday. And she called the police as soon as she could, and they sent a zone car to take her report, and the report landed on Martina's desk this morning because Grace was scored as high risk by the police and so here we all are. Grace has been out of the house for less than a day and doesn't quite know what comes next: the rest of her life or imminent death.

After he slapped her, Grace says, she fell to the floor and pretended to pass out. Then she mentions to Martina and Lynn Nesbitt, almost like it's an aside, how several years earlier she'd had a brain injury. She was fine now, for the most part, but she feared that his pounding on her would exacerbate that earlier injury and she'd die accidentally. As she lay on the floor pretending to have passed out, though, he saw right through her act, she says. He lifted her under her arms, banged her into the wall, and said, "You want to play dead? Okay. I'll shoot you right now if you want to play dead."

That's when Joey darts into the room and climbs up his mother's shins, snatches Martina's business card from his mom's lap.

"Joey," Martina says. "Joey, don't you take that card!" But she's smiling at the boy; she opens her clipboard case, takes out another one, and hands it to Grace.

Martina tells me later the thing that really signaled the dangerousness of Grace's situation was her pretending to play as if she'd passed out. "That to me is every sign of wrong," Martina said. "You got to play like you're passed out?" After a mass shooting, people often describe how they played dead to stay alive. In Sutherland Springs, for example, a victim named Rosanne Solis told the media, "I played dead and it saved my life."[3] During the Orlando Pulse nightclub shooting, a young man named Marcus Godden said he "lay on the ground. I could hear shots. I played dead."[4] In Oregon, in Tobago, in Mississippi, in Norway, in England, shooting victims use this exact phrase: "I played dead." For victims of intimate partner terrorism, it's an autonomous survival response. They play dead, and play dead, and play dead again.

Once Grace finishes her story, Martina goes back over the entire thing in detail, this time repeating it back to Grace to make sure she has it all right. "I don't want to put words in your mouth," she says. Was his first slap before or after he held the gun to you? Did he slam you onto the bed first or into the wall? Slaps or punches? What happened after? He made you swear you wouldn't call the cops on him or he'd take Joey? Okay. Okay. Okay. Martina's scribbling notes as Grace talks.

Grace mentions again the flowers he bought the next day. That's when she got really scared. Because he'd never bought her flowers before. He didn't apologize. But he bought her those flowers. It reminds me of a poster in Martina's office: *He beat her 150 times. She only got flowers once.* The pink and white flowers are atop a casket. Byron told her that if she ever called the cops on him, and he got picked up, he'd get a local gang after her. The Zulus. He told her they owed him.

"Dumbass," Martina says, of Byron. She knows all about the Zulus. "They're mainly a social thing, not like the Heartless Felons. I'm not worried about the Zulus from a police perspective, but that doesn't necessarily mean there's not an idiot in there that's crazy."

Grace nods but doesn't look convinced by this. Nesbitt asks if she's had a doctor check her (she hasn't). Joey is back and forth, running into the living room, the kitchen, the back bedroom, zooming like a lizard. Martina nudges Mark. "Why don't you take him in back for a minute?"

Once they're gone, she pitches herself on the edge of the couch, facing Grace. "This is the most dangerous time for you," she says, "so we're going to hurry up and get this warrant out." Even though it's Sunday, the warrant will be issued immediately. Martina writes down her cell number. It's her second cell, actually, a phone dedicated just to the victims she meets with. She tells Grace to call her any time of day or night. I will spend days with Martina, returning on several trips and visiting victim after victim, and to each one of them, she says this: call me any time of day or night, twenty-four seven. "So we are going to take Byron down," Martina says. "You're on my team. But this protection order is not knife proof. It's not bulletproof. So when you see him, you have to call the police. You have to let me know. It's okay to call me crying, and it's okay to call me and say you want to go back. As much as you love him, you have to call me when you get that urge."

Grace is nodding, crying in fear and relief. She swears she is not going back this time. She swears it.

Joey darts into the room, his head a swivel. "Joey! What's going on?!" Martina says, like he's a long-lost nephew. Mark skates into the room, grabs his brother, and out they go. Split second. Comic timing. Dynamic duo.

Nesbitt starts in now with a Danger Assessment on Grace. Has he strangled you? Beaten you while pregnant? Does he have access to a gun? Is he a substance abuser? Is he unemployed or underemployed? Are there children in the home that aren't his? Has he threatened to kill you? Threatened to kill himself? Threatened to hurt the children? Has he ever avoided being arrested for domestic violence? Have you left him after living together? Does he ever choke (strangle) you? Does he control all or most of your daily activities? Is he constantly jealous? Do you believe he is capable of killing you?

Yes, yes, yes, yes, yes. To every question, yes. To all of it. Yes. The answers pile up in emotional strength; her face crumples; she wipes repeatedly at tears as they fall, and I imagine her thinking of all the times she's returned, all the decisions she's probably blaming herself for, all the times she maybe didn't call the police. I can picture her thinking about her kids' faces, imagining maybe the angry face of Byron, wondering how she ever got to this place. No victim of domestic violence—man or woman, adult or child—ever imagines that they're the type of person who would wind up in such a situation. Whatever we envision when we envision a victim, there is one universal truth to each and every one of those images: none of us ever picture ourselves.

What we might conjure, if anything at all, is a punch. Someone we're dating, one punch, and we'd be gone. But that's not how it happens. It evolves over time. A partner who might not like your makeup. Or a suggestive outfit. Maybe he'll say it's for your own protection. Then a few months later, maybe he yells a little louder than you've heard before. Maybe he throws something, a fork, a chair, a plate. (It's worth noting that should that plate bounce off the wall and break into shards, and should a shard cut you in the face, the Supreme Court considers it "intentional" abuse.[5]) Then, in between weeks and months of some good times, and some not-so-good times, you might hear how he knows men look at you, he sees other men looking at you. You might even feel complimented by this. But then maybe he follows it up with a request that you stay home with him a little more. Maybe this, too, is for your "protection." And that one friend you have, the loud one? He knows she doesn't like him. And before you even realize it's happening that friend's falling away from your life. Then, a couple of years in, he loses his job, comes home in a mood, pushes you into a wall. And you know that's not him, not really. You've been with him awhile now. Anyone would feel bad, losing a job. And he apologized, right? Seemed truly remorseful. And then the next month it's a slap, a backhanded shove, another thrown plate. But neither the control nor the abuse tend to come at once, lit up like a punch. They leak out slowly over time like radon.

For battered men, who comprise anywhere from 15% to 40% of the victims in America (depending upon which study you read[6]), the stigma is even greater. Men rarely seek out shelter. They rarely call law enforcement. The culture that tells women to keep the family intact, to find love and be loved at all costs, is the same culture that emasculates and shames men in abusive situations, that tells men if they are victims, it is because they are weak and not real men. It is the same culture that tells them violence is acceptable as a response to any external threat or internal pain, but tears are not. It is a culture that limits both victim and perpetrator, the abused and the abuser.

Same-sex partners fare no better. They, too, rarely report their situations to police or advocacy centers, despite rates of violence being generally higher in LGBTQ couples compared to heterosexuals, with transgender individuals and bisexuals experiencing the highest rates of violence out of all groups.[7]

Grace's score is about as high as they come. Some victims need to be told what it means, the danger they're in. But not Grace. I can see by her tears, by her shaking her head, that she knows exactly what all those yeses mean. "What's wrong with me?" Grace says, quiet as a sigh. "Why do I feel empathy towards him? Like I feel bad that I'm talking about Byron?"

"It's okay to still love him," Nesbitt says, reaching her hand toward Grace's leg. "But we're involved now, and we're going to get you and your children the help you need." She tells a story then that might be true, might be apocryphal. This one detective, Nesbitt says, used to be on their squad, and he was lactose intolerant. Wouldn't you know it, his favorite food was ice cream. He loved ice cream. But every time he ate it, it made him sick. Luck of the draw. What were the chances? Didn't mean he still didn't want to eat it. Just that he knew if he ate it, he was going to get sick. Grace gets it.

"This is going to be the hardest thing you ever do," Martina says. "It's also the most courageous." And just then I think she's going to offer Grace a pep talk, a tough love diatribe about making sure she actually leaves. But she doesn't. Instead, Martina brings up the kids, the abuse they've witnessed, and how Grace has a responsibility to them. "The environment we put our children in will have a profound effect on who they are when they grow up," Martina says. "So these little boys, they may start to do this to others."

Grace wipes at her eyes. "I know, I know."

But Martina doesn't let her off the hook that easily. "You doing this is going to let them know it's not allowed, okay?"

Grace nods.

Later, I will ask Martina if she thinks Grace will really go through with leaving Byron, and she nods. She thinks she can sometimes tell when victims are ready; when they go from being victims to being survivors. Domestic violence literature talks about that average of seven tries before a victim actually leaves.[8] But it's not entirely accurate, because victims vacate emotionally first, sometimes years before they are actually physically able to leave. And for Grace, it seemed clear that whatever fear she was feeling about Byron, and whatever sadness may have set in about the breakup, the thought of leaving her children to be raised without her was now driving her decisions. Byron had tipped the scales.

But Martina doesn't take chances when it comes to these kinds of promises. She's seen victims return too many times. So when Grace's story is all finished, and Martina has filed her notes in her binder, she shifts on the couch and looks and Grace and says, "I'm going to tell you a story about my sister. True story. You can look it up."

Free Free

Martina had an older sister named Brandi. Brandi lived a few hours away from Cleveland in Warren, Ohio. The two hadn't been in touch much, but one day in the summer of 2015 Brandi's daughter, Bresha, showed up on Martina's doorstep. Bresha showered her aunt with stories of her father's years of abuse. Cruel and terrifying stories. He'd cut off Brandi and Bresha and the rest of the children from their family entirely; Martina recognized the tactic of isolation. And she'd known of some of the abuse. Years earlier, Brandi had wound up in the hospital with seizures and a stroke after a severe beating. She was in such bad shape that a priest had come to read her her last rites in the hospital. Martina visited Brandi at the hospital. "Her left side was all numb," Martina says, "and that girl doesn't even remember me being at the hospital visiting her."

After that, Brandi left her husband for six months, and stayed with her children at her mother's house. But then she'd eventually gone back, and Martina and the family had little contact, until the day Bresha showed up on Martina's doorstep and refused to return home. Bresha begged to stay with Martina, said her father would kill them all if she went back. Martina called social services. She called the police. She got all sorts of people involved.

Brandi's husband had broken her ribs and her fingers, given her black eyes.[1] Brandi said she believed he once broke her nose—for which she never received treatment. Jonathan controlled their money, their social lives, their work lives (the couple worked together). She didn't have a car of her own, had never had a bank account of her own. Brandi was so beat down she couldn't think for herself, didn't know how to make a decision, didn't know how to keep her children safe. Martina would come to call it the worst case of domestic violence she'd ever witnessed.

A year later, Bresha ran away again. "Now she's a little grownup and she comes to my house," Martina tells Grace. "And I notice she has cut marks. She's fourteen years old."

Martina says Bresha was suicidal, needed to be hospitalized. Bresha told everyone she'd rather be dead than go back home to her father. "July twenty-eight," Martina says, "she picked up her father's gun and she shot her dad and killed him in his sleep."

On that day, Martina got up early, let her little dogs out (Sammy, Barkley, Bosco), and noticed that she had text after text, missed call after missed call. It was 5:36 in the morning. Five thirty-six a.m. is the kind of detail someone who writes a lot of police reports would remember. She knew something was wrong, but she didn't want to find out what, exactly. Her family was still recovering from the accidental overdose of one of Martina's nephews; he'd been leaving Martina a voice mail when suddenly, his voice on the line just cut out. It turned out that he'd passed out, choked on his own vomit after taking some bad drugs, and died. Martina took it hard. The two of them had been close, and he'd left behind three little kids. Everyone, it seemed, in the whole family called Martina to help them out of their problems.

She let her dogs back in and saw her sister pull in the driveway. It was a sign of something truly terrible, something big enough that she felt a hammer of dread in her gut. Her sister gave her the news. Bresha had shot and killed her father.

Martina remembers stumbling backward, almost falling.

Minutes after she got the news, Martina's phone rang. It was Bresha on the line. "Don't you say a thing," she told Bresha, knowing anything she said could be used in court. "Not a word, not a single word. Don't even say my name. Do not talk until I get there."

Martina tore down the highway in her car to Warren. By the time she reached the police department, Bresha's story had hit the news. It spread immediately across Ohio, and before the end of the day, it would make major headlines, from the *New York Times* to the *Daily Mail* in the UK. Eventually, even outlets like *People* magazine and the *Huffington Post* covered it.

THE STORY IS SO powerful it sits like a vapor in Grace's living room. Grace's eyes haven't left Martina's freckled face. Finally, Martina breaks the silence. "So your children see all this . . . When I tell you this affects your children, you got to stay the hell out of that house . . .

You have to put them in a safe environment. If you cannot do that, I will step in."

Grace promises. "I've dealt with this for years. I'm done." She says part of why she stayed was that she was scared of shelters, and she had nowhere else to go. She's staying now with one of her exes; her friend lives upstairs.

"Don't let money or food make you go back," Martina says, promising her that's something they can help with.

"If you call me and tell me you changed your mind, which I expect you to, I am going to talk you out of it, but just know, I'm going to do my job. I'm going to call children's services."

For the first time, Grace half smiles. She tells Martina she is absolutely, one hundred percent sure. She is not going back this time.

THE STORY OF MARTINA's niece and sister populates half the conversations I ever have with her. It's as ubiquitous for her as her next-door neighbor's homicide, and as present in every moment as the air around us. She tells me how prosecutors wanted to try Bresha as an adult, but Martina knew it would be the end of Bresha's life if that happened. "She'd be just another young Black girl stuck in the system," she told me. She promised Brandi she'd do all she could for Bresha, everything in her power, but Brandi had to follow Martina's orders. Martina started a GoFundMe page to cover attorney's fees for her niece. She spoke to the press, to anyone she could, about how this had happened. The hashtag #FreeBreshaNow became a symbol not just of the racial injustice in the judiciary and law enforcement, but a rallying cry for Black Lives Matter. Demonstrations cropped up for months in front of the Cleveland courthouse and even nationally in cities across the United States.

Jonathan's sister, Talema Lawrence, in an interview with Vice News, said Bresha had killed her father in his sleep, when he was defenseless, which made her a murderer. But Jonathan's family also said she needed mental health counseling to grapple with "her issues" and with what she'd done. They were adamant that domestic violence had "nothing to do with" the murder since she hadn't killed him in the midst of an escalating fight. Advocates will recognize this scenario, the abused killing the abuser in his sleep. Sleep is that rare moment a fighter can't fight back. Sleep is when abused women who've finally worked up the courage to fight back sometimes kill their abusers. (Others kill in a violent moment out of self-protection.) Many women across the country today languish in jail cells because their histories of domestic violence were barred in court in their own defenses.

The evidence of Jonathan's violence had been substantial. In 2011, after the beating that landed her in the hospital, Brandi was granted a protection order. She spoke of his threats to kill her and kill the children if she ever tried to leave, his years of beatings, isolation, and control. She said she had to wake him in the middle of the night to ask if she could use the bathroom, so heightened was his paranoia that she was cheating on him. After the protection order was granted, she and her three children moved to where her parents were living by then, in Parma, Ohio. Those six months are the only time that Martina had much contact with Brandi at all.

Eventually, Jonathan convinced Brandi that things would be different. And the order of protection was dropped. Martina remembers her mother sobbing when Brandi returned. "We had just learned these horror stories of what he did to her . . . I was like, 'Mom, she is going to do this, like, ten more times,'" Martina said. "They always go back."

Martina knew she couldn't force her sister to stay away from Jonathan. Brandi didn't live in Martina's jurisdiction, where she could have built some protections around her sister, and the local police department didn't have a specialized domestic violence unit, or even one dedicated officer.[2] (They did have a courthouse advocate.) Martina talked to the police station in Warren, told them who she was, who her sister was, about the family's history. She elicited promises from them that they'd do what they could, drive by more often, make their presence known. Martina had little faith in this promise, but she felt there was not much she could really do until Brandi made the decision to leave. With every domestic violence expert I've ever spoken to, this is a crucial step: that a victim has to decide when enough is enough. "So for the next couple years we call [the police] to do checks," Martina says. "They question her in front of him. She doesn't say anything."

This is the long-term fallout from a lifetime of violence directed toward you: the rewiring of a brain geared solely and entirely toward survival. A brain that reacts to being under constant attack will continue to send danger signals; increased levels of cortisol, adrenaline and other stress hormones, contributing to a vast constellation of physical and mental health issues. Disassociation is one of the more common issues, but victims of chronic domestic violence can also have a wide and long-term range of problems, from the emotional to the physical. They may have long-term cognitive loss, memory problems or sleep disorders. They may suffer from inattention or irritability. Some researchers link a host of physical ailments to unresolved trauma, including fibromyalgia and severe digestive issues. In his book *The Body Keeps the Score,* the author Bessel van der Kolk writes, "The most important job of the brain is to ensure our survival, even under the most miserable conditions . . . Terror increases the need for attachment, even if the source of comfort is also the source of terror." Van der Kolk believes that while post-traumatic stress in soldiers garners the most attention these days, victims of trauma, including domestic violence, are "arguably the greatest threat to our national well-being."[3]

Domestic situations, Martina told me, aren't like any other calls that police get. With other situations, you take the call, make an arrest, write your report, and then you're more or less done with that person. "In a zone car, you only get called to people's nightmares," she says. "Domestic is not the same . . . I do less cases, but they're so much more involved." It's not uncommon for Martina to see a victim so often the two of them are on a first name basis. The cases are emotionally complicated for the victims, and often carry addiction issues and financial issues; Martina must take all of it into account when she advises clients or meets with prosecutors on any given case. Sometimes the barriers come from the victims themselves. There was a young girl, eighteen years old, that Martina and I visited one day. She'd scored a seven on her Danger Assessment. (The Cleveland team altered Campbell's twenty questions to suit their territory, so their assessment has eleven questions total.) It wasn't a particularly high score, but Martina knows how important it is to address violence when victims are young. Advocates have warned for years now about how often the cycle of abuse begins in one's youth— teenage years, even pubescent years. And here was a teenager telling a detective she didn't want to prosecute. Martina wanted to get face-to-face with this girl, even if she couldn't convince her to change her mind. In fact, her primary goal wasn't even getting the girl to court. Her primary goal was far simpler: she wanted this girl to hear from at least one adult that abuse was not normal.

The girl was still in high school, living at home with her mother. Her boyfriend's brother was in the house at the same time we were there. The girl had left a voice mail for Martina earlier that day telling her to mind her own business, cussing her out. Martina called her back anyway, said she was on her way over even if the girl didn't want to prosecute.

"If [your boyfriend] does something to you," Martina told her shortly after we arrived, "I look like a failure, okay?"

"Okay," the girl said. She had a large gash across her neck that she said was from a fight with a girl at school.

"Are you afraid of him?" Martina asked her.

"I mean, no," said the girl. "Only certain times when we fight, yeah. But that's normal. I went through it with my dad."

Martina stopped writing and stared at the girl. "That's *not* normal. Don't you say that to me," she said. "That is not normal. You listen to me. If you're scared, that's fine. You're *supposed* to be scared; you're a young girl. You take my card and you call me if that man touches you."

Then Martina turned to the brother, who was pacing in the other room. "That's your brother. What is wrong with you guys?"

"Not *you guys*," he said. "I got some problems, too."

"But he's crazy, right?" she said. She didn't roll her eyes, but she might as well have.

"Everybody's crazy," he said. "It's how you handle it."

The girl's mother was in the bathroom, getting ready for work. We were standing at the kitchen table, beside a living room entirely devoid of even a single piece of furniture. "You can't just be hitting people," Martina said to him. "Would you agree?"

"I would agree," he said. "Whatever you say."

Which sounded, of course, like he didn't agree at all.

IN THE END THE court, perhaps bowing to public pressure, tried Martina's niece as a child. She was held in a juvenile detention facility for a year and released in February of 2018. If she maintains good behavior, her records will be expunged when she is twenty-one. But for Martina, the story is ongoing. "The first fourteen years she was abused and then the last two she was incarcerated . . . so she hasn't really been *free* free," she says. She talks to her niece about once a week. And her sister Brandi is slowly learning how to operate in the world on her own. Martina has taught her basic finances, and she got her a car so Brandi could get herself back and forth to see her daughter, who was held several hours away from her home. Making sure Bresha doesn't wind up the victim in her own abusive relationship as an adult is a nagging kind of existential concern for Martina. And in that, only time will tell.

Brandi and Bresha are an immersion for Martina into the particular emotional and psychological dynamics of a criminal act. It's an unusual perch from which to see. Martina is not simply a cop sitting there telling a civilian what to do, pretending any of it is easy, pretending these problems aren't part of her world, too. She's grappled with this from nearly every possible angle: public, private, professional, personal. She sits in court and sees it. She sees versions of Brandi and Bresha and Jonathan every single day. Not just the crime and punishment, but the terrible and terrific toll of violence—the *whether* and the *how* you rebuild your life, and the *whether* and *how* you convince your children to make different choices than you made. The ancestral manifestation of emotional and physical terror.

BEFORE WE LEAVE GRACE'S house, Martina does a few minutes of safety planning. They talk about schedules, about Grace's job. About whether she can alter it some or alter her route to work or enter and exit a secured door so that Byron can't track her so easily. She calls Mark back into the room and says if he sees Byron on his way to or from school, he is to run as fast as he can to the nearest house and call the police. "You get the hell away from him. Open a door and go right in. Call the police. Be loud. Jump in someone's car. I don't care. But what I don't want—and not to scare you, Mark—is for him to grab you and then tell your mom. Then we got a big problem."

Joey flops his body from the kitchen onto the floor of the living room. "Joey?!" Martina says with a giant grin, "What's goin' on?"

He ignores her. Monkeys up his mother.

"He is going to kill you," Martina says to Grace. "I am telling you. This is the most crucial time. You have to figure, his whole world just came to an end, right? You were his punching bag, his target with that gun."

Grace wipes at Joey's face with her tissue. Mark does not seem at all taken aback by Martina's candor. His stepfather's violence is well known to him.

Martina gives Grace a bus ticket to get to court because she doesn't own a car. She has Grace program 911 into her cell phone speed dial for efficiency. She reminds Grace that she's on her way toward freedom, toward getting her life back. "Quit looking at the bad things you did. Look at the good things," she says. "You called the police. You agreed to meet with me. You let me take photos. We did the protection order.

We're getting the warrant out." By the time we leave, Grace is smiling, is making promises to Martina, and Joey's back in the kitchen, trampolining on the chairback.

Before she leaves, Martina stands at the screen door and turns around to Grace. She asks about the police who came when Grace called, the ones who first took the order. "Were they nice to you?" Martina asks her.

"Oh," Grace says, "they were very nice."

"Good," Martina says. She asks every client this same question. Were the police nice? Did they do their job? Were they polite? No one requires her to ask this question, she just does. The Cleveland police, she is well aware, have long had a reputation for corruption, for racial profiling. The Tamir Rice killing thrust the force into the national spotlight more than any other event in recent history. "The hardest thing to do is call the police on someone," she tells me later. "Everyone has a bad day, but it's important to me to know how people view the police. It should be important to the police to know how people feel."

"How do you feel now?" Martina asks Grace.

"I feel everything," Grace tells her. "Happy, sad, scared."

When Byron goes before the judge, he will be put on a GPS bracelet. And he'll face multiple charges in court that include felonious assault, endangering children, kidnapping, and intimidation, among others.

Later, over pizza, Martina takes a call from Grace. Byron has stolen her credit card and run up a bunch of charges. Martina goes through the steps of what Grace should do: call the credit card company, get a new card, cancel the old one, keep a record of it all. Martina says she'll add it to her report. It's the kind of thing that is maybe beyond the scope of her job, but she takes these calls anyway. "When I have to handle your case, there's a big problem," she says, as she hangs up with Grace. "But I try to be the detective that I wanted my sister to have."

More than a year passes, and I catch up with Martina on the phone late one winter afternoon. Grace held out for a long time, months, much longer than Martina thought she would. But then, just as Martina had predicted, Grace recanted. Instead of jail time, Byron got probation. And Grace? The last Martina heard she'd taken Byron back. Before we hang up, Martina makes one last prediction: "I'm sure I'll hear from her again."

Shadow Bodies

Washington, D.C., is completely still as I walk the perimeter of the main courthouse looking for the one door I was told would be open. It's after ten p.m. on a Saturday night, two weeks before Christmas. Snowfall is expected and, in typical D.C. fashion, an overly thick layer of salt has been poured in anticipation and now crunches under my shoes, an ominous reverberating sound in the eerie downtown quiet. I've spent plenty of time here during the day, when it's bustling, filled with attorneys and residents and often tourists who mean to be at the National Gallery but made a wrong turn somewhere around Pennsylvania Avenue and Fourth Street. There's little that feels creepier than a bureaucratic building in a major city in the wee hours of a weekend night. Plus, I can't find the one unlocked door.

I circle the entire city block that the courthouse takes up, and then retrace my steps. The building is made from smooth Indiana limestone, looming architectural squares with narrow windows built in. Finally I see the guard on duty, camped out behind the main entrance, obscured from view by the darkness and the door's frame.

"I saw you pass the first time," he says, teasing. He introduces himself as the "popcorn man." Provider of snacks to the unlucky folks required to be here at this hour. Indeed, the faint smell of popcorn lingers. "Hang on just a beat," he says, then dials an office upstairs.

WASHINGTON, D.C., IS A strange place to live. It carries an outsized reputation, given how relatively tiny it is (sixty-eight square miles, a third smaller than Boston, though both have about seven hundred thousand residents). When people from other areas talk about it, it's either staid and boring (New York and Los Angeles) or full of corrupt, morally bankrupt people (most everywhere else). I like to tell people that it's a lot like Los Angeles—another city that carries a single unshakable association to outsiders. But the reality is that in both cities you can carve a life entirely separate from that association. Aside from the one time my daughter's school trip was halted by a presidential motorcade, there's very little that daily reminds me I'm in the nation's capital. To me, the city's most enduring characteristic is the way in which it can often hold an absolute dichotomy: a national government that may or may not have anything at all to do with the residential context in which it is operating. Today is a case in point, where we have a government composed of a conservative majority, and a citizenship comprising the most politically liberal people in the nation.[1] Local government policies are so progressive that a friend of mine who works in government once joked to me that we were practically a socialist city.

To me this means that Washington, D.C., is the perfect city from which to view policy at the macro level and people at the micro. Here in this small urban area, where all the problems of any city—lack of affordable housing, crime, poverty, violence, gentrification—battle for extremely limited resources, Washington, D.C., incorporates many of the country's more recent innovative programs. D.C., like a growing number of other towns and cities across the country, has taken the philosophy of coordination and communication that advocates like Ellen Pence, Kelly Dunne, Kit Gruelle, and others have espoused for decades, and tried to graft it onto the domestic violence field here, all across the city. And that is why I've come here on this winter night to the eerie courthouse, to see the hinge upon which this operation rests, something called the response line.

The popcorn man gives me the thumbs-up, hangs up his phone, and directs me to the elevators. The minute the doors open onto the fifth floor, I am immediately lost in a series of symmetrical, identical corridors for what is clearly a long enough amount of time that I hear a lone voice around a corner call out, "Hello?" It's a woman, I learn, who has been here just shy of ten hours and who will be leaving momentarily. "Don't worry," she tells me. "Everyone gets lost."

DC Safe runs the response line twenty-four hours a day, seven days a week. They have thirty advocates in total, and in addition to whomever answers the response line, there are also another two advocates on call at home. The orders of protection they do here are all civil. Unlike High Risk Teams, or larger community coordinated responses, they focus on the very short term—just days, usually—in the hopes of getting a victim to a place where he or she can make clear-headed decisions for the longer term. Primarily, police are the ones calling from on-site situations of domestic violence in one of the city's eight wards. Advocates then formulate an immediate plan for victims and will most often call them back and discuss this plan in the minutes after a perpetrator has been arrested. This means that the response line is a fulcrum with a limitless number of spokes. Advocates can look up dockets for officers to find out if there are orders of protection in place, or warrants for arrest, or other pending cases. But they also help victims in an almost endless constellation of fairly small but significant ways. They have partnerships, relationships, and contracts with agencies all across town in various capacities: shelters, yes, but also locksmiths, grocery stores, victim services, hotels, attorneys. If an officer calls the response line, the advocate can arrange for shelter for a couple of nights, or get a bag full of diapers and formula out to a victim who's fled her house, or get her connected to a forensic nurse at a local hospital who is trained to find domestic violence injuries, or get her a grocery store gift card if an abuser controls all of their money, or pay for a taxi to get to safety. Advocates walk clients through the system of obtaining an order of protection, how to apply for transitional or longer-term housing, and how to access free legal assistance.

But DC Safe also has advocates ride along with police whenever possible. They go out on domestic violence calls with a dedicated officer, and can field victims' needs immediately. Many jurisdictions are embedding domestic violence advocates more and more often in police departments (New York City and its five boroughs aims to have them in every precinct by 2019), and some, like Cleveland, have been doing this for years. DC Safe is unique in that it wants to formalize the process of advocates being not just in police departments across all of Washington, D.C., but actually in cars on ride alongs with officers. They would eventually like to have an advocate in a zone car on every shift, as well, but at the moment, the organization simply doesn't have the personnel. The night I went on a ride along in a northeast ward, there was an advocate in another car—in a different ward—but we never crossed paths.

Natalia Otero, the cofounder of DC Safe, along with Elizabeth Olds, told me that in the throes of a crisis, victims are not in a position to make the kinds of informed decisions they often need to make to ensure their safety. Victims and abusers come to domestic violence services through police and crisis centers, of course, but also through emergency rooms, school administrators, coworkers, and clergy. So Otero's challenge was how to get victims over whatever hurdles kept them in place so that they could make better informed decisions. Police reports are full of victims fleeing with nothing, not even shoes, coats, identification. A woman I once interviewed in San Diego had spent a weekend imprisoned in her home; she and her boyfriend finally drove to a convenience store, and as he pulled back into their driveway, she opened the car door and sprinted to a car backing out of a neighboring driveway. She had no money, no identification, no cell phone. In the moment, she had one single thought: get away. She didn't think of where she'd go or how, or even who to call for help. It was just those two words: *get away*. Victims focus on small questions because the big ones are often too difficult to face in moments of chaos and fear. Otero told me that the biggest difference she sees when a victim has basic needs met for a day or two or a week is "their level of competence. They're in such a better position to make longer-term decisions."

Otero and I talked at a restaurant in Penn Quarter just a few minutes' walk from the courthouse. DC Safe has so many partner agencies, so many funding needs, and so many plans and programs going on that she is in constant motion. She tells me she knew early on of the High Risk Teams and Danger Assessments and Campbell. She'd worked in domestic violence for years, but her background was business. When she graduated from Georgetown University with a business degree, she was approaching the problem not so much as a social issue but a challenge for a business, a market with unmet needs. Washington, D.C., was getting thirty thousand domestic violence emergency calls annually with no way to categorize or address those calls. "We needed one central clearinghouse, one organization to be the entry point for all the many first responders across the city," she told me. And she wanted it to be in the courthouse, where access to records and to prosecutors and to judges could be procured. She began the response line full-time in 2011 and DC Safe now serves more than eight thousand clients a year.

I WANT TO BELIEVE all this is making a difference, coordinated community responses like DC Safe's program, the High Risk Teams, advocates partnering with police, abuser intervention. I want to believe that we're getting better at working with the victims and intervening with the perpetrators, that we're recognizing the vast and endless ways domestic violence devastates families and communities. And I want to believe all of this is a national call to action. Yet as I write this, I can't help but think of how I sat in that ghostly midnight courthouse fewer than six blocks from the United States Capitol where Congress just weeks ago in September failed to reauthorize the 2018 Violence Against Women Act. Instead, it gave VAWA stopgap funding for another three months and this time—unlike when VAWA first passed with bipartisan support—there is not a single GOP cosponsor.[2] And just today I got both an e-mail and a Facebook post alerting me to a new report from the Violence Policy Center that says that murder of women by an intimate partner has increased by 11% since 2014.[3] This report, I should note, only covers single incidents, not mass shootings, familicides, or any other combination of deaths. And then, just days after this report was released, our current president stood on the White House Lawn and said in the aftermath of a contentious Supreme Court hearing, "It's a very scary time for young men in America, where you can be guilty of something you may not be guilty of." He said this on October 2; two days into Domestic Violence Awareness Month, which he failed to mention.

There are other dismal signs, too. A high profile case came out of Cleveland, a former judge named Lance Mason with a known history of domestic violence killed his ex-wife, a beloved teacher named Aisha Fraser. It wasn't Martina's district; the murder happened in Shaker Heights. But it made me wonder just how much we can expect any one person to make a difference. Then, in another mass shooting in Chicago on Monday, November 19, 2018, at Mercy Hospital, the fact that it began as domestic violence was left out of nearly all media coverage. There were three victims at Mercy Hospital, but the target was Dr. Tamara O'Neal, the ex-fiancée of the shooter. A headline from Melissa Jeltsen at the *Huffington Post* captured it best: "Tamara O'Neal Was Almost Erased from the Story of Her Own Murder."[4]

There are other markers that worry me, too, especially those invisible ones. An uncomfortable misogyny creeping into areas that had, until now, seemed fully resolved to the idea of women's equality. Congress, for example. The White House, with our current "grab 'em by the pussy" president, for another. The Supreme Court, for a third. Kit Gruelle's quote about our current political situation haunts me more often than I'd like to admit: "We are leaping backwards at an obscene pace."

There is more cause for concern about gun violence. Despite federal law that gives states and jurisdictions the right to take guns away from convicted abusers, including stalkers, there is ample evidence that even in this we are failing. Between 2010 and 2016, the number of guns manufactured in the United States nearly doubled, from 5.5 million to 10.9 million—and the overwhelming majority of those guns stayed here on U.S. soil.[5] It is surely no coincidence that the states with the highest number of guns per capita also happen to have the highest rates of domestic violence homicide, including South Carolina, Tennessee, Nevada, Louisiana, Alaska, Arkansas, Montana, and Missouri.[6] In a study for his 2007 book, *Why Do They Kill*, David Adams asked fourteen men who were in prison for intimate partner homicide if they'd have done it were a gun not available. It's a common argument, that if someone wants to kill, he'll find a way. But eleven of those men said no, they wouldn't have killed if they hadn't had access to a gun.[7] In a study released in October 2018, the researcher April Zeoli looked at states where anyone served with a restraining order is automatically required to relinquish guns, and found there was a 12% drop in intimate partner homicides, yet only fifteen states required that guns in such instances be turned in.[8] Similarly, Zeoli found that in California, where broader restrictions for anyone—including both life partners and dating partners (California calls it closing the "boyfriend loophole")—convicted of a violent misdemeanor had to relinquish guns, there was an astonishing 23% drop in domestic violence homicides.[9] Fifty American women are shot and killed *every month* by intimate partners; a further untold number are threatened with those guns, kept in line, kept quiet. (And then there are those killed by other methods. Stabbed, strangled, pushed out of moving cars, poisoned.) The United States is the most dangerous developed country in the world for women when it comes to gun violence.[10] This is not an issue of partisanship, liberal versus conservative, though I understand many people view it that way; to me it is a moral imperative.

Why are our guns more important to us than our citizens?

I cannot come to any other conclusion than that retired nurse in Montana, knitting as she investigates on the fatality review team. *Get rid of the fucking guns.*

AT THE SAME TIME, I think there is reason to hope. I look around at my male friends, my colleagues, my brothers, my friends' husbands, and I see allies everywhere. I see men who care, who speak to an insecurity that I and many women feel, who will say, unabashedly, that they will refuse to be influenced by the craven misogyny filtering through the country and even the rest of the world. I see an awareness among the many LGBTQ people I know, among women and minorities, and I see it in my young university students. All of them know more than any of us knew twenty years ago.

And there are other hopeful signs, plenty of them. Multiple smartphone apps have been developed to help survivors in an emergency situation, or to assist teens and college students in danger, or give shelter options for the night, or to help bystanders figure out how to intervene. Dozens, in fact—and Campbell is involved in the formation of a number of them.[11] At the same time that the High Risk Team was forming, Casey Gwinn, the former city attorney in San Diego, began his transformative family justice centers. FJCs colocate as many different partnerships as possible into one location, from advocacy to counseling to legal services to law enforcement, so that victims don't have to tell and retell their stories. They have a single intake center for their clients: they can offer help filing an order of protection, for example. Or children's services, or job training, or police reports. So innovative was this program that the Bush Administration earmarked $20 million to replicate it and now there more than 130 centers in the United States and across twenty-five countries.[12]

Gwinn's most recent endeavor is Camp Hope, a summer camp with several locations around the country for children from violent homes; the camp's aim is to disrupt that cycle of violence.

Campbell's work is still helping to make strides. Former Maryland police officer Dave Sargent's nationally lauded program began when Sargent took Campbell's Danger Assessment, and whittled it down to three primary questions that a police officer could ask on scene to try to determine dangerousness quickly: 1. Has he/she ever used a weapon against you or threatened you with a weapon? 2. Has he/she threatened to kill you or your children? 3. Do you think he/she might try to kill you?[13] Answering yes to these three will trigger eight more questions, as well as a call from the responding officer to the local domestic violence hotline who will then connect with victims on-site. The timing is crucial; Sargent understood how often domestic violence homicides are situations that escalated quite suddenly to murder. Local media outlets, police reports, and prosecution files are overflowing with statements like "I didn't mean for her to die." Sargent dubbed his model the Lethality Assessment Program, sometimes referred to as the Maryland Model, and it's used in more than thirty states and in Washington, D.C., by first responders.[14]

There are other signs, too, that point to structurally deep social and cultural changes in how we address this particular type of violence. For example, the United States now has more than two hundred dedicated criminal domestic violence courts (New York and California are leading the charge). More and more of these courts are recognizing the particular psychology behind domestic violence, why victims recant or won't show up for court, for example, and the usefulness of having domestic violence advocates embedded both in the court itself and in prosecutor's offices.[15] Still, more than 40% of those courts still don't regularly order offenders to attend batterer intervention courses.

There is no doubt that we've made great strides in treating domestic violence as the public health crisis that it is. VAWA alone is often credited with reducing domestic violence by 64% between 1993—before it was authorized—and 2012.[16] Though Lynn Rosenthal, the former White House Advisor on Violence Against Women, warns against putting too much emphasis on this success. "The likelihood of a nineteen-year-old getting kicked across the room by a partner is essentially the same as when we started," she said. Stalking is now a felony charge in more than forty states.[17] Strangulation is a felony in forty-five.[18] The movement to keep victims out of shelter and in their communities is growing.

Rosenthal had just finished a listening tour called Youth Leads in high schools around the United States when she met me for lunch one day to talk about the broad view of all this. The aim of the listening tour, she said, was to try to determine best practices for addressing teen dating violence. A 2017 report from the Centers for Disease Control found that more than eight million girls experienced rape or intimate partner violence before the age of eighteen; for boys, the number was about half that.[19] Experts across the field note that the time to address dating violence starts as young as sixth and seventh grade. Rosenthal told me that in her sessions with high schoolers, she found herself heartened by the way young people, especially young men, talked about issues of domestic and sexual violence. "These young guys have a very different relationship to each other and to women," she said, comparing them to elder generations. "They have a lot of questions themselves about it . . . They're not going to let their peers engage [in sexual violence] without some sort of confrontation."

We were eating at a local place called Busboys and Poets, where the owner, Andy Shallal, is one of the highest profile activists in a city full of high-profile activists. On the screen behind Rosenthal was her former boss, Barack Obama, giving a speech in South Africa. Rosenthal said something surprising to me in that moment, something I'd not really quite thought about until she said it. "In some ways, men have been the biggest beneficiaries of the women's movement," she said. "Look at all the men who have a very different relationship [today] with their children. They go to school events; they talk to their kids. In my neighborhood, the guys are always walking their kids to daycare, to school. Look at how involved young fathers are. It's not perfect, and women still bear the burden in many ways, but they have experienced a change."

How a matter like family violence with such profound public consequences was *ever* considered a private issue is confounding in hindsight. Familial violence is not a problem in a silo. It is insidious, infecting so many other challenges we as a society face, in education and healthcare, in poverty and addiction, in mental health and mass shootings and homelessness and unemployment. Given the sheer span of issues that domestic violence intersects with, whatever solutions we imagine for the future must take this breadth into account. We cannot address homelessness without addressing the fact that domestic violence accounts for so many homeless families. We cannot successfully address educational disparity or poverty without addressing how much domestic violence can be a root cause of such problems. I think of the relatively minuscule funding we give to VAWA relative to other governmental expenditures, and remember Rosenthal's solution: to "invest everywhere." Her point was not about investing endless resources so much as acknowledging through our solutions the complicated ways that domestic violence launches so many of these other problems.

Rosenthal says the #MeToo movement is a sign of progress. It didn't just erupt out of nowhere, she tells me. This moment in our lives, in fact, reminds her of the time around the OJ trial, when suddenly conversations about domestic violence began to happen on a national scale. From those conversations came changes—substantive, groundbreaking, important changes, many of which show up in this book. "#MeToo came from years of laying the groundwork. Lots of people having these discussions and suddenly conditions were right for it to happen," she says.

David Adams, too, sees unique opportunities in this moment. "It's discouraging," he told me recently of our present time, "but I do think it's [energized] young people . . . And more and more people—especially women and minorities—are getting mobilized."

Throughout my reporting, it struck me how often I came upon such seemingly small changes that wound up making the difference between life and death, between a good decision and a bad one. A bag of diapers and grocery money, a laminated order of protection rather than paper, an afternoon court time rather than early morning, visiting a victim's house rather than waiting for a visit, taking a literal step back from an argument rather than a step forward. If I had to whittle down the changing world of domestic violence to just one idea that made all the difference, it would be communication. Across bureaucracies, certainly, but also political ideologies and programs, people and systems and disciplines. So many of the changes I saw when I traveled around the country came down to this one single act. The High Risk Teams, family justice centers, youth programs and batterer intervention and court initiatives, fatality review teams and police protocols and any number of other programs all shared this one absolutely free resource: they talked to one another.

THE NIGHT I VISIT the D.C. response line, a woman whom I'll call Naomi[20] was working the phone. Like many of her colleagues, she works four ten-hour overnights a week. And like many who work in domestic violence all across the country, Naomi witnessed violence first in her home. She and her mother were in and out of shelters when she was growing up. After she got older, she began volunteering for a shelter where she once lived as a victim with her mom. Some of the advocates still remembered her from when she was as a kid.

Tonight she sits in a cube in DC Safe's headquarters. Books line one wall: *Next Time She'll Be Dead. Loving to Survive. When Love Hurts.* The first call that comes in is from an officer at a house where a woman's grandson came home high, picked up a dining room chair, and crashed it into the floor until it was broken. This isn't the first time she's had this problem with her grandson. The officer gives Naomi birth dates, contact numbers, and names of the grandmother and grandson, then a synopsis of the incident. Naomi types it all into a database. Any high risk cases will get flagged in their system by Naomi (or whoever is on shift) for follow up by the advocates on shift tomorrow. Naomi's off the phone with the officer in just a couple of minutes (with less serious incidents, officers might wait till the end of their shift to call the response line). A few minutes later, Naomi calls the grandmother—I'll call her Irma—and introduces herself. "I'm calling to see if you're interested in filing an order of protection?" Naomi asks her.

Irma says she tried to get a stay-away order six months earlier, but was told that unless her grandson was actually violent, she didn't qualify. "I would like for him to get help," Irma says. "Maybe be evicted with whatever his problem is. I don't know how you go about doing that."

Naomi says that since the situation seems to be escalating, Irma may be granted an order this time, and that DC Safe can help her file it. She'll have to come to the DC Safe office Monday morning. Washington, D.C., has two dedicated domestic violence courts with judges assigned to cycle in annually.

"I was trying to give him a chance," Irma says, "to find out why he's so angry."

"It sounds like that's not really working," Naomi says.

"No, it's not. I'll have to go further."

"Part of the order will be him vacating the property," Naomi tells her. "You can also request that he do some kind of drug or alcohol counseling, or you can put just general counseling. The judge would grant it with those stipulations on there." Naomi gives her instructions on where to go Monday, what to say when she arrives. She tells her to bring a book and a snack and be prepared to wait a few hours. "The U.S. Attorney's Office is going to see if you want to assist them in pressing charges," Naomi says. "You just need to make sure your phone is on and the volume all the way up. They'll only call once and they won't leave a voice mail or anything. They'll call between eight and noon."

D.C. has an unusual order of protection that allows an abuser to stay in contact, to co-parent, to even sometimes continue to live together. Called HATS, the acronym stands for: no harassing, assaulting, threatening, or stalking. But abusers and victims can remain in the same house. This kind of protection order has obvious shortcomings, but in a city like Washington, D.C., where affordable housing is perhaps the greatest challenge to any social service agency,[21] it can help create, as Naomi put it, "a line in the sand saying I'm taking this seriously. This is a warning." Often, victims don't want an abuser to vacate the premises. They may need the financial and parenting support. "Clients are often like, 'We have kids together. We pay the bills together. I can't kick him out.' This makes them more willing to [file]."

Calls come in steadily as the minutes and hours stack up, most of them more or less the same relatively low level of violence as the grandmother and her grandson. The phone rings through the empty cubicles, a muffled sound. Midnights in the response line office are calm and quiet in a way I hadn't expected. I thought there'd be a whole phone bank of people, multiple conversations happening at once. But no, it's just this one woman, this one phone, this one cubicle. Naomi wears a red turtleneck that sets off her green eyes; textbooks sit on the desk beside her computer. If she has time and it's not a busy night, she studies for one of the classes she is taking by day. Her aim is to someday be a psychologist.

A call comes in from one of their clients who is currently in a shelter. The shelter's heating system is working, but the temperature is set to fifty-nine degrees and no one can access the locked thermostat box. Another call comes in that a woman with a protection order in place had her ex-boyfriend take the keys to her rental car and make off with it. The key ring also had her house key on it, and it's her only set. Naomi arranges to have her locks changed later tonight, then calls a maintenance man to access the shelter's thermostat.[22]

In the early morning hours, an officer phones in from one of the wealthier northwest districts of D.C. A woman has been strangled, but is alive and stable. He uses the word "choked." The couple had recently broken up and they'd gotten into an argument. The offender was arrested. The officer says he offered for the woman to have a forensic exam (a forensic nurse who works out of the Washington Hospital Center was on call) but she said she didn't need one. Naomi asks some questions about the woman. What was her demeanor? What did she remember of the event? He says the choking lasted only a couple of seconds, that the woman had been drinking, but he detected no signs of the strangulation. Her voice wasn't raspy. There were no marks.

Afterward, Naomi phones another advocate who's on call that night to discuss whether they should intervene more assertively to get the woman to see the forensic nurse. After a few minutes, they decide it's not a situation of high lethality and since he's been arrested, the woman's safety is not in question at the moment. She'd promised to come down to the courthouse to fill out an order of protection Monday morning.

It strikes me just how banal all of this is. These relatively minor acts of violence. The police call in and they speak to Naomi with the same dispassion as they would a dispatcher. This happened, then that. Off to the next incident. The response line is just part of their protocol. In other words, there isn't even a barrier to break down between systems and cultures any longer. The entire thing has become procedural. Its very ordinariness is perhaps its greatest success.

I spent so many years looking at the highest risk cases, looking at the men who killed their whole families, the fatality review teams who take up cases where it is already too late for the people involved, the families and advocates and law enforcement personnel who worked with Michelle and Dorothy and a thousand other victims who never became survivors. In fact, I spent so much time in this darkness, I nearly missed the significance of this night with Naomi entirely. It's what Kelly Dunne had told me so long ago and I had, for a long time, not really understood. That the best shot we have with domestic violence is to disrupt it in the misdemeanor phase before it becomes something bigger. These calls to Naomi, one after another, from officers or to clients, when I took the long view, were an incredible sign of progress.

Naomi went home early, and took a portable phone with her so she could continue working the line until her shift was over. She had to beat the snow. D.C. is prepared for a lot of things: terrorist attacks, political standoffs, government shutdowns. But snow is not one of them. It is nearly three a.m. when I walk out of the courthouse, that same echoing quiet, the crunch under my shoes. As I wait for my late-night Lyft driver, it strikes me that Naomi isn't just a symbol of progress because of what she does. She is a symbol of progress because of where she'd come from; she herself was a survivor, yes, but a survivor who'd found a way to disrupt the cycle in her own small way. A former hurt person helping to heal people. There is a place in the system for her now, just as there is for Jimmy. And maybe someday even for Donte. Like there was for Victoria, the woman I'd seen years earlier in the San Bruno jail whose father had once planned to kill her in a Denny's restaurant. Nearly everyone I'd ever met in the world of domestic violence had stories of abuse, as victims or perpetrators or witnesses. Hamish Sinclair and David Adams had abusive fathers. Suzanne Dubus was raped one winter night by two men. Jacquelyn Campbell had her former student, Annie; Martina Latessa had her sister, Brandi. Jimmy and Donte had the men they'd once been. Behind every one of them was this shadow of another body, a terrible story. But all of them were also the disruptors now, changing the future narrative.

It reminded me of a story. One evening several years ago, I sat in Dunne's office with her at dusk. It was summer and far past dinnertime. Dunne had always been so matter-of-fact when she talked to me about her work. I'd watched her in trainings play the 911 tape over and over from the night Dorothy died and she'd always focus on what the case showed, how you could graph Dorothy's story atop Campbell's research and you'd have a perfect fit. Mirror images of each other. All the risk markers and signs of escalation, yes, but the other things, too, so common in extreme violence. Their love at first sight, Dorothy's youth, William's morbid jealousy. You could graph all these onto Michelle and Rocky, too. Dunne never got emotional in these trainings. She was meticulous and impassive, a perfect picture of the lawyer she had almost once become.

On this night, she showed me something she'd written on a pink message sheet the day she met Dorothy, a note she keeps close: *Very lethal case.* I had heard about this note from Dubus, read about it in local news reports. I wanted to see it. I didn't tell Dunne, but Dorothy's death had haunted me, too. When I was writing about her years ago for the *New Yorker*, I used to get a sandwich for lunch and park on Green Street at Dorothy's house and sit eating it in my rental car. I don't know what I was doing, really. There was no evidence of her life or her death there now, but the street was quiet, idyllic. Sometimes I was sure I could smell the sea. A faded Big Wheel sat like a prop in the grass. It was a time when—between interviews and research—I could be reflective. Maybe Dorothy had become a shadow body in my life, too. So often when reporters write about issues, we are covering stories of the living, speaking to change makers, policy makers, who are alive and well. But in domestic violence, I suspect for many of us it is often the dead with whom we really commune.

I asked Dunne, sitting in her office, what she would say to Dorothy today, if she returned from the dead and walked right back into the office.

Dunne started to answer; then something stopped her, like her body suddenly hit an invisible wall. She bolted from her desk to a bank of filing cabinets, where I could not see her. I heard her short sharp breaths, a sniffle. "No one's ever asked me that before," she said.

I sat without speaking.

Dunne came back to her desk, wiped at her eyes. Then she looked at me and whispered, "I would tell her I'm sorry."

AUTHOR'S NOTE

During the last months I was writing and reporting *No Visible Bruises*, my stepmother went into hospice. She'd been diagnosed with colorectal cancer in the summer of 2015 and died in September of 2017. About three weeks before she died, I was sitting beside her hospital bed in the home she shared with my father, when she told me her first marriage and her childhood home had both been abusive. (This childhood abuse did not come from her mother, who raised her after her father left.) She and my father had been married for thirty-eight years; I'd been researching domestic violence in America for nearly eight years by then. I was utterly shocked.

For years we hadn't been close, but more recently we'd found a way to come together. Why had she never told me? Had I not made a safe enough space for her to talk about it? There were so many questions I wished I could have asked her, but she put me off, wisely. She didn't want to talk about it, and in fairness, by the time she'd divulged this information I knew far more about domestic violence than most people. Whatever memories she refused to share, I could imagine anyway. She knew she was dying, and she didn't want to think about any of the dark chapters of her life. She was entirely focused on my father, on the pain her death would cause us, and on not being able to see her grandchildren grow up.

If someone I'd known for thirty-eight years could keep her abuse from me, what did it say about how we deal with abuse in our midst today, the shame and stigma it still carries? When she finally died, my father and I stood in the kitchen sobbing. It was the second time I'd witnessed this specific scene, my father crying over a wife lost too young to cancer, but this time I was an adult and I understood so much more—of what she'd gone through, of what he was going through. He apologized to me that day and for the next weeks every time he broke down for "not being stronger." Here was a man who'd just lost his second wife to cancer and yet he didn't feel he had a right to public tears. Why? I told him his tears made him stronger, in my eyes, as a man, as a husband, as a father, that he didn't fear his full range of human emotion. It's a lesson I wish I could impart to all men.

It is for these reasons, these two moments, one with my stepmother and one with my father, that I dedicate this book to her. I am grateful I was able to tell her that I was doing so before she died.

ACKNOWLEDGMENTS

Whatever is required of any work of literary journalism, perhaps the foremost element is time. When you are telling someone else's story, and that story happens to be about the worst thing that ever happened to them, the time commitment can be extraordinary. For this reason, I am profoundly and deeply indebted to the families of Rocky Mosure and Michelle Monson for their time, their trust, and their faith. I would be lying if I said I did not cry alongside them at times. So my deepest gratitude is to Sally Sjaastad, Paul Monson, Sarah and Gordon Mosure, Alyssa Monson, and Melanie Monson. I would also like to thank those who gave me their time not just once or twice, but over and over, in some cases for years: Jimmy Espinoza, Donte Lewis, Hamish Sinclair, David Adams, Neil Websdale, Kit Gruelle, Sunny Schwartz, Reggie Daniels, Leo Bruenn, Ruth Morgan, Peg Hacksylo, Natalia Otero, Martina Latessa, Jacquelyn Campbell, Lee Johnson, Suzanne Dubus, Kelly Dunne, Robert Wile, Casey Gwinn, Gael Strack, Sylvia Vella, Joan Bascone, James Gilligan, Joan McCracken, Gary Gregson, William Kidd, Lou Johns, Maureen Curtis, and Lynn Rosenthal. Thanks to Nikki Allinson, who triple-checked my math. I would especially like to thank Matthew Dale, who did not live long enough to see this book come to fruition, but whose boundless work on behalf of victims sprouts through these pages.

For their generous support, I would like to thank the DC Commission on the Arts and Humanities, the College of Arts and Sciences at American University and especially the Columbia School of Journalism, and Harvard University's Neiman Foundation for the Lukas Work-in-Progress Award. You have all made possible what often felt impossible.

For me, the line of family and friend has always been extremely porous and I thank, as always: Ann Maxwell, David Corey, Andre Dubus III, Fontaine Dubus, David Keplinger, Stephanie Grant, Danielle Evans, Donald Rutledge, Soleak Sim, Lance Lee, Zac Fisher, Lisen Stromberg,

Ted Conover, Masha Gessen, Kate Woodsome, Elizabeth Flock, Julie Gibson, Yasmina Kulauzovic, Michelle Rieff, Tap and Mia Jordanwood, Lisa Eaves, Elizabeth Becker, Jen Budoff, Tom Heineman, Sarah Pollock, Katherine Ann Rowlands, Alison Brower, Marianne Leone, Chris Cooper, Richard Snyder, and Joshua Snyder.

The team at Bloomsbury is the most enjoyable, creative group of people I've had the pleasure of working with: Sara Mercurio, Jenna Dutton, Nicole Jarvis, Valentina Rice, Marie Coolman, Frank Bumbalo, Katya Mezhibovskaya, Cindy Loh, and Ellis Levine. They made sure I understood that the voice of the writer was always foremost in their endeavors. I am especially indebted to my editors, whose wisdom and grace mark every page in this book: Callie Garnett and Anton Mueller.

At American University, I am lucky to be supported in my intellectual and creative endeavors with colleagues who are a quiet source of inspiration. With a million thanks and gratitude to Peter Starr, David Pike, Kate Wilson, Patty Park, Kyle Dargan, Dolen Perkins-Valdez, Richard McCann, and Despina Kakoudaki. To the *New Yorker* editors who had the patience to work with me when I wasn't at all sure that anyone could shape for the outside world what I needed to communicate from my inside world: Alan Burdick, Carla Blumenkranz, Dorothy Wickenden, and Lauretta Charlton.

I say without hyperbole, this book would not be what it is without the tireless help of my research assistant, Molly McGinnis, who at times would ask: "Should I be supportive researcher today or authoritarian editor?" Remember her name; Molly has a big career ahead of her.

Susan Ramer, how lucky I am to have had you as an agent for twenty-three years. The decades speak to the fact that I would not be writing this today if not for you. Thank you for your belief in my words, your tireless drive to bring out my best. Yours is the fingerprint hidden inside every page of anything I write.

And, finally, for Jazz: everything I love and care most about in the world can be found in you.

NOTES

PREFACE

1. Formally, this is called the Extraordinary Chambers in the Courts of Cambodia, not to be confused with the International Criminal Court in the Hague, Netherlands. In informal conversation, we tended to refer to Cambodia's tribunal as, simply, the war crimes tribunal.

2. https://www.unodc.org/unodc/en/press/releases/2018/November/home-the-most-dangerous-place-for-women-with-majority-of-female-homicide-victims-worldwide-killed-by-partners-or-family-unodc-study-says.html.

3. https://www.un.org/press/en/1999/19990308.sgsm6919.html.

4. https://www.bbc.com/news/world-46292919. See also: https://www.unodc.org/unodc/en/press/releases/2018/November/home-the-most-dangerous-place-for-women-with-majority-of-female-homicide-victims-worldwide-killed-by-partners-or-family-unodc-study-says.html

5. Ibid. UNODC.

6. https://www.bjs.gov/content/pub/pdf/ipv01.pdf.

7. E-mail correspondence with Jacquelyn Campbell.

8. ". . . eight million workdays . . ." https://ncadv.org/statistics.

9. Sun, Jing et al., "Mothers' Adverse Childhood Experiences and Their Young Children's Development," *American Journal of Preventive Medicine* 53, no. 6 (December 2017): 882–91.

10. https://everytown.org/press/women-and-children-in-the-crosshairs-new-analysis-of-mass-shootings-in-america-reveals-54-percent-involved-domestic-violence-and-25-percent-of-fatalities-were-children.

11. https://www.politifact.com/texas/statements/2017/dec/02/eddie-rodriguez/domestic-violence-not-confirmed-precursor-mass-sho.

12. https://www.cbsnews.com/news/sutherland-springs-texas-church-gunman-devin-kelley-wife-speaks-out.

13. https://www.thestate.com/news/local/article25681333.html. See also: https://www.dailymail.co.uk/news/article-3131858/Charleston-killer

-Dylann-Roof-grew-fractured-home-violent-father-beat-stepmother
-hired-private-detective-follow-split-claims-court-papers.html.

14. This does not include the budget for victim compensation. https://www
.justice.gov/jmd/page/file/968291/download.

15. https://www.whitehouse.gov/wp-content/uploads/2018/02/budget
-fy2019.pdf.

16. https://money.cnn.com/2018/07/16/technology/amazon-stock-prime
-day-jeff-bezos-net-worth/index.html. My mad math skillz required that
I call my daughter's fifth grade math teacher to verify this percentage.
Thank you, Ms. Allinson!

17. https://jwa.org/encyclopedia/article/wifebeating-in-jewish-tradition.

18. Ibid.

19. Elizabeth Pleck, *Domestic Tyranny: The Making of American Social Policy
against Family Violence from Colonial Times to the Present* (Champaign,
IL: University of Illinois Press, 2004).

20. History of Domestic Violence: A Timeline of the Battered Women's Move-
ment. Minnesota Center Against Violence and Abuse; Safety Network:
California's Domestic Violence Resource. Sept. 1998 (copyright 1999).
See also: Mantel, Barbara, "Domestic Violence: Are Federal Programs
Helping to Curb Abuse?" *CQ Researcher* 23, no. 41 (November 15, 2013):
981–1004. http://library.cqpress.com/cqresearcher/cqresrre2013111503.
And: Pleck, *Domestic Tyranny*, 17, 21–22.

21. Davis, Jackie. "Domestic Abuse." Criminal Justice Institute. White paper.
https://www.cji.edu/site/assets/files/1921/domestic_abuse_report.pdf.

22. https://www.theclever.com/15-countries-where-domestic-violence-is
-legal.

23. https://themoscowtimes.com/articles/nine-months-on-russian-women
-grapple-with-new-domestic-violence-laws-59686.

24. https://www.justice.gov/eoir/page/file/1070866/download.

25. https://www.womenshealth.gov/relationships-and-safety/get-help/laws
-violence-against-women.

26. http://victimsofcrime.org/our-programs/stalking-resource-center
/stalking-information.

27. http://victimsofcrime.org/docs/src/analyzing-stalking-statute.pdf
?sfvrsn=2. In the UK, stalking was traditionally seen as simple "harassment" despite 120,000 women reporting stalking annually, a figure that
experts claim is about only a quarter of the real number. But unlike the
States, in 2012 the British government passed a law that allowed stalking
to be charged as a criminal act, and by 2015, prosecutions rose by 50%.

28. https://www.thehotline.org/about-the-hotline/history-domestic
-violence-advocates.

29. https://lethalityassessmentprogramdotorg.files.wordpress.com/2016/09
/development-of-the-lap1.pdf.

30. http://library.cqpress.com/cqresearcher/document.php?id=cqresrre 2013111503#NOTE[21]. Because the OJ trial predates the National Domestic Violence hotline (not to mention the Internet), the numbers weren't tracked nationally, but regionally across the country, shelters and hotlines reported record calls.

31. http://articles.latimes.com/1992-10-03/news/mn-266_1_domestic -violence.

32. https://www.cnn.com/2018/02/09/politics/rob-porter-trump-response /index.html and https://www.nytimes.com/2018/02/08/opinion/trump -porter-abuse-women.html.

BARNACLE SIBLINGS

1. Historians dispute this story, claiming that if there was a suicide by Crow warriors, it happened on the other side of the river. http://billingsgazette .com/news/local/sacrifice-cliff-the-legend-and-the-rock/article_fc527e19 -8e68-52fe-8ffc-d0ff1ecb3fea.html.

DADDY ALWAYS LIVES

1. In Maryland, stalking is always a misdemeanor. In Montana, a first offense is generally a misdemeanor, though a stalking law passed there in 2003 allows it to be charged as a felony. https://leg.mt.gov/bills/mca/45/5/45 -5-220.htm. See also: https://leg.mt.gov/bills/mca/45/2/45-2-101.htm. Though stalking is a crime in all fifty states, there are only about a dozen states that allow it to be charged as a felony if it's a first offense. https:// www.speakcdn.com/assets/2497/domestic_violence_and_stalking_ ncadv.pdf. See also: https://ncadv.org/statistics. Just over forty states allow for stalking to be charged as a felony, though only thirteen states allow stalking victims to sue their stalkers. http://victimsofcrime.org /our-programs/stalking-resource-center/stalking-laws/federal-stalking -laws#61a.

2. https://well.blogs.nytimes.com/2016/07/11/with-coercive-control-the -abuse-is-psychological.

3. Stark, Evan, PhD, MSW, "Re-presenting Battered Women: Coercive Control and the Defense of Liberty." Prepared for *Violence Against Women: Complex Realities and New Issues in a Changing World* (Les Presses de l'Université du Québec: 2012), http://www.stopvaw.org/uploads /evan_stark_article_final_100812.pdf.

4. https://www.gov.uk/government/news/coercive-or-controlling-behaviour -now-a-crime.

A BEAR IS COMING AT YOU

1. Some of the information about what Michelle wrote that night comes from a local newspaper article titled "That Black Night" written by Ed Kemmick of the *Billings Gazette* and published on November 23, 2002. Sally also shared with me Michelle's original note.
2. http://leg.mt.gov/bills/mca/45/5/45-5-206.htm.
3. Kelly Dunne, in-person interview. July 2011 in Newburyport, MA.

THIS PERSON YOU LOVE WILL TAKE YOUR LIFE

1. Campbell is counting women killed by more than just guns; a September 2018 report from the Violence Policy Center cites a statistic of fifty American women killed each month, but this number counts only those killed by guns.
2. Klein, Andrew. "Practical Implications of Current Domestic Violence Research. Part I: Law Enforcement." *NCJRS*. Unpublished. April 2008, 9. https://www.ncjrs.gov/pdffiles1/nij/grants/222319.pdf.
3. http://www.opdv.ny.gov/public_awareness/bulletins/winter2014/victimsprison.html. State of New York, Department of Correctional Services, "Female homicide commitments: 1986 vs. 2005" (July 2007).
4. Latina Ray pled to a sentence of eleven years before her case went to trial. Her story is recounted in the documentary *Private Violence*.
5. At the time of this writing, in 2013, homicide is number two, eclipsed only slightly by HIV/AIDS.
6. ". . . 60% . . ." Interview with Dr. Sylvia Vella. See also: Glass, Nancy et al., "Non-Fatal Strangulation Is an Important Risk Factor for Homicide of Women," *Journal of Emergency Medicine* 35, no. 3 (October 2007): 330.
7. Strack, Gael B. and Casey Gwinn. "On the Edge of Homicide," 2 ("gendered crime").
8. Strack, Gael B. and George E. McClane. "Violence: Recognition, Management, and Prevention." Interviews with Gael Strack, Geri Greenspan, Jackie Campbell, Silvia Vella, Casey Gwinn.
9. Also see: Strack and Gwinn, "On The Edge of Homicide."
10. Strack, Gael B., George McClane, and Dean Hawley. "A Review of 300 Attempted Strangulation Cases Part I: Criminal Legal Issues."
11. "penultimate abuse by a perpetrator . . ." Strack coined this the "continuum of violence."
12. Interview with Sylvia Vella.
13. E-mail correspondence with Neil Websdale, director of the Family Violence Institute at Northern Arizona University.

14. Interview with Gael Strack. The autonomic nervous system info was explained to me by Dean Hawley, who spoke on background only ("Cases . . . prosecuted as a misdemeanor"). See: Strack et al. "A Review of 300 Attempted Strangulation Cases."

15. http://www.strangulationtraininginstitute.com/about-us.

16. Background on Supreme Court sentencing provided by Matt Osterrieder. 202.502.4653. See also:

   - Page 53 of this link for sentencing guidelines on strangulation: http://www.ussc.gov/sites/default/files/pdf/guidelines-manual/2014/CHAPTER_2_A-C.pdf.
   - U.S. Supreme Court sentencing table (starts at level 14 for domestic violence): http://www.ussc.gov/sites/default/files/pdf/guidelines-manual/2014/2014sentencing_table.pdf.
   - "Acceptance of responsibility . . ." when they plead guilty they get 2 points off, page 371 of this: http://www.ussc.gov/sites/default/files/pdf/guidelines-manual/2014/GLMFull.pdf.

17. http://myemail.constantcontact.com/E-news-from-the-Training-Institute-on-Strangulation-Prevention.html?soid=1100449105154&aid=2vdIhXbn5lM.

18. See: http://www.azcentral.com/story/news/local/phoenix/2015/03/02/county-attorney-strangulation-protocol/24001897.

19. Note: the data for this says it went from 14% to 60%, but Sgt. Dan Rincon says the number is now 75%. So there's a descrepancy between this newer number and published work saying 60% (like here on page 2: http://www.ndvfri.org/newsletters/FALL-2012-NDVFRI-Newsletter.pdf), but in Rincon's trainings he now uses 75%—a number he got from the Maricopa County Attorney's Office.

20. Institute for Strangulation Prevention, Sept. 2017 newsletter: http://myemail.constantcontact.com/E-news-from-the-Training-Institute-on-Strangulation-Prevention.html?soid=1100449105154&aid=2vdIhXbn5lM.

21. Also see: David, Alice, "Violence-Related Mild Traumatic Brain Injury in Women: Identifying a Triad of Postinjury Disorders," *Journal of Trauma Nurses* 21, no. 6 (November 2014): 306–7.

22. E-mail correspondence with author.

23. Barriers to diagnosis and treatment came on background mostly from Dean Hawley. Gael Strack also verified, and Attorney Geri Greenspan discussed legal barriers.

SYSTEMS, ACCIDENTS, INCIDENTS

1. https://www.ndvfri.org/review-teams.
2. http://www.leg.mt.gov/content/Committees/Interim/2015-2016/Law
-and-Justice/Meetings/Sept-2015/Exhibits/dale-presentation-domestic
-violence-review-september-2015.pdf.
3. https://www.hopkinsmedicine.org/news/media/releases/study_suggests
_medical_errors_now_third_leading_cause_of_death_in_the_us.

PENANCE

1. This quote comes from an edited phone conversation between Hamish Sinclair and Ed Gondolf from April 2014 that Sinclair sent to me through private correspondence to explain his philosphy and curriculum. Gondolf is the author of *The Future of Batterer Programs* (Boston, MA: Northeastern University Press, 2012).
2. https://www.theatlantic.com/politics/archive/2018/02/porter/552806.
3. For the record, I raised my hand, but being an adult in an audience of hundreds of jiggly, giggly kids didn't warrant my inclusion. My daughter, meanwhile, was cringing in her seat, hoping I didn't embarrass her—which, of course, I would have.
4. This should not be confused with the NLP alternative medical practice that has been largely discredited—it was once erroneously hailed as a possible treatment for a range of diseases, from cancer to Parkinson's to the common cold.

WATCHING VIOLENCE IN A FISHBOWL

1. Her name has been changed. I do not know the identity of Victoria's father, and did not confirm her accounts presented at the jail that day. (The point for me was observing restorative justice in action.)
2. I am not allowed to record audio in the jail.
3. Schwartz's own memoir, *Dreams from the Monster Factory*, details much of the creation of the RSVP program.
4. Lee, Bandy and James Gilligan, "The Resolve to Stop the Violence Project: Transforming an In-House Culture of Violence Through a Jail-Based Programme." *Journal of Public Health* 27, no. 2, (June 2005): 149–55.
5. Ibid., 143–48. Gains came from, among other things, not having to re-arrest and prosecute those who may have otherwise re-offended, as well as general costs for housing inmates, among others.

6. Alissa Riker is the current director of programs at San Bruno. We spoke on background by phone in the spring of 2018.

7. Lee and Gilligan, "The Resolve to Stop the Violence Project," 143–48.

8. Peterson, Cora et al., "Lifetime Economic Burden of Intimate Partner Violence Among U.S. Adults," *American Journal of Preventive Medicine* 55, no. 4 (October 2018): 433–44.

9. National Center for Injury Prevention and Control. *Costs of Intimate Partner Violence Against Women in the United States.* Centers for Disease Control and Prevention (Atlanta, GA: 2003).

10. Report by Amy S. Ackerman, Deputy City Attorney. Domestic Violence Investigation—December 2001. Available here: https://sfgov.org/dosw /domestic-violence-investigation-december-2001.

11. Harlow, Caroline Wolf. "Prior Abuse Reported by Inmates and Probationers." Bureau of Justice Statistics (April 1999). https://www.bjs.gov /content/pub/pdf/parip.pdf.

THE FATAL PERIL CLUB

1. Her name has been changed.

2. In October of 2018, Hamish Sinclair had to stop giving his ManAlive classes at the Glide Community Center because the probation department determined that it could not have probationers—that is, peers who may still be on probation themselves, despite having successfully gone through ManAlive and facilitator training—with access to other probationers' files. Sinclair will be offering the classes at alternative facilities, though not with an affiliation to the San Francisco probation office. This does not affect the classes Espinoza and his Community Works colleagues teach—at San Bruno or at the satellite office.

CLUSTERED AT THE TOP

1. Though this has improved slightly in the years since Adams wrote his dissertation, women are still doing the bulk of childcare and household chores in the home, as well as what is referred to these days as the "invisible work" of managing a household. See: http://www.pewsocialtrends .org/2015/11/04/raising-kids-and-running-a-household-how-working -parents-share-the-load. See also: http://www.marketwatch.com/story /this-is-how-much-more-unpaid-work-women-do-than-men-2017-03-07.

2. This number comes from David Adams.

3. Gondolf, *The Future of Batterer Programs*, 237.

4. https://www.sun-sentinel.com/sports/bal-ray-rice-completes-pretrial -intervention-in-domestic-violence-case-in-new-jersey-charges-being -dismi-20150521-story.html

5. https://www.washingtonpost.com/opinions/im-done-helping-the-nfl -pay-lip-service-to-domestic-violence-prevention/2018/06/05/1b470 bec-6448-11e8-99d2-0d678ec08c2f_story.html?utm_term=.5313d65 ee95b.

6. Eckhardt, C., R. Samper, and C. Murphy, "Anger Disturbances Among Perpetrators of Intimate Partner Violence: Clinical Characteristics and Outcomes of Court-Mandated Treatment." *Journal of Interpersonal Violence* 23, no. 11 (November 2008): 1600–17.

7. Pence, Ellen, "Duluth Model," *Domestic Abuse Intervention Programs*, Duluth, MN. http://www.theduluthmodel.org.

THE HAUNTING PRESENCE OF THE INEXPLICABLE

1. Many familicide or domestic violence homicide offenders claim to "hear voices" and try to use the "not guilty by reason of insanity" defense. It almost never works. Juries are rightly skeptical of such defenses and the bar for proving insanity is very, very high.

2. Even the fact of these two instances in the headlines speaks to how issues of race dominate the headlines. It is shocking that a white middle-class man would kill his white middle-class wife and children. It is less headline-worthy when black women and children are killed. Though in the case of familicide, given that Caucasian men are primarily the perpetrators, it's difficult to draw exact comparisons.

3. I am skeptical about some of these images—in part because body bags are generally used out in the field and O'Hanlon was not in the field for those particular operations, and in part because they are a trope of war, short-hand for an emotional experience that is rarely excavated.

A SUPERHERO'S KNEECAPS

1. Jolin, A., W. Feyerherm, R. Fountain, and S. Friedman, "Beyond Arrest: The Portland, Oregon Domestic Violence Experiment, Final Report," Washington, D.C.: U.S. Department of Justice, 95-IJ-CX-0054, National Institute of Justice, NCJ 179968 (1998); Lyon, E., "Special Session Domestic Violence Courts: Enhanced Advocacy and Interventions, Final Report Summary," Washington, D.C.: U.S. Department of Justice, 98-WE-VX-0031, National Institute of Justice, NCJ 197860 (2002);

Lyons, E., Impact Evaluation of Special Sessions Domestic Violence: Enhanced Advocacy and Interventions. Washington, D.C.: U.S. Department of Justice, 2000-WE-VX-0014, National Institute of Justice, NCJ 210362 (2005).

2. Richard Ivone, chief of police. https://www.nj.com/news/index.ssf/2011/03/as_commander_of_swat_team_pisc.html.

3. Ibid. http://www.womenandpolicing.com/violencefs.asp.

4. Police Family Violence Fact Sheet. National Center for Women and Policing. http://womenandpolicing.com/violencefs.asp.

5. www.nytimes.com/projects/2013/police-domestic-abuse/index.html. See also: www.fdle.state.fl.us/FSAC/Crime-Data/DV.aspx

6. Townsend, M., D. Hunt, S. Kuck, and C. Baxter, "Law Enforcement Response to Domestic Violence Calls for Service." U.S. Department of Justice, 99-C-008, National Institute of Justice, NCJ 215915 (2006).

7. Meyer, Shannon and Randall H. Carroll, "When Officers Die: Understanding Deadly Domestic Violence Calls for Service," *Police Chief* 78 (May 2011).

8. Blair, J. Pete, M. Hunter Martindale, and Terry Nichols, "Active Shooter Events from 2000–2012." Law Enforcement Bulletin; FBI Jan 7, 2014. https://www.leb.fbi.gov/articles/featured-articles/active-shooter-events-from-2000-to-2012. See also: J. P. Blair, T. Nichols, and J. R. Curnutt, *Active Shooter Events and Response* (Boca Raton, FL: CRC Press, 2013).

9. Unpublished research commissioned by *Marie Claire* and conducted by Harvard University's Injury Control Research Center and shared with the author.

10. See Campbell, Jacquelyn et al., "Risk Factors for Femicide in Abusive Relationships: Results from a Multisite Case Control Study." *American Journal of Public Health* 93, no. 7 (July 2003).

11. https://www.nytimes.com/2017/11/06/us/politics/domestic-abuse-guns-texas-air-force.html.

12. https://www.everytownresearch.org/navigator/states.html?dataset=domestic_violence#q-gunmath_mcdv_surrender. These states included: Hawaii, California, Nevada, Colorado, Louisiana, Tennessee, Minnesota, Iowa, Illinois, Maryland, Pennsylvania, New Jersey, Massachusetts, Connecticut, Rhode Island, New York, and the District of Columbia.

13. Some states have written their own legislation to try and address the "boyfriend loophole," but there is currently no federal law that addresses it.

14. https://www.americanprogress.org/issues/guns-crime/reports/2018/03/22/448298/disarm-domestic-abusers/. See also: https://www.americanprogress.org/issues/guns-crime/reports/2014/06/18/91998/women-under-the-gun.

15. See Zeoli study from *Injury Prevention*.

16. See Vigdor study from *Evaluation Review.* Also: "When Men Murder Women: An Analysis of 2013 Homicide Data" from the Violence Policy Center (September 2015).
17. Interview with Teresa Garvey.
18. Thirty-three thousand annually, from Zeoli.
19. Interview with April Zeoli.
20. Adams, David, "Statement before the Joint Committee on Public Safety and Homeland Security." Sept. 13, 2013. www.emergedv.com/legislative-testimony-by-david-adams.html.
21. See transcript for Gruelle.
22. Some of the jurisdictions I did drive alongs with didn't allow for "media" to drive along, but only the general population, including my hometown of Washington, D.C. They allowed me to do ride alongs on the condition that I maintain the anonymity of the officers I interacted with on the calls I observed.

SHELTER IN PLACE

1. The National Domestic Violence hotline has a database of five thousand, but this number includes both shelters and domestic violence agencies.
2. The reader was Risa Mednick, executive director of Transition House in Cambridge, MA. https://www.newyorker.com/magazine/2013/08/05/mail-12.
3. https://www.dc.curbed.com/2016/6/23/12013024/apartment-rent-washington-dc.
4. https://www.mpdc.dc.gov/node/217782.
5. Desmond, Matthew. *Evicted* (New York: Broadway Books, 2016), 191–92.

IN THE FIRE

1. https://www.governor.pa.gov/governor-wolf-signs-tiernes-law-providing-protections-victims-domestic-violence.
2. Fagan, Jeffrey. "The Criminalization of Domestic Violence: Promises and Limits." Presentation at the 1995 conference on criminal justice research and evaluation. January 1996. www.ncjrs.gov/pdffiles/crimdom.pdf.
3. http://www.federalevidence.com/pdf/2007/13-SCt/Crawford_v._Washington.pdf.
4. Henderson, Brady and Tyson Stanek, *Domestic Violence: from the Crime Scene to the Courtroom*, Oklahoma Coalition Against Domestic Violence & Sexual Assault, 2008.

5. Brooklyn formed its own High Risk Team, but did not receive OVW funding, and would not allow me access to anyone on their team.

6. http://www.dispatch.com/news/20171004/115-deaths-in-year-paint -grim-picture-of-domestic-violence-in-ohio.

7. See: Domestic Violence Report from the Ohio Attorney General http:// www.ohioattorneygeneral.gov/Law-Enforcement/Services-for-Law -Enforcement/Domestic-Violence-Reports/Domestic-Violence-Reports -2016/2016-Domestic-Violence-Incidents-by-County-and-Age.

GRACE UNDER PRESSURE

1. "In their first year of operation . . . than eighty." https://www.cleveland .com/metro/index.ssf/2017/12/cleveland_team_tackles_high_risk _domestic_violence_cases_to_improve_safety_reduce_deaths.html.

CHAMBERING A ROUND

1. https://www.ncbi.nlm.nih.gov/pubmed/11604294.

2. Some of the details have been left out to protect the identities of Byron, Grace, and the children.

3. https://www.nbcnews.com/storyline/texas-church-shooting/shooting -survivor-could-see-texas-gunman-s-shoes-she-hid-n818231.

4. https://www.independent.co.uk/news/world/americas/orlando-attack -survivor-reveals-how-he-played-dead-among-bodies-to-escape-nightclub -killer-a7080196.html.

5. https://www.newyorker.com/news/news-desk/the-court-slams-the -door-on-domestic-abusers-owning-guns.

6. http://www.saveservices.org/2012/02/cdc-study-more-men-than -women-victims-of-partner-abuse/; https://www.reuters.com/article /us-usa-gays-violence/data-shows-domestic-violence-rape-an-issue-for -gays-idUSBRE90O11W20130125.http://web.csulb.edu/~mfiebert /assault.htm.

7. For a statistical breakdown of physical assault, rape, or stalking in LGBTQ couples or transgender individuals see: https://www.ncadv.org/blog/posts /domestic-violence-and-the-lgbtq-community.

8. http://www.thehotline.org/2013/06/10/50-obstacles-to-leaving-1-10.

FREE FREE

1. https://www.cleveland.com/metro/index.ssf/2017/05/bresha_meadows _cousin_says.html

2. As of 2016, the town of Warren, Ohio, had a population of just under forty thousand (https://www.census.gov/quickfacts/fact/table/warrencityohio/PST045217#PST045217). For a frame of reference, Amesbury, Massachusetts, where Robert Wile is the dedicated domestic violence detective, is less than half that, with sixteen thousand (https://factfinder.census.gov/faces/tableservices/jsf/pages/productview.xhtml?src=cf) according to the latest U.S. Census figures for each town, respectively.

3. Van der Kolk, Bessel. *The Body Keeps the Score* (New York: Penguin, 2014), 46, 61, 135, and 350.

SHADOW BODIES

1. No Republican has ever won the electoral vote in Washington, D.C. In the 2016 election, D.C. went 91% for Hillary Clinton. San Francisco, another liberal bastion, went 84%. https://www.nytimes.com/elections/results/president.

2. https://www.congress.gov/bill/115th-congress/house-bill/6545/cosponsors. The 1994 passage had fifteen Republic cosponsors: https://www.congress.gov/bill/103rd-congress/senate-bill/11/cosponsors.

3. http://vpc.org/studies/wmmw2018.pdf.

4. https://www.huffingtonpost.com/entry/tamara-oneal-chicago-shooting-domestic-violence_us_5bf576a6e4b0771fb6b4ceef.

5. https://www.npr.org/2016/01/05/462017461/guns-in-america-by-the-numbers.

6. Diez, Carolina et al., "State Intimate Partner Violence-Related Firearms Laws and Intimate Partner Homicide Rates in the United States, 1991–2015," *Annals of Internal Medicine* 167, no. 8 (October 2017): 536–43. http://annals.org/aim/fullarticle/2654047/state-intimate-partner-violence-related-firearm-laws-intimate-partner-homicide. See also: http://annals.org/data/Journals/AIM/936539/M162849ff4_Appendix_Figure_Status_of_state_IPV-related_restraining_order_firearm_relinquishment.jpeg.

7. https://www.emergedv.com/legislative-testimony-by-david-adams.html.

8. https://everytownresearch.org/guns-domestic-violence/#foot_note_. CA, CO, CT, HI, IA, IL, MA, MD, MN, NC, NH, NY, TN, WA, and WI.

9. Zeoli, April M. et al., "Analysis of the Strength of Legal Firearms Restrictions for Perpetrators of Domestic Violence and their Impact on Intimate Partner Homicide," *American Journal of Epidemiology* (October 2018). Note: Zeoli's study references "broader restrictions," meaning anyone convicted of a violent misdemeanor, not just domestic violence. As state law, this captures a larger portion of criminal behavior and thus even

someone not convicted specifically of a domestic violence misdemeanor, but *any* kind of violent misdemeanor is required to relinquish firearms.

10. https://everytownresearch.org/guns-domestic-violence/#foot_note_12.

11. For a fairly comprehensive rundown of smartphone apps, see this compendium from the National Network to End Domestic Violence: https://www.techsafety.org/appsafetycenter.

12. Critics of FJCs say they are expensive to replicate, impractical in rural areas, and often off-putting to victims who are intimidated by bureaucracy. There is also not a national model for FJCs to replicate; founders instead feel that areas interested in creating FJCs should feel free to adapt them for use in their own regions. Many FJCs, similarly, are not run specifically by crisis centers, which some suggest doesn't put the victim's voice and needs front and center. This number comes from private correspondence between the writer and Casey Gwinn in October 2018.

13. https://mnadv.org/_mnadvWeb/wp-content/uploads/2017/07/Train-the-Trainer-PowerPoint.ppt.pdf.

14. Lethality Assessment Program: https://lethalityassessmentprogram.org/what-we-do/training-and-technical-assistance.

15. Labriola, Melissa et al., "A National Portrait of Domestic Violence Courts." U.S. Department of Justice. Center for Court Innovation. February 2010. https://www.ncjrs.gov/pdffiles1/nij/grants/229659.pdf.

16. Rosenthal, Lynn, "The Violence Against Women Act, 23 Years Later," Sept. 13, 2017. https://medium.com/@bidenfoundation/https-medium-com-bidenfoundation-vawa-23-years-later-4a7c1866a834.

17. Data compiled by author and research assistant with technical support from AEquitas.com.

18. Data compiled by the Training Institute on Strangulation Prevention.

19. Smith, Sharon G. et al., "The National Intimate Partner and Sexual Violence Survey." 2010–2012 State Report. National Center for Injury Prevention and Control, Division of Violence Prevention. Centers for Disease Control. Atlanta, GA. April 2017. https://www.cdc.gov/violenceprevention/pdf/NISVS-StateReportBook.pdf.

20. The on-call advocates did not want their real names used for fear of reprisals from abusers.

21. Thousands of affordable housing units have been lost in D.C. in the past decade, and another 13,700 units are due to have their subsidies expire in 2020. In late 2017, the city established a $10 million fund to help offset the significant losses in affordable housing in recent years. https://www.washingtonpost.com/local/dc-establishes-10-million-fund-to-preserve-disappearing-affordable-housing/2017/11/26/242893ea-cbb7-11e7-aa96-54417592cf72_story.html?utm_term=.9e85c5cf2eda.

22. The woman has to show proof of ownership or her name on the lease.

INDEX

A NOTE ON THE AUTHOR

Rachel Louise Snyder's work has appeared in the *New Yorker*, the *New York Times Magazine*, the *Washington Post*, the *New Republic*, *Slate*, and elsewhere. Her other books include *Fugitive Denim* and the novel *What We've Lost Is Nothing*. She has been the recipient of an Overseas Press Award for her work on *This American Life*. *No Visible Bruises* was awarded the J. Anthony Lukas Work-in-Progress Award. An associate professor at American University, Snyder lives in Washington, D.C.